"Ingenious and revelatory, *Pyrotechnic Ci* apparatus of fire-safety regulation that I insights into the reciprocities of law and flickering threat of fire, will challenge ar new arrangements of governance, the bu~~ilt environment, and the social~~ contract."

Timothy Hyde, *Massachusetts Institute of Technology*

"In this radical reading of fire-safety standards, Liam Ross broadens the discipline of architecture to include concerns often unconscious to the designer's mind; the legal assumptions and agreements hidden within design codes. *Pyrotechnic Cities* provides a fascinating and truly new take on the 'lawscape' of cities and shows the productive side-effects of regulations."

Helena Mattsson, *KTH School of Architecture*

"Fire has often figured as the mythical beginning of architecture, and of the properly human, but it is also an agent and marker of its end. In this erudite book, Liam Ross addresses the relation between architecture and fire through a series of case studies that, taken together, build into an episodic cultural history of the way the threat of fire has been mediated through building standards and the particular effects – social, spatial, material, and technological – to which these have given rise. With a final section on Grenfell Tower, this is a topical and important study that throws light on the discursive construction of standards and the management and distribution of risk in our increasingly combustible world."

Mark Dorrian, *University of Edinburgh*

"*Pyrotechnic Cities* is an insightful study of building standardisation. Drawing on Science and Technology Studies, the book offers a much-needed rethinking of the role of incidents (like the Grenfell Tower fire) in revealing regulatory practices that were not visible before. Drawing on a range of local and global examples, analysed carefully in their historical or geographical specificity, the book puts forward a compelling argument about the social and technological networks of translation underpinning the production of standards in the built environment (with a focus on fire-safety standards). A must-read for every student, academic and practitioner in Architecture."

Albena Yaneva, *University of Manchester*

"All your burning questions answered: Liam Ross' book on the history of fire and architecture is not only erudite and witty, it's also extraordinarily informative. Through a range of urban settings, from twentieth century

Edinburgh to colonial Lagos, and contemporary London to Edo period Tokyo, *Pyrotechnic Cities* shows how fire has not only shaped the regulation of buildings, but the anatomy and economic fate of cities. There's an art to telling a fireside story, and Dr Ross has perfected it here, in a book that I believe will be a future classic for architects, historians and the curious alike."

Adam Jasper, *ETH Zurich*

Pyrotechnic Cities

This book explores the relationship between architecture, government and fire. It posits that, through the question of fire-safety standardisation, building design comes to be both a problem for, and a tool of, government. Through a close study of fire-safety standards it demonstrates the shaping effect that architecture and the city have on the way we think about governing.

Opening with an investigation into the Grenfell Tower fire and the political actors who sought to enrol it in programmes of governmental reform before contextualising the research in current literature, the book takes four city studies, each beginning with a specific historic fire: The 1654 Great Fire of Meirecki, Edo; the 1877 town fire of Lagos; the 1911 Empire Palace Theatre fire, Edinburgh; and the 2001 World Trade Centre attack, New York. Each study identifies the governmental response to the fire, safety standards and codes designed in its wake and how these new processes spread and change.

Drawing on the work of sociologists John Law and Anne Marie Mol and their concept of 'Fire Space', it describes the way that architectural design, through the medium of fire, is an instrument of political agency. *Pyrotechnic Cities* is a critical investigation into these political implications, written for academics, researchers and students in architectural history and theory, infrastructure studies and governance.

Liam Ross is an architect and senior lecturer in Architectural Design at the University of Edinburgh. He studied at the University of Edinburgh and the Architectural Association, and completed his doctoral dissertation under the supervision of Prof. Mark Dorrian. Through his research he responds 'to a call to study boring things', paying attention to taken-for-granted aspects of design practice that nonetheless have pervasive effects. Over the past six years his work has focussed on fire-safety standards; he has sought to foreground the contingencies that underpin these universalising codes, and to illustrate their often surprising side-effects. That work has been published in *Arch +, arq, Architectural Theory Review, Candide, Gta Papers* and *Volume*, was exhibited at the British Pavilion at the 13th Venice Architecture Biennale, and features in the edited collections *Industries of Architecture* and *Neoliberalism on the Ground*. At present he is working on a study fire of metaphors, considering them part of the conceptual infrastructure of architectural theory.

Routledge Research in Architecture

The *Routledge Research in Architecture* series provides the reader with the latest scholarship in the field of architecture. The series publishes research from across the globe and covers areas as diverse as architectural history and theory, technology, digital architecture, structures, materials, details, design, monographs of architects, interior design and much more. By making these studies available to the worldwide academic community, the series aims to promote quality architectural research.

Architecture of Threshold Spaces
A Critique of the Ideologies of Hyperconnectivity and Segregation in the Socio-Political Context
Laurence Kimmel

Pyrotechnic Cities
Architecture, Fire-Safety and Standardisation
Liam Ross

Architecture and the Housing Question
Edited by Can Bilsel and Juliana Maxim

Architecture and the Housing Question
Edited by Can Bilsel and Juliana Maxim

Mies at Home
From Am Karlsbad to the Tugendhat House
Xiangnan Xiong

For more information about this series, please visit: https://www.routledge.com/Routledge-Research-in-Architecture/book-series/RRARCH

Pyrotechnic Cities

Architecture, Fire-Safety and
Standardisation

Liam Ross

Routledge
Taylor & Francis Group

LONDON AND NEW YORK

Cover image: Spectres of Edo Castle, Max Ochel and Liam Ross, 2020

First published 2022
by Routledge
4 Park Square, Milton Park, Abingdon, Oxon OX14 4RN

and by Routledge
605 Third Avenue, New York, NY 10158

Routledge is an imprint of the Taylor & Francis Group, an informa business

© 2022 Liam Ross

Every effort has been made to contact copyright-holders. Please
advise the publisher of any errors or omissions, and these will be
corrected in subsequent editions.

British Library Cataloguing-in-Publication Data
A catalogue record for this book is available from the British Library

Library of Congress Cataloging-in-Publication Data
A catalog record has been requested for this book

ISBN: 978-0-367-45967-3 (hbk)
ISBN: 978-1-032-21474-0 (pbk)
ISBN: 978-1-003-02629-7 (ebk)

DOI: 10.4324/9781003026297

Typeset in Sabon
by codeMantra

To my parents

Contents

Figures

Acknowledgements

This book developed from my doctoral research supervised by Mark Dorrian and Dorian Wiszniewski at the University of Edinburgh, and I would like to thank them both for their guidance. For their comments on the work as it developed I would like to thank Tim Anstey, Tilo Amhof, Nick Beech, Adam Bobette, Paul Carter, Beatriz Colomina, Catherine Ingraham, Karin Matz, John Macarthur, Helen Runting and Finn Williams. For providing opportunities to present the work, my thanks to Saloman Frausto, Adam Jasper, Douglas Spencer and Brady Burroughs. For editorial comments on previously published material, thanks to Katie Lloyd Thomas, Adam Jasper, Helena Mattsson, Catarina Gabrielsson and to the anonymous reviewers at *Architectural Theory Review* and gta Verlag.

The original research on Lagos was conducted with Tolulope Onabolu and was supported by the British Council as a contribution to *Venice Takeaway* at the British Pavilion, the 13th Venice Architecture Biennale. Thanks to Vanessa Norwood, Vicky Richardson, Ojoma Ochai and Tolulope Ogunlesi at the British Council, and to Fred Coker, Afolabi Aiyeola, Morenike Medun, Tunji Odunlami and the Onabolu family for their support. The original research on Tokyo was made possible by a research exchange with Kindai University, Japan. Thanks to Shinichi Ogawa for his support, and to Ai Sekizawa at the Tokyo University Graduate School of Global Fire for comment on the work. This research would not have been possible without the technical and sociological expertise of colleagues in fire-safety engineering and the Institute for the Study of Science, Technology and Innovation at the University of Edinburgh; my thanks in particular to Luke Bisby, Barbara Lane and Grahame Spinardi.

This work has also been conducted in parallel with studio teaching at the University of Edinburgh, and sustained by the creative engagement of students. In particular I would like to acknowledge Vsevelod Kondratiev Popov, Hironori Kaseda, Sigurd Norsterud, Jens Walter, Anthony d'Auria, Anna Raymond, Bronagh Sweeney, Sophie Humphries, Maria Esteban Castena, Nicola Grant, Lauren Potter, Michael Dargo, Hannah Dalton, Max Ochel, Alistair Hume and Yida Zhou whose engagement has informed the current work. My thanks, as ever, to Siobhan and Hugo for their constant support and insight.

The material presented in Chapter 3 is reproduced with the permission of Routledge, appearing in reduced form in Liam Ross, 'Regulatory Spaces, Physical and Metaphorical: On the Legal and Spatial Occupation of Fire-Safety Legislation', in *Industries of Architecture*, ed. Tilo Amhoff, Nick Beech, and Katie Lloyd Thomas (Routledge, 2015).

The material presented in Chapter 4 is reproduced with the permission of Taylor & Francis, appearing in reduced form in Liam Ross, 'On the Materiality of Law: Spatial and Legal Appropriations of the Lagos Set-Back', *Architectural Theory Review 20*, no. 2 (4 May 2015): 247–65.

The material presented in Chapter 5 is reproduced with the permission of gta Verlag, appearing in reduced form in Liam, Ross. 'Spectres of Edo Castle'. In *Grand Gestures: Gta Papers 4: Volume 4*, 64–85. Zürich: gta Verlag/ETH Zürich, 2020.

The material presented in Chapter 6 is reproduced with the permission of University of Pittsburgh Press, appearing in reduced form in Liam Ross, 'Creative Uncertainty: Arup Associates, Fire Safety and the Metaengineering of Government'. In *Neoliberalism on the Ground: Architecture and Transformation from the 1960s to the Present*, 270–93. University of Pittsburgh Press, 2020.

1 Introduction

Gathering around fire

1.1 Coincident rainbows

The Aggregate Night Bomb Census for the period of 7 October 1940 to 6 June 1941 records four bombs falling on the future site of the Grenfell Tower, North Kensington. During that period, known as the Blitz, high explosive bombs were recorded falling on streets now part of the Lancaster West Estate: Bomore Road, Treadgold Street, Whitchurch Road and Grenfell Road. Those explosions were recorded by the Research and Experiments Branch of the Ministry of Home Security, who documented bombings in an attempt to identify and predict patterns in the German attack. Their findings are collated graphically through the London County Council's *Bomb Damage Maps*.[1] In tones of black, purple, magenta, orange and yellow those maps code every building in the city in terms of damage suffered, classifying severity from "total destruction", "damaged beyond repair", "repairable at cost" to "not structural" or "minor in nature". While most of Kensington remains blank or is coloured yellow, the future site of Grenfell Tower and the Lancaster West Estate appear as blackened impact sites rimmed by rainbows of peripheral damage: explosions of colour pixelated by the tenure pattern of London's typical pre-war terraced housing (Figure 1.1).

The LCC's *Bomb Damage Maps* paint a picture that is surprisingly similar to a different survey of the same city, completed 40 years earlier. Working at the same resolution and with a similar palette, Charles Booth and his volunteers coloured every building in the city either black, dark blue, magenta, orange or yellow. But the *Descriptive Map of London Poverty*, completed in 1889, looked for different kinds of patterns.[2] Here those colours classified the tenants of buildings as being either of the "Lowest class. Vicious, semi-criminal", "Very poor", "Mixed", "Middle class" or "Wealthy". The patterns of Victorian poverty in Kensington, though, are similar to those of the Second World War bomb damage. Notting Dale, the electoral ward of the future Grenfell Tower, is peppered with black spots surrounded by bruising of dark blue, purple and red. Neighbouring Notting Hill was struck less often, and appears mostly yellow. That patterns

DOI: 10.4324/9781003026297-1

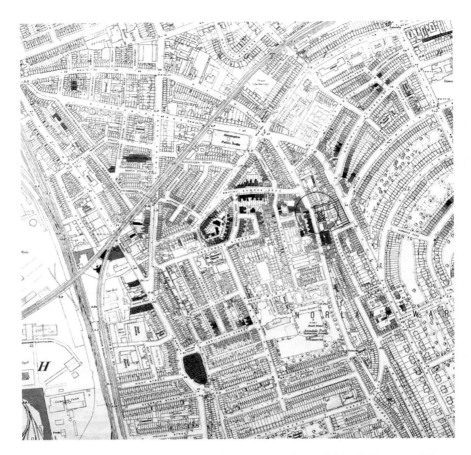

Figure 1.1 **Detail, Sheet RM59, London County Council Bomb Damage Maps.**
Grenfell Road and the future site of the Lancaster West Estate are at
the centre of the image. Source: *London County Council Bomb Damage
Maps*, 1939–1945, London Metropolitan Archives LCC/AR/TP/P/039/036. Reproduced by the permission of the London Metropolitan Archives

of poverty might predict patterns of bombardment is not so surprising. In
the 19th century, Notting Dale was a site of local industry as well as working class housing. Crossed by railway lines and canals, during the Second
World War that area also became home to a Rolls Royce engine factory as
well as a Barrage Balloon depot. Military and industrial facilities, as well
as the housing and labour force that surround them, are forms of critical national infrastructure and hence strategic targets. Black and blue in
both maps, the site of the future Lancaster West Estate was defined by
the coincidence of "very poor" and "total destruction". Or to put that in

contemporary language, the site was defined by the coincidence of multiple deprivation, home to a population that was vulnerable both economically and militarily.

The urban fabric that today survives in Notting Hill, and has been largely replaced in Notting Dale, was itself the product of an earlier catastrophic fire. The Great Fire of London, which occurred in 1666, destroyed as much of the city as did the Blitz, burning out the medieval centre as far as its defensive walls. The effects of post-fire regulation, from the 1667 Reconstruction Act through to the 1774 Fire Prevention Act, were more wide-reaching. Often cited as the first act of building regulation in the UK they shaped the urban form, construction materials and detailing of London in ways that are still visible today. Outlawing timber construction they made mandatory the use of London's now familiar brick; requiring non-combustible and protruding party walls they defined the height and roof profile of much of the city; controlling the separation between windows as well as their depth, they designed the future cities facades; regulating the width of plots to facilitate the standardised production of structural components, they reshaped patterns and types of land and property ownership. The terraced houses through which London expanded during the 18th and 19th centuries were "more or less the clauses of [those] building regulations turned into bricks and mortar", and those regulations were shaped most profoundly by a particular way of thinking about and mitigating fire-risk.[3] Three-hundred years later, when the Blitz tore holes in that fabric, it cleared the space not only for new buildings but also for new ways of thinking about fire risk and building regulation. The German bombing campaign also accelerated ambitions for "slum clearance" ongoing since the time of Charles Booth. Where those bombs fell, towers later rose. Like slow-motion dust plumes, post-war rebuilding replaced low-rise, private brick construction with new building types and technologies: the reinforced concrete frames and pre-cast panels of point-towers and slab-blocks, often lined with asbestos. And those new forms of construction likewise depended on new forms of regulation; the Second World War was itself the prompt for the UK's first national building code; the exigency of post-war reconstruction displaced a patchwork of local authority by-laws with a unitary national code. That is, the Great Fire and the Blitz didn't just pave the way for isolated building projects; through those regulatory frameworks designed in their wake, they prompted programmes for reconstruction that were city-wide, indeed national in scope.

1.2 Archaeologies of fire

Looking at the LCC's *Bomb Damage Maps* and the *Descriptive Map of London Poverty* we might be reminded of Thomas Pynchon and *Gravity's Rainbow*. The Londoners who inhabit that novel are also engaged in experimental research, consulting and comparing maps for patterns that might predict German bombardment. They do so because they are weighed down by a particular fear, that of dying without warning. Supersonic bombs of the type that struck Notting Dale during the Second World War arrive before they can be heard; they become audible only at the moment of impact. In the sonic boom that follows the history of their approach is broadcast in a reversed and condensed form: a tell-tale sign that arrives exactly too late.[4] Looking at those maps today we might also see signs of an approaching catastrophe – the fire that would break out at the Grenfell Tower on 14 June 2017, killing 72 people. The coincidence of those two maps places the Grenfell fire on a longer historical trajectory, an arc that we can begin to trace by picking apart the built fabric of that tower.

The rapid spread of the 2017 fire occurred externally, and has been attributed to polyethylene present in the building's aluminium composite cladding. That cladding had been installed one year prior to the fire, part of a 2016 refurbishment project. Resident groups within the tower raised safety concerns about that refurbishment before the fire, but felt those concerns were being ignored.[5] Further, some felt that the cladding was not for the residents at all, but was installed as a means to hide the building from more wealthy neighbours, a view supported by planning documents that describe the refurbishment as a means to leave "living conditions of those near the development suitably protected".[6] That refurbishment had come after a number of proposed and realised developments that had left many residents feeling unwelcome: an Academy school built in on the grounds of the Tower leaving residents without amenity space (as well as limiting fire-tender access to the burning façade), but also a proposal to demolish Grenfell Tower and the Lancaster West Estate, making space for new-build market-rental properties, causing concern that social tenants might be "decanted" out of London, or left homeless.[7] That social tenants might feel precarious in Kensington and Chelsea is not surprising; the borough has claims to be the most unequal in Britain, and Grenfell has become a flashpoint within broader concerns over health and wealth disparities. But in the current political and economic climate, there are a number of reasons why the demolition and sale of the estate might be attractive to a majority Conservative council. The site is one a dwindling number of capital assets that the council might sell in order to balance budgetary requirements without raising taxes. Likewise, it is one of a dwindling number of council-owned sites that might be cleared to make space for new, higher-density housing, allowing the borough to increase the total number of homes available. That is, the fact that bombardment and state-led re-development cleared this site of private ownership claims also renders it vulnerable to future re-development. More generally, though, high-rise post-war social-housing towers have had their critics, often being perceived as failures both architecturally and socially, and Grenfell itself has been a prompt for further demolition.[8] Nonetheless, to an earlier government the original concrete tower – whose structure survived the fire relatively intact – had seemed an effective solution to pressing problems; housing commissioned, maintained and owned by the local authority was a means to address not just the urgent post-war housing crisis but also the long-standing poverty of London's pre-war working-class housing. The Blitz ripped through existing patterns of building ownership and construction, providing post-war governments with the opportunity for such a solution. Though patterns of Victorian poverty and war-time bombardment were not the cause of the 2017 fire at Grenfell Tower, both play a part in constructing these conditions of possibility.

Like the Great Fire and the Blitz, Grenfell is today prompting change within the UK's fire-safety legislation, bringing particular scrutiny to those concerned with the testing of materials, and the use of combustible cladding at height. A ban on combustible cladding over 8 m has already been imposed, requiring the re-cladding of other buildings, many of them also post-war towers now found to be unsafe. Further regulatory changes are expected, and these will extend the impact of that single fire well beyond its original site. That is, the Grenfell fire will leave marks on cities across the UK, if not the world. But as we have seen, the marks of many fires are also legible within the built fabric of that one building. Overlaid on Grenfell Tower and its site we have already seen a number of different programmes for the reform of urban fire-safety: those forms of testing now problematised for allowing highly flammable materials to be certified as safe and installed at height; those post-war building standards that supported new building types and modes of construction, but seen as problematic by subsequent governments; and those prescriptive urban and architectural rules that, imposed in the wake of the Great Fire, would replace London's previously timber buildings. Our cities are an archaeology of fire; they are formed from successive acts of regulation, each prompted by and learning from particular building fires, each seeking to re-shape our built fabric and its legal frameworks in different ways. The study of those exchanges between building and governance is the topic of this book.

1.3 First fire

To recognise the foundational role played by fire in human history is not novel; fire has often been conceived as the *fons et origo* of civilisation, if not humanity. Limiting ourselves to this one site, we could extend our archaeology further back in time to find evidence of the pre-historic significance of fire. The environmental historian Stephen Pyne tells us that, during the Blitz, London was subject to a "Bracken Invasion".[9] In the shattered basements, scorched earth and rubble of war-torn London bracken spread with a rapidity contemporary commentators found hard to believe. Pyne explains that, lying dormant beneath the city, the spores of that plant were the biological record of earlier human settlement. Bracken flourished in the UK with the arrival of its earliest human settlers, spreading in their wake, sprouting vigorously following fires used to clear native forest. In turn, that plant provided them with construction material and fodder for animals. Bracken was an integral part of the "fire-regime" of early Britain; it helped structure the pattern, frequency, scale and intensity of free-burning fires, allowing fire to do certain kinds of work for those humans, but also for other fauna and flora. The presence of bracken on the British Isles reminds us that what we think of as our "native" and "natural" habitat is, in fact, the product of a long and active cooperation between human and non-human actors, fire key among them. And prior to written records, it is often fire that provides evidence for that process of construction. On the British Isles bracken provides the earliest record of fire, in the form of fossilised charcoal deposits preserved in the Wealden coals, as well as evidence of Neolithic pioneers and their settlement practices. That is, the history of our built and "natural" environments is written, sometimes quite literally, in fire.

Fire is also present from the very beginning of the beginning of architectural theory. In "Of the Origin of Building", Chapter One of Book Two in *De Architectura*, Vitruvius describes a fire. In Gwilt's translation this tells that "[a] tempest, on a certain occasion, having exceedingly agitated the trees in a particular spot, the friction between some of the branches caused them to take fire".[10] Finding the warmth comfortable, those in the neighbourhood developed "signs and gestures" allowing them to cooperate in maintaining the fire, inviting others to join them:

> Thus the discovery of fire gave rise to the first assembly of mankind, to their first deliberations, and to their union in a state of society.[11]

Vitruvius is here following a tradition common to Greco-Roman culture; in Greek and Roman myths, and through the work of thinkers from Aristotle to Lucretius, fire is thought of as a fundamentally civilising element. In his own account, Vitruvius adds kindling to that story by suggesting that this first assembly was also the first building site, the site of the first shelter, and, as such, conceives of architecture and the city as part of a chain reaction which, from that first spark, will grow to form our culture and society. This aspect of his account is already surprising; it implies that the first occupant of building, the first thing that needed shelter, was fire, not humans. It suggests that the environmental pressure those first buildings were subject to was internal than external; they were means to keep the warmth in, to sustain fire, rather than keep the coolth out. But Vitruvius uses fire in other ways, too; following the Pythagoreans in their elemental theory he explains the properties of familiar building materials – brick, lime, pozzolana, timber – as an effect of the quantity of earth, air, fire and water contained within them. Larignum, or Larch wood, is thought not to burn because it contains very little fire or air. "It is, on the contrary, full of water and earth; being free from pores, by which fire could penetrate, it repels its power".[12] These properties explain the failure of Julius Cesar to burn down the wooden fort at Larignum, and recommend Larch as a material for fire-proofing the eaves of Roman houses. That is, in *De Architectura*, fire appears as an essential explanatory tool, one that can be used to understand the origin and social function of architecture, but also its material being.

The foundational role of that first fire has been fanned and spread by later interpreters. In her visual analysis of the illustrations of *De Architectura*, Olga Medvedkova notes how artists have expanded the metaphoric significance of fire in that treatise.[13] In Baldassare Peruzzi's *The Discovery of Fire by Primitive Men*, the agitated tree, burning fire and first shelter are drawn in like manner. A tree can be drawn to look like a fire, a shelter can be drawn to look like a tree; in its formal likeness to caves, trees or fires, Peruzzi seems to suggest, architecture maintains a mimetic bond with its origin. Raphael and Cesare Cesariano, Jean Goujon and Walther Hermann Ryff suggest a more literal connection. Through paired illustrations of the first fire and first building site, these authors and artists suggest a similarity between the building of fires and the building of shelters. Carpentry, and so construction, began with the bonfire; both are arts of branch-breaking (Figures 1.2 and 1.3). But beyond *De Architectura* there are no shortages of other theorists who have returned to this same mythic scene to kindle their own concerns. Corbusier went there to develop his own neo-humanism, drawing from Classical thought a revised elemental theory that likewise concerned the balancing of opposites including fire and water, hot and cold, dry and wet.[14] Reyner Banham went there in order to identify and describe contrasting environmental strategies; in the hut he saw a technology that modifies environments through the energy embodied in construction, in fire a technology that modifies environments by releasing that energy through combustion, suggesting that the history of architecture was over-burdened with huts, and could learn more from the fire.[15] Lisa Heshong went there to reflect on the affective power of heat, to discover the architecture of "thermal delight".[16] Joseph Rykwert went there to study "Adam's House" in paradise, and again to locate the origin of urban foundation rites.[17] More recently Luis Fernandez-Galiano went there to recount the loss of fire in the contemporary built environment, relegated from the centre of our lives and spaces into systems of mechanised heating, but also to use fire as a prompt for reflections on entropy, time and memory.[18] That is, architectural theory is rich with references to this first, civilising fire. Along with the primitive hut, the first fire is one of architecture's "primal scenes", a place the discipline returns to repeatedly, as to a psychoanalyst's couch, hoping to begin again by discovering what it always already was. Or perhaps better, we might say that architecture culture is "focussed" on this image of fire as a constructive technology, central to our settlement practices, "focus" being the Latin for fire-place, for hearth, making fire a synonym for home.

Figure 1.2 **Jean Goujon, illustration depicting the first fire**. Source: Vitruvius, Marcus Pollio. Architecture, *Ou, Art de Bien Bastir de Marc Vitruve Pollion, Autheur Romain Antique; Mis de Latin En Francoys Par Ian Martin*. Paris: Jacque Gazeau, 1547. c. 15r.

1.4 Absent fire

As we have seen, though, fire is not always constructive. Accidental fires occur periodically, razing buildings and cities to the ground. Enemy forces and arsonists employ fire to the same effect intentionally. Of all the man-made and natural disasters to befall our cities, fires are perhaps the most physically damaging. Architectural discourse has had less to say about this destructive, free-burning fire. In one of the few edited collections dedicated to this topic, *Flammable Cities: Urban Conflagration and the Making of*

Figure 1.3 **Jean Goujon, illustration depicting the first building.** Source: Vitruvius, Marcus Pollio. *Architecture, Ou, Art de Bien Bastir de Marc Vitruve Pollion, Autheur Romain Antique; Mis de Latin En Francoys Par Ian Martin*. Paris: Jacque Gazeau, 1547. c. 15v.

the Modern World, editors Greg Bankoff, Uwe Lübken and Jordan Sands reflect on this paucity of literature.[19] Among architectural historians, they suggest that only Zeynep Çelik, in her account of Istanbul, acknowledges the extent to which fire acts as shaping force in city form.[20] More detailed accounts of fire and its effect on urban design have come from other disciplines, from history, economics, urban studies and environmental studies, even comparative literature. They include Christine Meisner Rosen's account of the Great Fires of Chicago, Boston and Baltimore, and their effect on city growth and infrastructure expansion[21]; Eric Jones and Lionels Frosts analysis of the impact of urban fire on the durability of property and economic development in the US and Asia[22]; Cathy Frierson's cultural history of fire and arson in Imperial Russia[23]; Stephen Pyne's encyclopaedic "Cycle of Fire", documenting the way that naturally occurring and anthropogenic fire have shaped and maintain our distinct regional ecologies[24]; and Ross Miller's account of the Chicago fire by way of its impact on architectural design and literary culture.[25] To that literature the authors of *Flammable Cities* add a range of studies that describe the way fire has shaped the legal and urban fabric of cities including Amsterdam, Beirut, Buenos Aires, Cleveland, Edo, Hamburg, Istanbul, Jakarta, Lagos, Lisbon, Manila, Montreal, Moscow, San Francisco, Singapore and Valparaiso.

Given the strong connection already identified between urban conflagration and urban renewal, we might be surprised at this relative lack of architectural literature. Beyond London, "grand" urban designs follow in the wake of "great" urban fires with such regularity that we might see the two as co-dependent. Indeed, some have suggested we recognise "fire [as] the ultimate locus of urban utopia".[26] Bankoff, Lübken and Sands suggest one reason that might explain that lack. Destructive fires, just like those in the hearth, are a less frequent feature of contemporary cities; they have disappeared from our experience and our thought.[27] The work of Lionel Frost and Eric Jones provides some support for this suggestion. Specifically concerned with the frequency and extent of urban fires, they use that frequency as an index of urban "modernity". For those authors the prevalence of urban fire is a problem that is clearly associated with the "pre-modern" city; indeed, its relative lack is what defines the "modern" city as such. We might recognise that historical trajectory without interpreting it in the same way that those authors do; given the way fire frequency patterns in relation to climate, to use it as an index of "modernity" would seem to reinforce an association between that term and north-Atlantic biomes. Further, reductions in frequency and extent do not map directly onto reductions in harm; the Great Fire of London destroyed over 13,000 properties, but it did so slowly, leading to six reported fatalities. Limited to a single building, the Grenfell Tower fire was more than ten times as deadly, due to a rapidity of spread only possible due to the combustibility of contemporary building materials, particularly plastics. The relationship between fire and "modernity" is therefore not easily summarised. A reflexive nuance is offered to that explanation elsewhere in the same collection. Stephen Pyne suggests that just as industrialisation removed open fires from our everyday lives, so too the Enlightenment sought to marginalise fire from our thought.[28] Associated with out-dated practices, fire-prone colonies, unreason and mysticism, fire has long ceased to be the informing concept it was for Lucretius or Vitruvius, having come to be thought of as a subsidiary problem for physics and engineering. While accounting for the way industrial society has sought to partition fire, to isolate it within carefully controlled spaces, Pyne charts the way fire-thinking has been removed from scientific thought, showing us that fire is today both out of sight and out of mind by design.

1.5 Fire and prohibition

The absence of fire in our buildings and cities is, of course, carefully constructed, the result of successive programmes of urban and architectural fire prevention. If the contemporary city is characterised by an absence of free-burning fire, then that lack is an index of the success of those measures. In that sense, fire is present in our cities by way of this absence; the less we see it around us, the more we know our circumstances have been shaped by a concern for fire-safety. That concern is the topic of this study; that absenting of fire is its "focus". The signs that point to it are familiar and pervasive, those features that seek to suppress fire and our exposure to it: fire-exit signs, fire-escape routes, fire-doors, fire-stairs and muster points; maximum room sizes and occupancy numbers; fire-lifts, fire-hoses and fire-extinguishers; measures to control flammable substances; enclosed gas combustion boilers, their pipes and ducts. We are surrounded by the designed absence of fire to such an extent that we have stopped noticing. But:

> [i]f you are looking for it you can see fire engineering, particularly in a modern building, absolutely everywhere ... the manufacture of the carpet, the things that are covering the walls, the latches on the windows, the plugs, the fire alarms, the sprinklers – everything about the room.[29]

Fire is likewise present in our thought by way of its absence. Legislators and architects, those who design the fire-safe environment, think less about the physical character of that element, more about its margins of safety; they handle fire by way of its negation, through permissible clearance times, maximum egress lengths and widths, through ratings for fire-resistance, combustibility, and surface spread of flame, through fire-safety regulations, codes, standards and norms. This mode of thinking makes fire marginal in another sense; because fire-safety knowledge is carried by standards and norms, its implications are pervasive, ubiquitous. Those who work with such standards come to take them for granted; they find those norms "normal". That is, by way of its standardisation, fire-safety shapes our environment without being foremost in the minds of those who design and build our buildings. The implications of fire-safe design have become "part of the woodwork"; they are invisible on account of their familiarity. Fire-safety standards make up part of what we might call architecture's "infrastructural unconscious" – those patterns of thought that shape design practice, without being at the forefront of designer's minds.[30] Or, in other words, fire-safety standards make up part of what Andreas Philippopoulos-Mihalopoulos calls our 'lawscape", that set of legal agreements and assumptions that are embedded within, and normalised by, the built environment. They form part of an incestuous intimacy that is constructed by our standards, codes and the built environment. Two kinds of normativity coincide and reinforce each other in the lawscape, that which is prescribed by law

becomes habitual and familiar in the environment. Law is the city's measure and the city is law's "megaphone"; the built environment enacts law,
at the same time sublimating it, such that "in the city law's presence is
magnified to a deafening extent – so much so that one no longer feels its
presence".[31] To study the "lawscape" of fire-safety is therefore to look for
the assumptions and assertions embedded in restrictions and proscriptions
existing in the world around us.

Fire is something we experience through its absence, through our distance from it, through rules, regulations and laws; this observation is not
particular to architecture and urban design, nor is it particularly "modern". Indeed, if we follow Gaston Bachelard we might consider them as
fundamental to a phenomenology of fire. In one of his many reflections
on this element, Bachelard reminds us that fire is not something we experience directly, for good reason; to handle fire is to risk getting burned.
Fire is something that is difficult to know about "objectively", its nature
and physics are obscure to most of us. Rather, what we think we know
about fire are those myths and legends, practices and conventions, rules
and regulations that surround it, those structures intended to ensure we
maintain a safe distance from it. As such, fire has a close association with
prohibition; what we first learn about it, usually from our parents, is that
we mustn't touch it. And when we do get burned, Bachelard suggests, what
we learn has less to do with fire and more to do with the legitimacy of
parental prohibition:

> [T]he natural experience comes only in second place to furnish a ma-
> terial proof which is unexpected and hence too obscure to establish an
> item of objective knowledge.[32]

Our distance from fire is, for Bachelard, a fundamental part of our relationship to it. Fire is not something we can understand as a natural object;
rather, fire is a properly social phenomenon, one that appears to us already
wrapped up in networks of care and concern. As such, our understanding
of this element is riddled with assumptions, unknowns, superstitions and
rules of thumb. We might wish to unpick those assumptions, and know
those unknowns, but opportunities to do so are rare. When fire suddenly
presents itself, within our buildings and cities, within our minds, it does so
unexpectedly, by surprise. What we learn from those moments – the Grenfell Tower fire, the Blitz, and the Great Fire of London – we always learn
too late. The understanding they offer is always already "forensic", partial, politicised, often limited to proving or disproving existing assumptions
and prohibitions. Those who would grasp fire directly are either half-mad
or half-God: Prometheus stealing power from Olympus, or Empedocles
throwing himself into Etna. For the rest of us this element must be approached with caution, by and through those networks of proscription and
prohibition that have already been drawn around it.

1.6 Architectures of fire-safety

This book explores how fire and the problem of fire-safety have shaped our built environment. It does so by describing a number of instances through which individual events and individual buildings come to be prompts for widespread programmes of urban change, particularly those enacted through changes to regulatory frameworks. It charts the effects of those programmes over time, considering the impact that specific regulations have on buildings, but also the way regulations themselves change, often in response to later fires. As illustrated by the opening reflection on the Grenfell fire, the way that our approach to this common problem develops across time, through a two-way dialogue between the city and law. Studying those moments in which fire breaks out in our buildings and cities, being momentarily thematised by designers and government, it considers our conscious response to this common phenomenon. But by considering the way that that response comes to be standardised, and taken for granted, it also illustrates the surprising side-effects of fire-safety regulation, the unintended problems created by governmental solutions. As such, the studies included here have a reflexive dimension; they seek to illustrate how, by way of standardisation, government has a shaping effect on building, but also how that effect bends back on its cause, such that buildings and fire exert a shaping effect on government.

The book is structured through a series of chapters that present distinct "city studies". They consider Edinburgh, Lagos, Tokyo and London. Those cities are chosen because, at particular moments in their history, they are shown to have had a particular proclivity to fire, giving them a regional importance in the development of fire-safe design. But those cities are also shown to form nodes within a global network of fire-safety knowledge, and attention is paid to the way fire-safety standards afford the movement of knowledge to and from those cities. Each city study begins with an account of a particular historic fire, an event that prompts a programme of fire-safety regulation. Those studies start by analysing the way those rules draw upon details of those particular fires, the governmental intent embedded within them and the way that intent is translated into design. Studying how those rules are applied by building designers, those studies continue to reflect on the way fire-safety intersects with other factors in building design, on the way standards come to be interpreted differently in different contexts, often coming to be "captured" by other interests. Perhaps most importantly, they seek out those moments in which fire-safety thinking is tested by later fires; that is, they are concerned with the way that fire itself challenges and problematises those governmental assumptions embedded within our built fabric. As such, those studies seek to demonstrate not only the close relationship between particular urban and legal environments but also how the two co-produce each other in complex and often surprising ways.

This book does not attempt to think about fire as either a physicist or an engineer might; it does not offer insight into the physical properties of fire, nor empirical analysis of the way built structures respond to fire. It approaches fire through the tools of the architect, that is, through those fire-safety standards that building design is subject to. The concerns and methods of the book are also shaped by this disciplinary perspective. The studies gathered here tend to focus on standards that provide organising principles for building design: spatial limitations on urban layout and the internal arrangement of buildings, and limitations on the use of combustible material. Those studies also employ by-design analysis as a means to understand the implications of particular legal frameworks, and their relation to the built fabric of particular buildings and cities. Many of the figures included in this book are active parts of the research process: analytic diagrams used to explore the spatiality inherent within certain standards, and survey drawings used to assess the compliance of those codes with as-built construction. However, unlike this introduction, the book seldom refers to the work of architectural historians or theorists. Rather, its ambition is to learn from other disciplines, particularly those that have engaged more closely with problems of urban fire and building standardisation, opening the work of those scholars to an architectural audience. The city studies work from historical accounts of particular fires and fire-safety regulations drawn from literatures in history, economics, urban studies and environmental studies. In analysing those programmes, though, this book is also informed by scholarship in two other fields. Drawing concepts and methods from Governmentality Studies, it seeks to understand the mentality embedded within our codes and standards, but also the way that mentality is transformed as it is translated into built fabric. Drawing from the field of Infrastructure Studies it outlines a schema through which we might assess the success of programmes of standardisation. Additionally, each city study is taken as an opportunity to bring historical material into dialogue with theoretical concerns; the city studies not only reflect upon but also seek to contribute to a range of concepts, including those of "Regulatory Space", "Seeing like a City", and "Governing through Uncertainty", as well as the broader discourse on "Risk". The concluding chapter engages with Law and Mol's term "Fire-Space", identifying a fire-like quality in standardisation itself. Using this term, the book concludes by reflecting on standardisation as a vector through which governmental ideas move and change.

1.7 Studying standardisation

Key terms and concepts employed in the city studies are introduced in more detail in the Chapter 2, through a review of recent literatures on standardisation. Developing a term from the late work of Michel Foucault, studies of governmentality show standards to be an important facet of governance in the post-war liberal democracies of Europe and America. The governmentality literatures are shown to focus on the discursive character of government; within the work of these scholars, standardisation is not taken to offer universal solutions to given problems, but is rather seen as a mode of problematising through which the scope and purpose of government comes to be constituted rationally, epistemologically and technically. With reference to Mitchell Dean's *Governmentality: Power and Rule in Modern Society*, this section introduces the key features of an "analytics of governance" – an analysis of the assumptions, rationalities, technologies and identities created by governmental programmes. A recognition of the "utopian" character of standards is seen to be key to that analysis; Dean suggests that the critical purchase offered by governmentality studies stems from the identification of gaps between the intent and effect of governmental programmes – gaps that emerge between the "governmental rationalities" that motivate an initiative and the "governmental technology" that it employs.

This chapter continues to review a further set of literatures on standardisation from scholars associated with actor network theory and infrastructure studies. These literatures are shown to complement and extend the critical ambitions of neo-Foucauldian scholarship. Their authors likewise highlight the difficulty of translating governmental ambitions into effective "technical delegates". Their focus on the material character of standardisation shifts analysis away from the stated intent of governmental programmes to concentrate on their often unintended consequences. As noted, the work of Susan Leigh Star is shown to be of particular relevance for this study in a number of ways. Her work reflects on a methodological challenge already implicit above – the difficulty of studying the impact of standards that are so pervasive, so "normal". In order to counter the normalising effect of norms, Leigh Star develops a methodology she refers to as "infrastructure inversion"; at certain moments the assumptions, rationalities, technologies or identities embedded within regulations and standards are suddenly "figured", becoming apparent in their partiality and contingency. In the case of this book, urban fire events provide such moments, moments in which the intents and effects of existing fire-safety standards are suddenly called into question, demonstrated as partial, politicised. Within those moments, Star prompts us to identify the "residues" of standardisation, its "textures", "mess-trajectories", "indeterminacy" and "practical politics", prompts which the following city studies take up in turn. Finally, through her concept of the boundary object, Leigh Star is shown to offer a schema of standardisation, one that suggests that the success of a standard depends on its ability to accommodate, among those gathered by a particular problem, different kinds and different levels of understanding. This schema is adopted as a means to assess the success of specific regulatory measures studied.

1.8 The shape of the British National Anthem

The first city study (Chapter 3) focusses on Edinburgh, using that city as a means to reflect on the close relationship between standards and the physical context within which they emerge. It does so first by recounting the details of the 1911 Empire Palace Theatre fire, showing how details of a particular building have, since that event, come to be reproduced across the world, being incorporated within *BS 9999:2008 Code of practice for fire safety in the design, management and use of buildings*. While recognising the contingent basis of this standard, the ambition here is less to criticise and more to demonstrate the complex network of concerns and factors that came to define "travel distance" as a governmental concept. This single standard is then situated in a broader historical trajectory. The chapter offers a brief overview of the development of Edinburgh's fire-safety legislation, charting a series of reflexive exchanges through which built fabric and legal framework came to co-produce each other. The city and its legislation are presented as an archaeology of "governmentality", of that process through which contemporary liberal governments have come to understand their role as one of ensuring the health, safety and well-being of the population. This case-study is then used as an opportunity to contribute to contemporary literatures on regulatory governance, here specifically to the concept of "Regulatory Space". Defined by Leigh Hancher and Michael Moran, this concept is shown to recognise – within discourses on public policy – how legislative frameworks are shaped by historically and geographically specific stakeholders. The contribution made by this chapter is to take Hancher and Moran's metaphor literally, and to reflect on the role of non-human actors – space, stone, gravity, water and fire – in shaping such frameworks. The chapter concludes by reflecting on what happens when codes and standards travel; it does so by studying the globalisation of travel distance – through British Standard 9999 – as an example of the way governmentalities move, and come to be reinterpreted in new contexts.

1.9 The flight of a muzzle spark

The second city study continues that exploration of the way that codes transform as they travel, moving here from Britain to Nigeria. It again begins with a specific fire, occurring shortly after the cession of Lagos, and its importance in justifying the importation of British legal frameworks to this colonial dependency. Specifically, it studies the first British by-law imposed in Lagos, the setback code of 1863. This regulation is shown to outlaw existing building practices and to justify forced demolition – requiring a fire-safety separation between buildings and the street – as well as requiring the importation of specific British building products. It is also shown to shape the contemporary character of the city, enforced today through Lagos State Physical Planning Department Regulation 15. The ambition of the chapter, however, is not to critique the colonial origins of the rule, but rather to track the way that its intent and effects have transformed, tacitly and explicitly, in the intervening period, becoming associated with a wide range of other problems, from infection control and environmental regulation to aesthetic concerns. This case study is again used as a prompt for broader reflection, here on the political ambivalence of any governmental technology, standards included. This reflection engages with the work of Marianne Valverde and Warren Magnusson – particularly their concept of "Seeing Like a City" – and their recognition that this ambivalence is necessary, a means through which the sovereign violence that underwrites law is gradually "recycled" into the everyday life of the city. Again, the ambition here is to extend this argument, highlighting the role that architecture and the built environment play in that process of appropriation.

1.10 Spectres of Edo Castle

The third city study uses Tokyo as a means through which to reflect on the historical imaginaries of fire, and the way they shape attitudes to risk. It begins by describing three catastrophic fires that have shaped the city of Edo/Tokyo: the Great Fire of Meireki, the Great Canto Earthquake and the Great Tokyo Air Raid. It identifies two urban-regulatory measures developed by the Shogun in response to the first of those events – the promotion of fire-safe construction and of land ownership adjustment. It goes on to study the dramatic way in which these two practices have come to shape the fabric of that city, and its ways of thinking about governing more broadly, coming to be considered the "mother of urban design" in Japan. Nonetheless, it notes their limited application, and their failure to stop repeated catastrophic fires within that city. Indeed, it identifies a series of "mess-trajectories" which these governmental programmes appear to construct. Ulrich Beck's *Risk Society* analytic is drawn on as a means to reflect on the tendency of governmental programmes to reflexively sustain problems they purport to address. Beck's analysis is likewise used to support a reflection on standards and historical imagination; this chapter outlines a number of historical circumstances through which a fire-prone built environment has come to be understood and appreciated as essentially "Japanese". Nonetheless, the chapter concludes by suggesting that fire is responsible for a process of "enforced cosmopolitanism" in contemporary Tokyo, one that brings with it new construction technologies, fire-safety approaches and modes of tenure.

1.11 Engineering uncertainty

The final two city studies both focus on London. The first of those turns to the question of deregulating fire-safety, considering the opportunities and problems this poses for the liberal governmentality. It begins by recounting the New York World Trade Center attack and subsequent debates over the building's structural collapse, and the collateral effect those debates have had on the UK's legislative context. This chapter focusses not on a specific code, but rather on a number of initiatives pioneered by Arup Associates to computationally model the dynamics of fire, smoke and crowd behaviour, and the ways these have been used to circumvent prescriptive legislative frameworks. It situates these initiatives within the emergence of fire-safety science and its ambition to develop "performance-based" standards. Identifying epistemological and practical difficulties within this ambition, it suggests that they be recognised as an attempt to meta-engineer the legislative frameworks of UK professional practice. It reflects on this attempt through Pat O'Malley's notion of "governing by uncertainty", and Foucault's "environmentality" of government. Concluding with a close analysis of one of the key instruments of fire-safety engineering – Arup's MassMotion software package – it returns to the problem of egress time, noting how this software black-boxes assumptions identified in *BS9999*.

1.12 Trial by fire

The final study continues a reflection on fire-safety and deregulation here in relation to the Grenfell Tower fire. It begins by tracing the route that fire took, on the 14th of June 2017, through the physical fabric of that building, charting a series of failures in particular construction details that allowed for its fatal spread. It goes on to draw out a parallel legal trajectory, studying the processes of standardisation intended to assure those construction details were safe. In doing so it presents fire as a "trial", a means of testing the strength of both our physical structures as well as our governing mentalities. In doing so, it offers a critique of Dame Judith Hackitt's *Building A Safer Future*, and the need to individuate the "ownership" of risk. With reference to details of the Grenfell fire, it considers the difficulty in attributing a single actor – social or technical – responsible for that event, arguing that fire is a risk that spreads whether we like it or not. Rather, it suggests that we understand that fire as the compound effect of a wide range of deregulatory agendas. It concludes by reflecting on the obduracy of the Tower itself as an example of what happens to the artefact of building as it is stripped of its governmental rationalities.

1.13 Fire space

The concluding chapter begins with a summary of the standardisation stories told so far. Within each chapter it seeks to identify key moments of exchange through which fire prompts new ways of thinking about building and governing. In the process of abstracting new rules from existing buildings, or of concretising existing codes in new structures, our ways of thinking about building and governing change. In this exchange between the material and the discursive, the general and the particular, neither the object of government nor its technical delegates remain static – flickering, unpredictable, changing, spreading, the process of standardisation is described here as being fire-like in character. This concluding observation is extended with reference to the work of Gaston Bachelard, John Law and Anne Marie Mol. For these scholars, fire will be shown to act as an explanatory metaphor for the "spatiality" of science and technology. Appropriating a term from Law and Mol, this section seeks to describe a spatial character proper to those standards studied. What we discover when we study standards is not the emergence of a set of universal or transferable logics or practices, but rather a flickering exchange between facts and artefacts, abstractions and concretisations, localities and networks. This spatial understanding is offered as a means to reflect on standardisation in general, but also particularly fire-safety standards. The conclusion ends by noting some of the material characteristics of fire that make this problem, and those programmes of regulation that follow in its wake, particularly decisive for urban design.

Taken together, this collection hopes to contribute a series of studies on the historical impact of fire on urban and architectural design, but also to make a timely and novel a contribution to architectural theory. In particular, it sees itself as part of a turn towards the study of those "infrastructures", both material and conceptual, that underpin architecture as a discipline and a practice.[33] To that discourse this study offers a reflection on the shaping effect of fire, regulation and standards on contemporary design practice.

Notes

1 Laurence Ward, *The London County Council Bomb Damage Maps 1939–1945*, 01 edition (London: Thames & Hudson, 2015).
2 Charles Booth, *Charles Booth's London Poverty Map* (London: The British Library, 1898), Maps C.21.a.18. (295). SE sheet.
3 Andrew Saint, 'Lessons from London', in *Cities for the New Millennium* (London: Taylor & Francis, 2001). p. 159.
4 Pynchon, *Gravity's Rainbow* (New York: The Viking Press, 1973).
5 'Grenfell Resident Who Raised Fire Concerns Labelled Troublemaker, Inquiry Told', *The Guardian*, 21 April 2021, http://www.theguardian.com/uk-news/2021/apr/21/grenfell-resident-who-raised-fire-concerns-labelled-troublemaker-inquiry-told.
6 'Grenfell Tower Was Covered in Material to Make It Look Better. That's Being Blamed for Multiple Deaths', *The Independent*, 8 August 2017, https://www.independent.co.uk/news/uk/home-news/grenfell-tower-cladding-fire-cause-improve-kensington-block-flats-appearance-blaze-24-storey-west-london-a7789951.html.
7 Edward Dafarn and Francis O'Connor's blog recounts in detail the history of their concerns as regards fire-safety at Grenfell Tower, and local opposition to estate redevelopment. See 'Grenfell Action Group', Grenfell Action Group, accessed 17 August 2021, https://grenfellactiongroup.wordpress.com/.

8 Simon J. Jenkins, 'The Lesson from Grenfell Is Simple: Stop Building Residential Towers', *The Guardian*, accessed 29 June 2018, https://www.theguardian.com/commentisfree/2017/jun/15/lessons-grenfell-tower-safer-cladding-tower-blocks.

9 Pyne, *Vestal Fire: An Environmental History, Told Through Fire, of Europe and Europe's Encounter with the World*, Reprint edition (Seattle: University of Washington Press, 2000). p. 368.

10 Marcus Vitruvius Pollio and Joseph Gwilt, *The Architecture of Vitruvius, Book II* (Cambridge: Cambridge University Press, 2015). p. 33.

11 Pollio and Gwilt. p. 33.

12 Pollio and Gwilt. p. 69.

13 Olga Medvedkova offers this visual analysis of Vitruvius' illustrators in O. Medvedkova, '4 In the Beginning, There Was Fire: Vitruvius and the Origin of the City', *Wounded Cities: The Representation of Urban ...*, 2015.

14 Corbusier's elemental thinking is addressed in Esra Sahin's doctoral dissertation. See E. Sahin, *'Exchange of Forces: Environmental Definition of Materials in the Works of Vitruvius, Alberti, Le Corbusier, and Peter Zumthor'* (Philadelphia: University of Pennsylvania, 2009). pp. 130–191.

15 Banham, *Architecture of the Well-Tempered Environment* (Chicago: University of Chicago Press, 1984).

16 Lisa Heschong, *Thermal Delight in Architecture* (Cambridge, MA: MIT Press, 1979).

17 Joseph Rykwert, *On Adam's House in Paradise, Second Edition: The Idea of the Primitive Hut in Architectural History* (Cambridge, MA: MIT Press, 1981); Joseph Rykwert, *The Idea of a Town: The Anthropology of Urban Form in Rome, Italy and the Ancient World* (London: Faber & Faber, 2013).

18 Guillén Fernández and Luis Fernández-Galiano, *Fire and Memory: On Architecture and Energy* (Cambridge, MA: MIT Press, 2000).

19 Greg Bankoff, Uwe Lübken, and Jordan Sand, *Flammable Cities: Urban Conflagration and the Making of the Modern World* (Madison: University of Wisconsin Pres, 2012).

20 Zeynep Çelik, *The Remaking of Istanbul: Portrait of an Ottoman City in the Nineteenth Century* (Oakland: University of California Press, 1993).

21 Christine Meisner Rosen, *The Limits of Power: Great Fires and the Process of City Growth in America* (Cambridge, New York: Cambridge University Press, 2003).

22 L. E. Frost and E. L. Jones, 'The Fire Gap and the Greater Durability of Nineteenth Century Cities', *Planning Perspectives* 4, no. 3 (1 September 1989): 333–347; Lionel Frost, 'Coping in Their Own Way: Asian Cities and the Problem of Fires', *Urban History* 24, no. 1 (May 1997): 5–16.

23 Cathy A. Frierson, *All Russia Is Burning!: A Cultural History of Fire and Arson in Late Imperial Russia* (Seattle: University of Washington Press, 2002).

24 The 'Cycle of Fire' is a series of six books, published by Weyerhaeuser Environmental Books, through which Pyne explores how fire has shaped specific national and regional ecologies. The cycle concludes with *Vestal Fire*, which explores the exportation of European fire-regimes through colonial expansion and globalisation. See Pyne, *Vestal Fire*.

25 Ross Miller, *American Apocalypse: The Great Fire and the Myth of Chicago* (Chicago: University of Chicago Press, 1990).

26 O. Medvedkova, '4 In the Beginning, There Was Fire: Vitruvius and the Origin of the City', in *Wounded Cities: The Representation of Urban ...*, 2015: 76.

27 Bankoff, Lübken, and Sand, *Flammable Cities*. pp. 5–6.

28 Stephen Pyne, 'Fire on the Fringe', in *Flammable Cities: Urban Conflagration and the Making of the Modern World*, vol. 390–396 (Madison: University of Wisconsin Press, 2012); Stephen Pyne, 'Fire in the Mind: Changing

Understandings of Fire in Western Civilization', *Philosophical Transactions of the Royal Society B: Biological Sciences* 371, no. 1696 (5 June 2016).

29 Luke Bisby quoted in Nick Collins, 'Professor of Fire: Safety Laws "Absurd"', 22 October 2013, sec. News, http://www.telegraph.co.uk/news/science/science-news/10393435/Professor-of-Fire-safety-laws-absurd.html.

30 I'm borrowing here a phrase from Vandertop in Caitlin Vandertop, 'Travel Literature and the Infrastructural Unconscious', in *Smethurst, Paul, and Julia Kuehn, eds. New Directions in Travel Writing Studies* (London: Palgrave Macmillan, 2015). pp. 129–144.

31 Andreas Philippopoulos-Mihalopoulous, *Law and the City* (London: Routledge, 2007). p. 9.

32 Gaston Bachelard, *Psychoanalysis of Fire* (Boston: Beacon Press, 1977). p. 10.

33 By this turn I refer most directly to the work of Aggregate Architectural History Collaborative, whose work intentionally turns away from the high-culture and politics of architectural modernism to consider seemingly mundane concerns: the ways in which the built environment is used to establish protocols, rules and structures that regulate the basic aspects of our social lives, so conducting our conduct. In their first published compendium, *Governing by Design*, they present that work as a collective response to the Foucauldian concept of "Governmentality". In the UK, the work of Katie Lloyd Thomas, Nick Beech and Tilo Amhof has likewise been particularly informative, through symposia and conferences published in *Architectural Research Quarterly 16* "Further Reading Required" and Routledge's *Industries of Architecture*. The work of Adam Bobbette, which often also studies fire, has likewise extended this notion of "infrastructure" to consider the material and environmental media on which architecture culture depends. Beyond the Anglo-American sphere, the work of Caterina Gabrielsson and Helena Mattsson, whose work likewise engages with the question of regulation and Governmentality, should also be noted as influential to the current study.

2 Context

Studying standardisation

2.1 The architect and standardisation

2.1.1 Ambivalent identities

The role of the architect has, at points in history, been very close to that of the legislator and regulator. For Vitruvius the writing of books was a more effective way to shape the built environment than the design of individual buildings. His *Ten Books* are, in effect, an early form of legislation, providing detailed prescriptions for the design of buildings intended to govern a diverse range of concerns: visual affects, physical and thermal comfort, acoustic phenomena, environmental control, the regular distribution of water and hence the accurate measurement of time. Medieval Cathedral building programmes were important laboratories of building design as well as social organisation; built prior to the existence of common units of measurement, their masons played an important role in defining the need and means of metric standardisation. More recently, Corbusier's *Le Modulor*, developed for the French National Organisation for Standardisation, proposed a new metric standard that sought to embed harmonic proportions and anthropometric measure not only in his own buildings but pervasively within the products of industrial standardisation. However, for contemporary architects, at least in the UK, regulations and standards appear less as a means to expand the scope of their design practice, more as an impediment to it. In *Architectural Design and Regulation* Rob Imrie and Emma Street interview practicing architects in order to gauge their attitude to planning requirements and building standards. The prevailing view saw regulation as a barrier to innovation, leading to mundane and repetitive designs, associated with technical inertia and bureaucratic management rather than the public good. While many offered a more nuanced view, a majority of UK practitioners agreed that "Architecture is subject to too much regulation", and that "Architecture is too bound up in red tape and prescriptive standards". There was strong agreement with the sense that "Regulation is becoming more complex", and that "Regulation is becoming more difficult to deal with". Likewise, architects felt disengaged, agreeing with the

DOI: 10.4324/9781003026297-2

statement "I am rarely consulted by government about planning control and building regulations".[1]

In explaining these views, Imrie and Street suggest that regulations are experienced by architects as a threat to their role in design and construction. When asked to talk about codes and standards, many architects expressed concern about,

> a dissolution of professional identities and a dispersal of functions to contractors and others not traditionally part of the design and construction process. There is ambivalence about professional identity and role ascription, so that it is no longer easy to identify who does what, or who, precisely, is the architect.[2]

This concern is easy to understand. If Vitruvius or Corbusier seem to embody the role of the architect as the "commander, chief, or captain" that governs construction, today building design appears to be regulated by an increasingly complex and diverse array of governmental requirements: acts of parliament and the mandatory standards they enforce, codes of conduct required by professional bodies, bi-lateral agreements under contract law, the industrial standards and technical guidelines that underwrite warranties and assurances, as well as voluntary modes of performance certification promoted by the marketplace. These frameworks relate to a range of governmental concerns broader than those covered in the *Ten Books*. They include the need to safeguard the health and safety of construction workers and the public, the definition and enforcement of professional accountability, ambitions to increase industrial efficiency through cross-platform compatibility, and the desire to limit the environmental cost of buildings and their operation. In practice, such rules can and do conflict with the design intent of clients and architects. Tasked with ensuring compliance, architects have mixed feeling about such regulations, which define but also de-limit their position of authority.

2.1.2 *Usurp, subvert, invent, comply*

The ambivalent relationship between architecture and regulation is addressed by a number of recent academic publications, and their contents illustrate similar concerns. *Hunch 12* addressed the theme of "Bureaucracy", using architectures interaction with governmental regulation as a means to demonstrate the contingent character of the discipline, its dependence on criteria and demands defined by others.[3] *Perspecta 35* was dedicated to the theme of "Building Codes", likewise suggesting that architecture today is bounded, shaped and directed by codes and standards, but also noting that these are seldom the focus of its critical or creative inquiry.[4] Through the theme of "Further Reading Required", *Architectural Research Quarterly 16* considered the disciplinary consequences of written specifications in product literatures and governmental regulation, here suggesting that this topic is often overlooked by scholarship.[5] *Volume 38* sought to sketch out "The Shape of Law", asking a range of architects and academics, "how to deal with the law?" In response to this presumed problem, they record a diverse set of strategies adopted by architects to re-define, avoid or subvert existing legal frameworks.[6] Similarly, *Architectural Theory Review* 20/2 studied "Corruption", gathering together stories of legislation, planning, tax rules, price cartels and safety restrictions all understood as limits that spur forms of creative interpretation and work-arounds.[7] *ARCH+ 50*, titled "Legislating Architecture", reminded architects that law itself is designed, enthusing architects to engage with the design of regulation as a mode of practice, evidently assuming this was not the norm.[8]

The work documented in these literatures often celebrate those moments in which the architect exhibits their authority in opposition to imposed governmental frameworks. The work of Spain's "guerrilla architect" Santiago Cirugeda, for instance, offers a critique of the way that governmental regulations, enforced by architects, frustrate the capacity of individual citizens to improve their own environment. His website *Recetas Urbanas* provides a repository of the ways in which codes and standards can be subverted, re-directed to novel ends. He instructs the public on how to use a scaffolding permit to construct an extension, or a skip permit to create a temporary urban park.[9] The work of Arno Brandlhuber and collaborators wrestles with rules in a variety of ways, sometimes breaking them, sometimes seeming to comply excessively. The "2.56" building in Cologne contravenes a German building code that requires every building to be self-supporting. Seeking to make best use of a 2.56 m wide gap-site, the practice brokered an owner's obligation to cover the cost of compartment wall retention in the event of demolition. As such, the new structure was permitted to bear upon the neighbouring buildings, setting a legal precedent in Germany. By contrast, the "Krystal" building in Copenhagen adheres exactly to local clearance and setback ordinances. Like the diagrams of Hugh Ferris, its built form is surprising and novel, while emerging from and complying with local norms.[10] The work of Luigi Snozzi perhaps best demonstrates the architect's fraught relationship with building codes. As part of a masterplan for the Swiss town of Monte Carasso, Snozzi was offered the chance to re-write local building by-laws. He proposed a set of seven rules (known as the "Snozzi 7"), intended to replace the existing two-hundred-and-forty clause code. Clause 1 stated that "any intervention must come to terms with the structure of the place", while Clause 2 defined the need for a "local structure" expert to adjudicate project compliance. Snozzi nominated himself as the only qualified expert to take on that role.[11] As such, an attempt to simplify the rules collapsed into mystification, and a bald assertion of personal sovereignty. That is, architectural literatures on regulation – be they interviews with practitioners, or reflection on celebrated works – are often overshadowed by a central concern. If *arché* is the first principle or rule, then architecture is the physical expression of rule, of the government of building. As such, the architect is rule personified. Thought as such, the dispersal of building design decisions to an increasingly complex and widespread regulatory framework appears as a threat to the autonomy of architecture, and to the traditional role of the architect.

That concern is not the subject of this book. Rather, this study recognises that in contemporary practice authority for design decisions is radically dispersed. It understands regulation and standardisation as modes of governance designed to facilitate that circumstance of distributed authority. Its ambition is the study of regulation and standardisation as modes of design in themselves. To make that study, it steps away from architectural literatures, and from the subject-position of the architect. Rather, it seeks to draw insight into practices of building regulation by drawing on concepts and methods from other fields, particularly those that have contributed to recent literatures on standardisation as a mode of government. This chapter offers a brief introduction to Governmentality Studies, Science and Technology Studies, and Infrastructure Studies, summarising the contributions they have made to the study of standardisation. In each case it outlines the particular problems they raise with respect to standardisation, the key concepts and methods used in their analysis, as well as the ambitions and limits of that analysis. Each section concludes by noting the ways in which concepts and methods drawn from those fields inform the work gathered in this volume.

2.2 Governmentality and standards

2.2.1 *Regularity and contingency*

The concept of "Governmentality" is associated with the work of Michel Foucault, particularly his late work at the Collège de France. In Foucault's work it names both that circumstance of dispersed and decentralised authority that exists in liberal democracies today, but also a way of thinking about governing that recognises this as an activity we are all involved in, all the time. But the question of how to conceive of a decentred and distributed model of authority is common to all of Foucault's work. He is associated with a repeated call to "cut off the king's head" in political theory. We hear this in *Power/Knowledge*,[12] and again in the *History of Sexuality,* where he suggests that any attempt to theorise "power" is necessarily connected with its legitimation:

> At bottom, despite the differences in epochs and objectives, the representation of power has remained under the spell of monarchy. In political thought and analysis, we still have not cut off the head of the king. Hence the importance of the theory of power of right and violence, law and legality, freedom and will, and especially the state and sovereignty.[13]

Foucault's work shifts focus away from authority and its self-theorisation, instead studying "practical systems", practices and technologies that embed relations of power within everyday life.[14] His celebrated studies of the prison and the clinic, for instance, argue that authority claims develop and are channelled through diverse and contingent social and epistemological frameworks, as opposed to being legitimated by any singular source of "sovereignty". For Foucault, positions of authority emerge in contingent and ad hoc fashion. Underpinned by violence, they come to be limited, gaining homogeneity and stability, through discourse. Through the analysis of discourse, he suggests, we can see how the problems and concerns of politics or science are themselves governed, at any given historical moment, by particular epistemic codes, or "rules of formation".[15] His work traces the mutually supportive relationship between these knowledge frameworks and the practices they rationalise, identifying "discursive regularities" that occur across disciplines within a given period (his archaeological method), and the transformations that occur within them over time (his genealogical method).

The critical ambition of Foucault's work is perhaps most succinctly illustrated through what he called the "paradox of the relations of capacity and power".[16] If knowledge and power are mutually supporting, then increased understanding might seem connected to increasing subjectification, even subjugation. We might recognise this "paradox" in the concerns already noted by practicing architects above; through developments in science and technology, our construction capabilities are greater than they have ever been. Nonetheless, in our interactions with increasingly complex systems of production, we might experience that increase in overall capability as a reduction in individual autonomy. Our own activity might tend to become more rule-bound. Foucault's work asks, "[h]ow can the growth of capabilities be disconnected from the intensification of power relations?"[17] Throughout his work, Foucault intentionally avoids an attempt to offer trans-historical principles of good government, not wishing to lend his own authority to any one mode of governance. In terms that resonate with the architectural literatures summarised above, his work asks, "in what is given to us as universal, necessary, obligatory, what place is occupied by whatever is singular, contingent, and the product of arbitrary constraints?" By identifying the assumptions and contingencies that underpin relations of knowledge and power, his work seeks to demonstrate their "fault lines" and "powers of consolidation", rendering them open to change.

2.2.2 *"Shifting the centre of gravity of governmental action downward"*

While Foucault's most celebrated works address the institutions of the early modern period, his later work at the Collège de France turns to focus directly on the discursive regularities of contemporary government.

In *Security, Territory and Populations,* and then more fully in *The Birth of Biopolitics* he offers a genealogical study of Liberalism, conceived not as a coherent philosophy, but as a means of critiquing government, a process of self-limitation within government. He charts those transformations in political thought – from Machiavelli to Wilhelm Ropke – through which theoretical questions of sovereignty and Right come be supplanted by practical questions concerning the management of the national economy.[18] As in his earlier studies, this genealogy seeks to demonstrate how novel ways of knowing and governing emerge together; new ways of knowing a population give rise to new governmental problems, and new technologies of governance. Across the series as a whole, he describes a process of "governmentalising" power, a process that involves "shifting the centre of gravity of governmental action downward" from reflections on legitimacy, to an increasing practical and technical imbrication with the health, safety, welfare, education and economic productivity of the population.[19]

Foucault uses the term "governmentality" to name this shift, one that he suggests occurs within government, but also within his own tools of analysis. That is, in Foucault's work the term has two distinct but related connotations. On the one hand it denotes his object of study, not "government" as a singular point of authority, but rather the "mentality to govern" itself. He uses the term to direct attention away from the exercise of state authority by those in positions of political power, towards a more diverse and disparate array of practices and technologies that "conduct conduct" in one way or other. He studies the way these operate at the scale of the individual, family, or institution, through modes of other-government, underpinned by law and violence, but also ethical concerns, practices and technologies of self-government.[20]

Foucault also uses the term to periodise a particular way that the state, in conditions of liberal democracy, comes to think about governing. He suggests that what characterises the mentality of a specifically neo-liberal government is its heightened awareness of the self-governing capacity of the population. The result of the liberal critique of government, he suggests, is that state power increasingly attempts to operate on and through diverse, disparate and emergent govern-mentalities. What "governmentality" names is a particular form of government, one that takes the population as its object, conceives its role as capacitating rather than disciplining, and measures its success in terms of economics – both national economic performance and the economy of government itself. He suggests the term as a label for the state of liberal thinking in post-war Germany, France, Britain and the US, where dispersed modalities of authority – particularly scientific and statistical analysis of the national economy, and questions of health, safety and security – come to predominate over direct assertions of sovereign right, or active techniques of discipline and punishment.[21]

2.2.3 Non-subjective intent

The term governmentality has subsequently been adopted by a number of Anglophone neo-Foucauldian scholars who have defined it more precisely as both a means and object of study. In *Governmentality: Power and Rule in Modern Society*, Mitchell Dean offers a succinct summary of the work of such scholars, with a view to outlining their characteristic assumptions and modes of analysis. The work of these scholars often focusses on practices of regulatory governance, and Dean's summary is useful to define a number of terms that will be used more widely within this study. Studies of Governmentality, Dean suggests, usually begin by identifying concrete "problems". Governmental programmes – be they practices of self-government or authoritarian practices – begin with a desire to change a given circumstance. The first question to consider with respect to such programmes is to identify who problematises that circumstance, and why? Like Foucault, Dean suggests that governmentality scholars assume that governmental problems do not pre-exist their discursive formation. There are no universal problems; all have contingent historical origins and trajectories. The first object of analysis for these scholars is to identify the particular way that, within liberal democracy, such problems tend to emerge and come to be shaped.

Dean suggests that we can understand how those problems are shaped through the interaction of four key parameters. Governmental programmes are typified by their "rationality"; that is, the liberal discourse on government is one that requires authority, particularly state authority, to constantly justify and rationalise itself. Authority positions are not conceived as sovereign, or Right; the rules they impose are subject to constant negotiation, and understood as means to limit the action of government, as well as the population. The rationality of government is itself dependent on specific forms of "visibility"; in order to govern an aspect of a population, one must first know about that aspect, render it visible and knowable. Governmentality is therefore a mode of authority through which the rationalities of government are themselves de-limited epistemologically. Ways of seeing, knowing and acting are, in turn, technologically mediated. Governmental programmes always come with their own "techne", with material practices and technologies that describe limits of knowledge and action. Finally, govern-mentalities produce and depend upon "identities"; as opposed to disciplinary forms of authority, they depend upon the willingness of individuals to engage in self-government, assuming or renouncing particular subject-positions.[22]

The critical dimension offered by these scholars often begins by recognising a "utopian" dimension within a given govern-mentality. All governmental action, Dean recognises, contains an irreducibly utopian intent; an assumption that the conduct of conduct is possible, that a different world can be constructed. But programmes of governance are also utopian in another way; they often tend to simplify reality, to seek out positive reinforcement of their own action, and to be blind to their side-effects, or to other concerns. Without imposing principles of good government, governmentality scholars often study disjunctions between the intent and effects of governmental action. By identifying the "non-subjective intentionality" of government, the things it does without meaning to, we can get to grips with a circumstance of "headless" rule.[23]

2.2.4 The utopia of standards

The work of Marianna Valverde, cited by Dean, applies this form of analysis to questions of urban regulation.[24] In *Seeing Like a City: The Dialectic of Modern and Premodern Ways of Seeing in Urban Governance* Valverde demonstrates the utopian character of comprehensive zoning in the US. Walking around her native Toronto in the company of a planner, she is shocked to learn of the prevalence of "legal non-conforming use" as a zoning code, a means to legally recognise non-compliance within the law. Finding that up to 50% of the city is subject to formal or informal exceptions, she shows that conventional critique of such zoning laws fail to understand the reality of that practice.[25] In *Everyday Law on the Street,* again focussed on Toronto, she considers that city's claim to be the world's most "diverse". Examining programmes intended to support democratic engagement she finds that instruments such as mandatory public consultations often disadvantage the marginalised groups they are ostensibly designed for, who are less likely to attend. As such she argues against the rhetorical localism advocated by the city.[26] Dean cites the work of Pat O'Malley's as an example of a neo-Foucauldian approach to the discourse on risk. Dean suggests that O'Malley's work demonstrates the political polyvalence of this concept, describing how it can be invested with different political purposes, associated at times with an increased socialisation of hazards, at other times working towards individualisation and the development of "practices of the self".[27]

The work of these scholars is drawn upon explicitly in particular chapters of this book. Valverde's work is engaged with in Chapter 4 as part of a reflection on the intents and effects of urban fire-safety policies in Lagos. O'Malley's work is engaged with in Chapter 6, through a reflection on uncertainty within the computational modelling of occupant egress. Beyond those specific references, though, this book suggests that the study of building regulations can be informed by governmentality studies more generally. The work of these scholars supports a shift focus in focus away from concerns over the architect's authority, towards a concern for the ways in which our built environment is shaped through forms of decentred authority. These literatures suggest that we recognise building standardisation as one of those "practical systems" through which positions of authority and forms of knowledge are co-constructed. They suggest that we recognise such practices are historically specific and politically polyvalent. Indeed, Dean's "analytics of government" can be applied directly to the study of building standards; regulations and standards are means of rationalising governmental action, dependent upon specific means of knowing and seeing the population, shaped by intervening technologies, and resulting in the formation of specific professional identities. Most importantly for this study, Valverde and Dean's work suggests that critical insight can be offered by drawing attention to divergence between the intents and effects of building regulation.

2.3 Standards in science and technology

2.3.1 *Technology and actancy*

If one group of recent literatures on standardisation are informed by the concept of governmentality, another group draw concepts and methods from the Sociology of Scientific Knowledge, and more specifically from Actor Network Theory (ANT). In *Calculating the Social: Standards and the reconfiguration of governing*, Vaughan Higgins and Wendy Larner gather together and reflect on this literature. Summarising the approach taken by these scholars, Higgins and Larner note a number of features common to those we have identified in the governmentality literature. The work presented in *Calculating the Social* draws attention to the importance of standards as a particularly contemporary technology of governance. Standards are understood as means to "conduct conduct" in widely diverging circumstances, across public and private sector organisations, in relation to legal or voluntary frameworks. Higgins and Larner likewise note that critical attention should be paid to the way that governmental intents and effects diverge; indeed, they place a particular emphasis on the interpretative flexibility of standards, their capacity to be turned to novel ends.[28]

It is the emphasis placed on this last issue that perhaps characterises ANT-informed studies of standardisation. Higgins and Larner dwell on this explicitly in their editorial, outlining what they perceive as the limits of Foucauldian scholarship. They suggest that the governmentality literature offers useful concepts and methods for analysing the discursive formation of government, recognising regulations and standards as epistemological devices, means by which concepts – safety, convenience or sustainability – come to be constituted, awarded the force of law, and marked out in the social and physical world. However, they suggest that these literatures remain too focussed on the "mentality" of government, and pay too little attention to practical problems that emerge when applying codes and standards in practice.

> While studies of governmentality draw attention to how standards are constituted as objects of knowledge, and the consequences for practices of governing, this body of literature can be criticized for focusing primarily on rule at the programmatic level. This arguably limits the capacity for governmentality studies to engage in a meaningful way

with the complexities of how governing works and achieves particular effects. Such a limitation can be traced to the distinction between rationalities and technologies of governing. Technologies are conceptualized as the technical means for making (discursive) rationalities of rule possible in a programmatic form. What is overlooked, however, is the material problematics of making such programmes workable in practice.[29]

If Foucauldian scholarship tends to focus on discourse, on what government says about governing, ANT-informed scholarship is more concerned with what actors do, rather than what they say.[30] And where governmentality studies identify a distinction between the "rationalities" and "technologies" of government, ANT-informed scholarship sees a more fundamental schism. Their scholarship is often concerned with the difficulty of translating a particular rationale into an effective "technical delegate", but they insist that technology never simply represents what we want it to, rather always brings its own "actancy". This set of literatures offer useful concepts for the study of standardisation, again drawn on later in the book. The following section introduces some of those concepts, contextualising these specific concerns within actor network theory itself.

2.3.2 Material stability, discursive flexibility

Though Actor Network Theory developed in the field of Science and Technology Studies (STS), its addresses concerns analogous to those of Foucault, but offers distinctly different findings. Contributing to debates on the politics of science and technology, the work of these scholars seeks to shift attention away from the truth claims of science, and towards the effects that it has in the world. In doing so they suggest that though scientific work depends upon the collaboration of a wide variety of people and things, this collaboration does not produce or depend upon a common "episteme". They suggest that, even in terms of its self-understanding, the scientific community is riven with controversy. Furthermore, in terms of its social practices, they suggest that we recognise it depends upon and is shaped by a wide range of actors, each of whom bring with them their own agendas and concerns, be they personal, commercial or political. In trying to explain how science holds together this diverse constituency, they give less significance to the formation of "discursive regularities", and more significance to the development of material and technical consistencies, particularly the standardisation of techniques and practices. They suggest that, by agreeing on consistent ways of acting, diverse communities are capable of "collaboration without consensus", working together without sharing a common knowledge-framework or "ontology".[31]

Actor network theory, developed by Bruno Latour, Michel Callon and John Law at the Centre de Sociologie de l'Innovation, Paris, in the early

1980s, is a schema for describing how such collaboration occurs.[32] In Latour's *Re-assembling the Social*, or Law's *Sociology of Monsters*, these scholars describe how "actors" with different and divergent objectives work together by forming "networks" of collaboration; how they translate their individual concerns into common terms; how they seek to embody those concerns within "technical delegates", such as social practices and material artefacts; and so how the materiality of those means reflexively informs the ends of their activity.[33] This schema closely parallels aspects Mitchell Dean's analytics of government, but with subtle differences. Perhaps the key difference is that, from an ANT perspective, the formation of a network does not hinge on the production of "identities". ANT scholars place less emphasis on processes of subjectification, as they are keen to recognise the contribution made by non-human actants; by the materials, technologies and animals that science – and other forms of human endeavour – depend upon, with or without their agreement.[34] Additionally, ANT scholarship places particular emphasis on the difficulty of translating governing-mentalities into technologies of government; indeed, this might be thought of as its primary object of study. Scholars associated with this field often focus on the difficulty of "enrolling" particular animals, materials and technologies (as well as other humans) within scientific work. They note how these actants are always more than the rationale they are taken to represent, that they often behave in unexpected ways, telling us things we didn't want to know, re-directing our attention to novel ends. This fraught process of translation is given such significance because, for ANT scholars, it is what holds communities of practice together. They suggest that scientific and technological cultures are not stabilised by an overarching episteme, by a "general theory", but rather describe science as a community gathered around common "things" in an attempt to make shared use of them.

In Latour's terminology, the things around which such practices stabilise are called "immutable mobiles". He outlines this concept using a map as his example in *Visualisation and Cognition: Drawing Things Together*. He asks, what is novel and scientific about the map that La Perouse brought back from his travels to China? Its novelty cannot lie in the quality of information it holds; it is not more truthful, more accurate, than those which precede it, being simply a compilation of sketches made by the people he encountered on his voyage. However, he contends that its novelty is precisely this ambition to "gather" disparate information within a singular thing. Latour suggests that the properly "scientific" character of the map is its ability to develop common codes – agreed conventions for measurement, projection – that hold together and make compatible a diversity of concerns: local observations, commercial interests, imperialism and the thirst for knowledge, facilitated and shaped by geometric projections, marine clocks, record keeping practices and engravings.[35]

What makes such objects work well, he contends, is their material consistency and their interpretative flexibility. A map is "immutable" to the degree that it exhibits characteristics that allow for consistent reproduction and apprehension: physical durability and reproducibility, conventions of scale, codes of legibility and so on. However, such objects must also be "mobile", both literally and metaphorically. They must be able to be moved from place to place, used in different contexts, but also used in different ways; they must afford a degree of interpretative flexibility, providing some kinds of information to one group, another to others.[36]

2.3.3 Boundary objects

An alternative schema, more directly related to practices of standardisation, is offered by Susan Leigh Star. Through the concept of the "Boundary Object", Leigh Star pays particular attention to the way different kinds of understanding intersect in the common "objects" that communities gather around. She first outlined this concept in *Institutional Ecology, 'Translations' and Boundary Objects: Amateurs and Professionals in Berkeley's Museum of Vertebrate Zoology, 1907–1939*, co-authored with James Griesemer. That paper studied the standardisation of processes and practices at a zoological museum, describing how a wide group of stakeholders – game catchers, amateur naturalists, professional scientists from differing disciplinary backgrounds, patrons, administrators and hired assistants – came to develop common ways of working, without sharing the same ends or world-views.[37]

In that paper Leigh Star and Griesemer outlined a schema of standardisation, one that occurs in three stages. It begins when a group of people are gathered together by a common concern, a shared problem or opportunity for those involved. In this particular case, it is the collection of a zoological museum, its care, extension and use. Working together around this "thing", those actors attempt to translate their diverse interests and understandings, navigating not only between different ways of knowing but also different levels of understanding. All individual actors, she suggests, have a detailed understanding of their own concerns, which might be more or less complex; their local knowledge is "well-structured" in her terms. However, their understanding of other people's understanding is limited, vague, "ill-structured". The common "thing" that gathers these actors is riven by competing concerns, agendas and epistemologies, of which no-one has a complete or transparent knowledge. Nonetheless, the group create a "boundary object", between them, the intersection of their well- and ill-structured ways of knowing. Again, the business of working together, they suggest, does not require consensus; one form of knowledge does not need to dominate over others. What is important for collaboration is agreement over common terms and practices that allow different ways of thinking and acting to co-exist.

This is where, for Leigh Star, the standardisation of practices, terms and techniques becomes important. They define the point of contact between detailed, local concerns and broader, more general forms of understandings. For Leigh Star, those standards do not *represent* the mentality of any of the particular actors; technologies do not represent rationalities. Rather, what makes a standard work well is its ability to facilitate the co-existence of well- and the ill-structured understandings, offering them sufficient purchase on their common "thing"; they fail when they cannot enrol their human and non-human participants in organised action, usually by becoming too detailed, too formalised, or by failing to provide adequate specificity.[38]

2.3.4 Gathering around things

This emphasis – which gives "things"[39] a central role in the formation of knowledge frameworks and social practices – lends ANT scholarship a particular focus. Despite its title, the ambition of ANT scholarship is less to theorise, more to describe; these authors offer "thick descriptions" of scientific and technological cultures, descriptions that trace the social and technical networks that subtend to truth claims. Latour suggests that this goal is achieved through textual descriptions that reveals the "string of actions in which each participant is treated as a full-blown mediator".[40] This descriptive character does not make their work a-political. From the early work on the sociology of Scientific Knowledge, to Latour's on-going work on the "controversies" of science, the work of this field has been an attempt to render science political, to make science and technology the subject of democratic discussion. Individual scholars bring with them their own concerns, also. The work of Susan Leigh Star, for instance, is grounded in gender studies and feminism; studying the hard work that it takes to produce and maintain social practices is, in her work, a means of identifying forms of "shadow-labour" or "invisible work" that systems of governance construct, but also sublimate.

Nonetheless, the critical ambition of this field might be seen to differ from that of Foucauldian scholarship. Latour reflects on this difference in "Why Has Critique Run Out of Steam: From Matters of Fact to Matters of Concern". He suggests that late 20th-century intellectual culture – pointing to critical-theory, deconstruction, as well as his own early work – has been a victim of its own political ambivalence, developing critical tools that are supportive of a radical relativism.[41] A focus on truth claims leads only, he suggests, to the identification of epistemological aporia. If a sociology of science is to positively shape what science does, he argues, it must shift in focus from "matters of fact" to "matters of concern"; it must move away from the deconstruction of truth (or "sovereignty"), to a focus on how we build shared concerns. In doing so, he outlines a programme for criticism that might be read not only as self-reflection but as a tacit critique of Foucault:

> The critic is not the one who debunks, but the one who assembles. The critic is not the one who lifts the rugs from under the feet of the naïve

believers, but the one who offers the participants arenas in which to gather. The critic is not the one who alternates haphazardly between antifetishism and positivism like the drunk iconoclast drawn by Goya, but the one for whom, if something is constructed, then it means it is fragile and thus in great need of care and caution.[42]

2.3.5 *Sociology of standards*

For ANT scholars, then, to critique the impact of science and technology on society is to describe it, particularly to describe it in a way that recognises those forms of actancy that might otherwise be ignored. This emphasis can be seen in a number of recent publications on standardisation, not least those by Leigh Star herself. In *Standard's and their Stories: How quantifying, classifying and formalizing practices shape our everyday lives*, Leigh Star and Martha Lampland gather papers that study the way that standards codify and naturalise particular ethical positions. The focus of this collection is on the hard work of making standards operate "on the ground". Through ethnographic studies of the way in which local user groups work with, and work around, systems of standardisation, she identifies within them representational problems, distributional inequalities but also opportunities for resistance.[43]

In *Standards: Recipes for Reality*, Lawrence Busch contributes to the sociology of standards, focussing specifically on the unintended side effects of standardisation. He describes the path-dependencies that standards create, the way they "black-box" the assumptions they are based on, again becoming open to misuse.[44] In *The Ad Hoc Collective Work of Building Gothic Cathedrals with Templates, String and Geometry*, David Turnbull offers a contribution specifically focussed on building standards.[45] Turnbull draws attention to these buildings as important sites of standardisation. Built prior to the existence of common units of measurement, without recourse to published architectural or structural treatise, and initially without measured plans, he considers how their masons coordinated action on site. Particularly important, he suggests, was the development of a "standard", a fixed metal or flexible string ruler, posted at the gates of cathedral towns, allowing peripatetic builders to calibrate their tools. Used in tandem with cutting templates such standards coordinated the improvisation of individual masons. Leigh Star cites Turnbull's work, suggesting that we see these "standards" as exemplary "boundary objects". Allowing practical flexibility rather than discursive fixity, these standards stabilised cathedral building practice, permitting the collaboration of diverse groups without establishing an overarching plan.[46]

The work of these sociologists offer important prompts for the study of building standardisation, taken on in this study. The governmentality literatures alerted us to the *techne* of government, noting that material and technological factors shape governmental outcomes. ANT scholars place even greater emphasis on such "non-human actants", considering them the means through which governmental problems emerge, and come to be stabilised. The studies in this book pay particular attention to the way in which buildings – in their technical and material properties – reflexively shape governmental agendas. Susan Leigh Star's work is of particular importance, though. Through her concept of the Boundary Object she offers a general schema through which to reflect on the process of standardisation, one adopted in this study. Building standards are here considered exemplary boundary objects, entities that are both discursive and material in nature, the intersection of a set of concerns, problems and opportunities, gathered by a physical thing. In each of the following chapters it is the city, and particularly the city on fire, that gathers actors. The process of standardisation is understood as a means by which those stakeholders attempt to come to common terms and shared practices concerning urban fire safety. Those terms and practices are not assumed to represent the rationality of any particular group, nor to mark out a consensual "discursive regularity". Rather, this study suggests that we see them as a means to hold together different concerns, different ways of thinking and acting. The process of design and construction – of building buildings in accordance with rules – is conceived of as an important part of this governmental process. It is only by being enacted that standardisation can succeed, or fail, to enrol human and non-human actants in some form of collaboration. As such, the following chapters study not just regulations themselves but the way they are interpreted by those who use them, and the physical effects they have on the city, particularly where those effects are unintended or counterproductive.

2.4 The infrastructure of standards

2.4.1 *Universalising, ubiquitous, familiar, invisible*

The final section of this chapter considers a third set of literatures that intersect closely with STS literatures, indeed that might be considered a subset of them. "Infrastructure Studies" is an emerging field of study which shares many concepts and methods outlined in the previous section, but applies them specifically to ways of knowing and governing that are "below" us, that form our technological "ground". The progenitor of this field is perhaps Thomas Hughes, and his work on Large Technical Systems and their governmental role.[47] In these studies – such as *Networks of Power*, a comparative history of electrification – infrastructures are conceived of physically. Hughes studies the large-scale fixed technologies through which the modern nation-state was formed; airports and runways, the power grid and the telephone, road and rail networks, and the public institutions of schools, post-offices and prisons.[48]

The term infrastructure, however, also has a broader meaning. Systems such as e-mail, electronic banking and standards for meta-data content, or life-assurance qualification requirements, even the metrical basis of particular musical styles and the underlying structure of given language-groups, might be understood as "infrastructures". More recent literatures in the sociology of scientific knowledge have sought to study infrastructures that are not necessarily physical, nor necessarily associated with the state; they study practices, concepts and techniques, as much as physical technologies, and concern themselves with the governing and self-governing practices of private companies, NGOs, industry and professional bodies. That is, through this broader conception of infrastructure, the history of technology comes to focus on an object that overlaps the concerns of governmentality scholars and Actor Network Theory.

In their *Agenda for Infrastructure Studies*, authors Paul Edwards, Geoffrey Bowker, Stephen Jackson and Robin Williams seek to define what makes a technology "infrastructural".[49] The first thing they suggest is scale; infrastructure studies are not concerned with the design of small or bespoke objects or systems for use by clearly de-limited social groups. Rather, these scholars study technologies that are big in spatial and temporal ambition, universalising and systematic in their logic. Infrastructures typically aim to be global in application and future-proof in ambition. The second quality of such infrastructures are their being taken-for-granted by those who work with them; scholars of Infrastructure Studies are not typically concerned with technology as it is consciously thematised by a society, but rather as something that has become its naturalised ground, as something that has become invisible through frequent use.[50] The singular work of architecture – a spatially limited construction, on a specific site, for a particular client – is not an infrastructure. It does, however, depend upon and reproduce a wide range of infrastructures; shared professional practices, disciplinary concepts and techniques, material supply chains and tacit social norms, as well as the formals codes, regulations, rules and standards that are the subject matter of this study.

2.4.2 Residues, textures, indeterminacy, mess

Processes of standardisation are then, for these scholars, exemplary forms of infrastructure, and their work suggest particular ways of studying building standardisation. In *Sorting Things Out*, Leigh Star works with historian Geoffrey Bowker to study those codes, conventions and standards that are embedded within our electronic equipment or online information, the forms of agreement that allow our technologically mediated life to unfold "as if by magic". To study these codes and standards, they suggest, is to gain access to the epistemologies and politics that sub-tend to the "smooth" quality of contemporary experience. Together they chart the way in which such processes of formalisation butt up against folk-classificatory, non-formalised aspects of everyday life.

In that book they also identify particular challenges associated with the study of "infrastructures" such as standards. The problem of studying standards is that they are so *normal*. What the categorical logics of meta-data standards and the legal requirements of fire-safety codes have in common is that they have become embedded in our everyday reality, transparent, invisible through use. How do we see the impact they have had, or imagine them otherwise? Beyond those question raised in the preceding sections, then, the additional methodological challenge these scholars identify is that of countering this naturalisation. How do we understand the contingent basis of a universalising rule, the partiality of a norm, the hard work behind the smoothness of standards? Bowker and Star name their method for doing this "Infrastructural Inversion".

The premise is as follows: in certain circumstances, infrastructures make *themselves* visible. Through a kind of gestalt switch, systems that are usually part of a naturalised ground suddenly stand out into sharp relief. Bowker and Star use the "computer says 'No'" moment in the BBC comedy *Little Britain* as an example; in the process of completing an application via computer, this apparently transparent, facilitating technology reveals itself as a stand-in with its own agency. These moments of "inversion" often occur when Infrastructures break. Heidegger's 'broken hammer' is an example of this; our non-reflexive use of a tool is interrupted when its materiality – fragments of wood and metal – suddenly stand out as obtrusively "present".[51] We can think of other comic examples; the leaky faucets and ill-fitting boots that make up Grandville's *Petites Misères de la vie Humaine*, or the homeless bobbin *Odradek* that laughs at Kafka's family man, offer other moments in which everyday objects appear to assume a kind of uncanny agency.[52] But Infrastructures also become visible while continuing to work. Bowker and Leigh Star cite Howard Becker's sociology of art as rich in examples. Becker recounts, for instance, the challenges of staging an eight-hour concert performance, which required the producers to become embroiled in the practicalities of negotiating varied working hours for unionised labourers, thus revealing the ordinary indebtedness of artistic forms to complex networks of social agreement.

2.4.3 *Ticklish nose*

Leigh Star offers a series of her own examples in *This is Not a Boundary Object*. In this paper, she recounts the development of her own research practice through a series of often humorous anomalies – each a moment of infrastructure inversion – that prompted changes in her thinking.[53] Having been served David Ferrier's notebooks on a silver platter, in the lushly carpeted archives of the Royal College of Physician's, she finds the pages covered in scrawled handwriting, marked by the bloody finger-prints of an ape, upon whose brain Ferrier has induced a lesion; she is prompted to reflect on science's dependence on non-human actants, and the work that goes to in obscuring that dependence. Reading between Ferrier's notebooks and his published reports, she finds the margin-notes written by caretakers of

epileptics, but not included in the official findings; she is prompted to reflect on the folk-knowledge that medical science depends upon, but silences.
Leafing through the archives of the Museum of Vertebrate Zoology, a dead
bird falls out of a manila folder, accompanied by a hand-written note from
a birder; she is prompted to study how the Museums categorical systems
are shaped by the practical requirements of working with amateurs and
hired-hand researchers.

Such moments are of methodological significance for Leigh Star. In her
lectures and papers, she uses them as object lessons for her own students.
She asks them to look "for things that strike them as strange, weird, and
anomalous... [and asks] What is causing them doubt? How may it become
enquiry?"[54] She describes the need to cultivate a nose that is tickled by
anomalies within categorical systems, by discrepancies between what people say and do, an interest in the counter-intuitive and often humorous
struggles between actors and the constraints and conventions they work
within.

Bowker provides a set of methodological pointers for researchers on
standards, suggesting ways to detect such anomalies. To begin she suggests
we look out for the "residues of ubiquity". Infrastructures are large, nested
systems that can appear to be ubiquitous. But they usually define outsiders,
exclude specific people from their concerns. Who or what are the "others"
that a standard creates, and what effect does it have on these groups? She
suggests, likewise, that standards often create "cumulative mess trajectories". While trying to solve one problem, governmental technologies often
create new problems that, in turn, legitimate further governmental action.
Sometimes the side effects of governmental action pile up to such an extent
that it is no longer possible to remember what the original problem was.
She suggests looking out for situations where standards have become so
embedded that the actors who work with them no longer remember their
original purpose. Her work likewise focusses on the "materiality and texture" of infrastructures: Leigh Star reminds us that not only are standards
ideational, or symbolic, but they also have materiality; they always require
material delegates, such as drawings, pieces of paper, software formats and
so on. While they frame broad problems for a network at large, they bring
a specific "texture" and "character" to that problem that is best understood
by the actors who work closely with them. The warp and weft of a standard is a space within which some actors carve out a certain space of freedom, redirecting given means to novel ends. Leigh Star likewise highlights
the fact that infrastructural systems such as standards are never built *de
novo*; they rely upon existing systems, which they build upon, and recode.
Working with infrastructures therefore requires a certain kind of historical
imagination. Infrastructural designers, she suggests, need to recover the
"multivocality of the past", and of things, and be aware of how narratives
of universality are constructed. Finally, she draws attention to the "practical politics of visibility". When designing infrastructures, actors are faced

with decisions in terms of the degrees of visibility to include in the system. Does it always benefit an actor or a group to be included within a system, to be seen by it? In some cases, invisibility might be more conducive to co-existence.

2.4.4 Infrastructure inversion

The premise of the studies collected in this book is that urban fires are often moments of "infrastructure inversion". They are moments when aspects of our built environment – its safety – suddenly stands out as taken-for-granted. In the event of a fire, ordinarily facilitating features such as walls, stairs, lifts, insulation, suddenly demonstrate new characteristics, they turn against us. Such fires often prompt reflection as to whether the codes and standards that shape that built environment are fit for purpose. Under close scrutiny, these codes and standards can often appear partial and contingent, failing to account for particular actors or particular circumstances. Such moments can often prompt the re-design of both our buildings and regulatory frameworks, rethinking assumptions that underpin existing buildings, generating the need for widespread reconstruction. This book is structured by the study of such moments; it studies a number of historic fires and the process of re-regulation and re-building that follow in their wake. In studying those moments, it follows cues offered by Bowker and Leigh Star above. Repurposing those prompts for the study of building standardisation, its sets itself the following broad questions.

> *Exceptional Standards*: We often presume that standardisation creates uniformity, but it also creates 'others', the practices that are outlawed. What happens to those practices? Are they transformed, or do they continue to be permitted, tacitly or explicitly? What is the field of difference constructed between such legitimate and illegitimate practices, how is it calibrated, and to what effect?
> *The Messiness of Order*: Building standards are rational documents. However, as they intersect with other shaping concerns in the built environment, they become enmeshed with other rationalities, sometimes to surprising and contradictory effect. What are the 'mess-trajectories' of building standards? What new governmental problems do they produce, and what new governmental actions do they legitimise?
> *The Materiality of Law*: Building standards are not *only* rational; they are always mediated by text, by drawings, by buildings. How are their effects shaped by that mediation? Does the texture of this media create specific pockets of agency for those who work closely with it?
> *Re-coding Norms*: Programmes of standardization, and programmes of urban renewal, are rarely built from scratch; they adapt and build upon existing physical and legal infrastructures. How do contemporary governmental standards re-construe the infrastructures that they

build upon? What conflicts and congruences emerge between the differing govern-mentalities embedded within generations of buildings and building legislation? How do architects and legislators discover a multivocality within law, and the city, in order to innovate?

While all of these questions are important for each of the case studies presented here, it is possible to suggest that each city-study was prompted by a particular set of these questions. In Chapters 3 and 6, which study the cities of Edinburgh and London, I focus particularly on the *texture* of fire-safety codes, the way that they create specific opportunities for those who work closely with them. In Chapter 4, which studies Lagos, I outline a *mess-trajectory* constructed by urban fire-safety legislation, and the *practical politics* of its application. In Chapter 5, which studies Tokyo, I consider the kinds of *historical imagination* that are invoked by programmes of fire-safety legislation in that city. As such, the whole of this study might be framed as an attempt to work-through, in the field of architectural theory, the methodological prompts offered by this emerging field of research.

It is worth noting in advance some of the limits of this methodology. As others have pointed out, the technique of infrastructure inversion is itself politically ambivalent; it is as useful for climate change denialists seeking to discredit climate science and delay governmental action, as it is for sociologists concerned with the hegemonic effect of techno-science.[55] That is, like Foucault's genealogical method, this approach might be seen to only reveal contingent historical impurities within broader processes of scientific and governmental rationalisation. But it is precisely by doing so, I want to suggest, that we see the shaping effect of the *built* for governmentality. In highlighting moments where building standards fail, this study does not attempt to offer an assessment of the effectiveness of standardisation per se. What it offers is a series of episodic sketches, charting the processes through which governmental authority becomes enmeshed within the problems and opportunities of building design. What we can generalise from these sketches is the way that buildings act, both in prompting and translating govern-mentalities. The forthcoming case studies are therefore presented as didactic lessons on the mutability and contingency of contemporary norms, but also as rich and instructive descriptions of the opportunities and stakes of thinking things otherwise.

Notes

1 See Section 5.3 "The Interrelationship between Regulation and the Practices of Architects". Rob Imrie and Emma Street, *Architectural Design and Regulation* (Chichester: Wiley-Blackwell, 2011).
2 Rob Imrie and Emma Street, 'Risk, Regulation and the Practices of Architects', *Urban Studies* 46, no. 12 (1 November 2009): 2555–2576.
3 Salomon Frausto, Bureaucracy, Hunch: No. 12 (Rotterdam : NAi Uitgevers/ The Berlage Institute, 2009).

4   'Perspecta 35 "Building Codes"', MIT Press, accessed 30 July 2017, https://mitpress.mit.edu/books/perspecta-35-building-codes.

5   Tilo Amhoff, Nicholas Beech, and Katie Lloyd Thomas, 'Further Reading Required', *Arq: Architectural Research Quarterly* 16, no. 03 (2012): 197–199.

6   Liam Ross, 'Just Joking', ed. Arjen Oosterman, *The Shape of Law*, 38 (2014) 134–137.

7   Adam Jasper, ed., 'Corruption', *Architectural Theory Review* 20, no. 2 (4 May 2015).

8   Arno Brandlhuber, ed., Legislating Architecture, vol. 50, ARCH+ (GmbH: Verlag, 2016).

9   'Recetas Urbanas: Santiago Cirugeda: Arquitectura Social', accessed 30 July 2017.

10 Perhaps the most explicit example of an architecture derived from buildings standards are Hugh Ferriss's analysis of the 1916 'set-back' code, which predicted the 'set-back' skyscraper to come. See Hugh Ferriss, *The Metropolis of Tomorrow, Facsimile of a 1929 Edition* (Mineola: Dover Publications, 2005).

11 'The Snozzi 7 | Legislating Architecture', accessed 30 July 2017, http://legislatingarchitecture.org/the-snozzi-7/.

12 Michel Foucault, *Power/Knowledge: Selected Interviews and Other Writings, 1972–1977*, ed. Colin Gordon, 1st American Edition (New York: Vintage, 1980). p. 121.

13 Michel Foucault and Robert Hurley, *The History of Sexuality, Vol. 1: An Introduction*, Fifth or Later Edition (New York: Vintage, 1990). p. 88.

14 Foucault outlines this object of study in 'What is Enlightenment', in Michel Foucault, *The Foucault Reader: An Introduction to Foucault's Thought*, ed. Paul Rabinow, New edition (London: Penguin, 1991). p. 38.

15 Foucault outlines his own research methodology in *The Archaeology of Knowledge*. Chapter 3 introduces the concept of "discursive formation". His contention is that the "objects" of discourse – madness, sexuality, criminality – do not precede their discussion, but are rather formed by those "rules", those conceptual possibilities, through which we think about them. See Part 2 of Michel Foucault, *The Archaeology of Knowledge* (London: Routledge, 2002).

16 Foucault, *The Foucault Reader*. p. 38.

17 Foucault. p. 38.

18 Michel Foucault, *The Birth of Biopolitics: Lectures at the Collège de France, 1978–1979: Lectures at the College De France, 1978–1979*, trans. Mr Graham Burchell (New York: Palgrave Macmillan, 2010).

19 I'm quoting here Foucault's paraphrasing of Wilhelm Ropke, from the *Gruntexte zur Sozialen Markitwirtshaft*, 1950. Ropke is not here outlining the theme-programme of Liberalism per se, but his own specific project in establishing a "social market society" in post-war Germany. Here questions of free-trade and economic planning are explicitly seen as means to displace economic protectionism and national socialism. What Ropke calls for specifically is,

> decentralisation in the widest and most comprehensive sense of the word; to the restoration of property; to a shifting of the social centre of gravity from above downwards; to the organic building-up of society from natural and neighbourly communities in a dosed gradation starting with the family through parish and county to the nation; to a corrective for exaggerations in organisation, in specialisation, and in division of labour ... ; to the bringing back of all dimensions and proportions from the colossal to the humanly reasonable; to the development of fresh non-proletarian types of industry, that is to say to forms of industry suitable to peasants and craftsmen; to the natural furtherance of smaller units of factories and undertakings ... ; to the breaking-up of monopolies of every kind and to the struggle against

concentrations of businesses and undertakings, where and whenever possible; ... to a properly directed country-planning having as its aim a decentralisation of residence and production.

It is striking that this political project reads, in terms of its "technologies" as a programme for town and county planning; the political here is identical to the architectural. I use this phase here because within Ropke's ambition Foucault identifies the basis of a "Vitalpolitic" or "Biopolitics" in which questions of Sovereign right are fully displaced by those of household management. See Foucault. pp. 148, 157.

20 Mitchell Dean, *Governmentality: Power and Rule in Modern Society* (London: SAGE, 2009). pp. 18–19.

21 For purposes of clarity in this text I chose to disambiguate between these two meanings of the word. When speaking of the diverse means of conducting conduct we employ and experience in our daily lives, I use the term "govern-mentality" (hyphenated). When speaking of the specific period of liberal government in Europe and America Foucault discusses, I use governmentality (non-hyphenated).

22 Dean. pp. 41–43.

23 Dean. p. 22.

24 Dean. pp. 157–158.

25 Mariana Valverde, 'Seeing Like a City: The Dialectic of Modern and Premodern Ways of Seeing in Urban Governance', *Law & Society Review* 45, no. 2 (1 June 2011): 277–312.

26 Mariana Valverde, *Everyday Law on the Street* (Chicago: University of Chicago Press), accessed 11 August 2015.

27 Dean, *Governmentality*. pp. 220, 227.

28 Higgins, Kitto, and Larner, *Calculating the Social*.

29 Higgins, Kitto, and Larner, *Calculating the Social*. p. 5.

30 Latour set out his methodological dictum that science and technology must be studied "in action", in chapter one of *Science in Action*. Bruno Latour, *Science in Action: How to Follow Scientists and Engineers Through Society*, New Edition (Cambridge, MA: Harvard University Press, 1988).

31 I take this description of scientific collaboration from Griesemer and Star (1989), but the term "collaboration without consensus" is now in broader circulation, as in Flyverbom (2011). Susan Leigh Star and James R. Griesemer, Institutional Ecology, 'Translations' and Boundary Objects: Amateurs and Professionals in Berkeley's Museum of Vertebrate Zoology, 1907–39', *Social Studies of Science* 19, no. 3 (1 August 1989): 387–420; Mikkel Flyverbom, *The Power of Networks: Organizing the Global Politics of the Internet* (Cheltenham: Edward Elgar Publishing, 2011).

32 For an introduction to Latours work and its relevance to architectural research see "Albena Yaneva, Latour for Architects (Abingdon, New York: Routledge, 2022).

33 John Law, *A Sociology of Monsters: Essays on Power, Technology, and Domination* (London: Routledge, 1991). Bruno Latour, *Reassembling the Social: An Introduction to Actor-Network-Theory* (Oxford: Oxford University Press, 2005).

34 I am here casting forward to an argument that will be made explicitly with reference to the work of Vaughan Higgins. See Vaughan Higgins, Simon Kitto, and Wendy Larner, *Calculating the Social: Standards and the Reconfiguration of Governing* (London: Palgrave Macmillan, 2010).

35 See Bruno Latour, *Visualisation and Cognition: Drawing Things Together*, in Long and Kuklick. pp. 4–7.

36 Latour in Long and Kuklick. pp. 7–8.

37 Star and Griesemer, Institutional Ecology, 'Translations' and Boundary Objects.

38 Star offers defines and then reflects upon this concept in two related papers; S. Leigh Star, 'This Is Not a Boundary Object: Reflections on the Origin of a Concept', *Science, Technology & Human Values* 35, no. 5 (1 September 2010): 601–617; Susan Leigh Star, 'The Structure of Ill-Structured Solutions: Boundary Objects and Heterogeneous Distributed Problem Solving', *Distributed Artificial Intelligence* 2 (1989): 37–54.

39 This role is perhaps most explicitly stated within Latour's concept of the "parliament of things". In the post-script to this dissertation we will return to this topic explicitly, when considering the way that objects might "judge". Bruno Latour and Catherine Porter, *We Have Never Been Modern* (Cambridge, MA: Harvard University Press, 1993). pp. 142–145.

40 Latour, *Reassembling the Social*.

41 Bruno Latour, 'Why Has Critique Run out of Steam? From Matters of Fact to Matters of Concern', *Critical Inquiry* 30, no. 2 (1 January 2004): 225–248.

42 Latour. p. 236.

43 Martha Lampland and Susan Leigh Star, *Standards and Their Stories: How Quantifying, Classifying, and Formalizing Practices Shape Everyday Life*, Edited by Martha Lampland and Susan Leigh Star, Cornell Paperbacks (Ithaca : Cornell University Press, 2009).

44 Lawrence Busch, *Standards : Recipes for Reality/Lawrence Busch, Science, Technology and Society* (Cambridge, MA; London: MIT Press, ©2011).

45 David Turnbull, 'The Ad Hoc Collective Work of Building Gothic Cathedrals with Templates, String and Geometry', *Science, Technology and Human Values* 18, no. 3 (1993): 315–340.

46 Susan Leigh Star uses these standards as an example of a "Boundary Object", a term we will touch upon later, referencing the work of Turnbull, himself a sociologist of scientific knowledge. See Geoffrey C. Bowker and Susan Leigh Star, *Sorting Things Out : Classification and Its Consequences/Geoffrey C. Bowker, Susan Leigh Star*, Inside Technology (Cambridge, MA: MIT Press, 1999).

47 Slota and Bowker make this argument in their essay "How Infrastructure Matters", in *The Handbook of Science and Technology Studies*, edited by Ulrike Felt et al. (Cambridge, MA: MIT Press, 2016). p. 532.

48 Thomas Parke Hughes, *Networks of Power: Electrification in Western Society, 1880–1930* (Baltimore: JHU Press, 1993).

49 Paul N. Edwards et al., 'Introduction: An Agenda for Infrastructure Studies', *Journal of the Association for Information Systems* 10, no. 5 (May 2009): 364–374.

50 I am taking this definition from Edwards et al.

51 The "broken hammer" is used by Heidegger to distinguish between the ontological categories of present- and ready-to-hand; "Pure presence at hand announces itself in such equipment, but only to withdraw to the readiness-in-hand with which one concerns oneself — that is to say, of the sort of thing we find when we put it back into repair". Martin Heidegger, *Being and Time*, New Ed edition(Malden: Wiley-Blackwell, 1978). p. 73.

52 Agamben connects Kafka's story and Grandville's etchings, as part of a sketch on the uncanny property of the commodity. His observation that under Grandville's pen "objects lose their innocence and rebel with a kind of deliberate perfidy" might reminds us of Latour's notion of "Reality" as "that which resists". Giorgio Agamben, *Stanzas: Word and Phantasm in Western Culture* (Minneapolis: University of Minnesota Press, 1993).

53 Leigh Star, 'This Is Not a Boundary Object'. pp. 606–609.

54 Leigh Star, 'This Is Not a Boundary Object'. p. 605.

55 'On the Uses and Abuses of Infrastructural Inversion | Serendipity', accessed 18 June 2014, http://www.easterbrook.ca/steve/2010/08/on-the-uses-and-abuses-of-infrastructural-inversion/.

3 Edinburgh

The shape of the British National Anthem

3.1 The 1911 Empire Palace Theatre fire

3.1.1 A lantern of oriental design

On 9 May 1911 there was a devastating fire at the Empire Palace Theatre in Edinburgh. Three thousand spectators were packed into the building, watching part of a two-week sell-out show performed by The Great Lafayette, the highest paid performer of his day. Lafayette, whose real name was Sigmund Neuberger, was an eccentric quick-change artist who travelled the country in a private train-carriage, accompanied by his beloved and be-jewelled dog Beauty – a gift from Harry Houdini – who he indulged with dangerous quantities of rich food. The show that night was set to a Persian Harem theme and involved a cast of fire-eaters, jugglers, contortionists and midgets, as well as a 15-year-old girl who operated a mechanical teddy-bear, a live lion and Lafayette's prize stallion, Arizona. During its finale, The Lions Bride, a young woman in oriental dress entered the Lion's cage. The animal stopped pacing, approached the woman, and roared. But just as it was about to pounce, its skin suddenly fell away to reveal Lafayette, who had mysteriously changed place with the beast. At the end of this act, which was to be the magician's own swan song, a lantern (Figure 3.1) "of oriental design, made of wood, with gelatine transparencies of various colour … lighted by seven 8 candle- power lamps",[1] fell from the rigging, setting fire to the rich draperies of the scene (Figure 3.2).

The audience, who were in a state of suspended disbelief, were slow to react. They were only saved, according to newspaper reports, by a quick-witted conductor, who roused the band to a rendition of God Save the King. This brought the patriotic crowd to their feet and snapped them out of their trance. All of the fee-paying guests escaped unharmed. A different fate, however, awaited the performers. An automatically deployed fire-curtain became trapped inches above the stage, creating a powerful draught that fanned the flames. And Lafayette had locked the back-stage doors, in order to guard his professional secrets. Both of these precautionary measures backfired; all 10 cast-members were killed, and Lafayette's charred remains

DOI: 10.4324/9781003026297-3

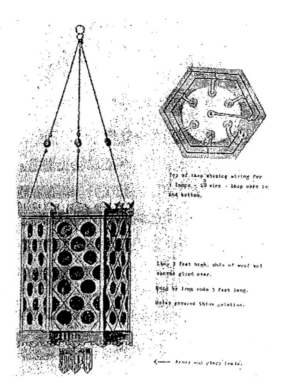

Figure 3.1 **"Detailed Drawing of the Lamp".** Source: British Fire Prevention Committee. 'A Report on the Fire at the Empire Palace Theatre on May 9th, 1911, Whereby Ten Lives Were Lost'. Redbooks of the British Fire Prevention Committee, 1911. Fig. 19.

were discovered twice, revealing his use of a body double. The ashes of both men were sprinkled between the paws of his dog Beauty, who had died portentously, of apoplexy, only a week earlier. A quarter of a million people gathered at Piershill Cemetery in Edinburgh for his funeral in crowds greater than those who welcomed George V on his royal visit, the following month (Figure 3.3).[2]

As remarkable as this story is – being rich in Edwardian tropes of empire and patriotism, mesmerism and fate – what's perhaps more remarkable is the fact that details of this event form the evidence-base of a number of contemporary building standards. The 1911 fire was the subject of a dedicated report by the British Fire Prevention Committee. That report was influential, for instance, in establishing the mandatory use of fire-curtains, despite their tragic consequence in this instance. It also established "clearance time" as a regulatory concept. Contemporary

Lamp here

Figure 3.2 **"View of the Scene (reproduced from a model)".** Source: British Fire Prevention Committee. 'A Report on the Fire at the Empire Palace Theatre on May 9th, 1911, Whereby Ten Lives Were Lost'. Redbooks of the British Fire Prevention Committee, 1911. Fig. 14.

newspaper accounts suggested that the audience escaped within the time it took the band to play the national anthem. While that song varies in length, depending on the tempo and number of verses, an official three-verse, andante rendition takes about two-and-a-half minutes to play, and it is this time that has since been taken to define our requirements for safe clearance time.

3.1.2 Space-time continuum

The regulation of "clearance time" supports, in turn, a number of spatial standards. The 1952 report Post-War Building Studies no. 29 Fire Grading of Buildings, for instance, uses it to standardise the width of exit doors and stairs, and to define the maximum occupant capacity of rooms and floors. Citing the Fire Prevention Committee's 1911 report, this document suggests that if buildings can be evacuated within 2.5 minutes "there will be no serious risk of panic".[3] But recognising that clearance time cannot be controlled directly, it suggests that "this factor is controlled indirectly by

The Last Act

Funeral of The Great Lafayette,
Some Floral Tributes

Figure 3.3 **"Escape routes 45 degrees or more apart".** Source: *BS9999:2008 Fire safety in the design, management and use of building.* British Standards Institution, 2008. Clause 16.3.2 Fig. 7.

the requirement for exit width". Citing studies by the French Fire Brigade and the US National Bureau of Standards it offers an average value for the rate at which people file through exits ("discharge rate"), and develops a new integer of measurement, based on average shoulder width (a 21 inch "unit of exit"). By multiplying these values by 2.5, it defines the maximum permissible number of occupants within a room, or storey:

> The discharge values of exits of different widths from a single floor may now readily be calculated. On the basis of a discharge rate of 40

persons per unit per minute and a clearance time of 2.5 minutes, each unit of exit width could deal with 40 x 2.5 = IOO persons.[4]

This same set of relations is today defined by British Standard 9999: Code of Practice for Fire Safety in the Design, Management and Use of Buildings.[5] This offers the more nuanced W = ((N/2.5) + (60S))/80, relating occupants (N), doors (W) and stairs (S). The constant remains a target clearance time of 2.5 minutes (Figure 3.4).

Where these concerns intersect most directly with architectural design, though, is through the regulation of travel distance. This concept is outlined in the post-war building studies and British Standards but is also enforced by UK law. In Scotland, it is defined by Building Standard 2.9.3 as "the distance that occupants have to travel to a protected door". This distance is again limited to ensure that occupants can escape "before there is a noticeable accumulation of smoke in the route of escape".[6] This dimension is perhaps the most spatially and economically significant of building standards. It establishes the maximum permissible plan depth of a building, and the number of stairs it requires, effectively setting a national ceiling for gross-net ratios, which, in turn, sets the bottom-line for speculative developers. The actual distance permitted varies significantly depending upon the type of building, its "occupant profile" and the number of available means of escape: from 9 metres in the case of a residential care homes with one escape stair, to 100 metres for a roof-top plant-room with at least two.

BRITISH STANDARD   **BS 9999:2017**

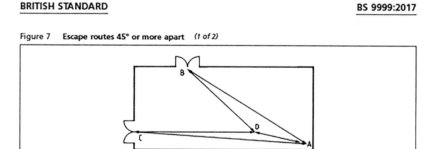

Figure 7   Escape routes 45° or more apart   *(1 of 2)*

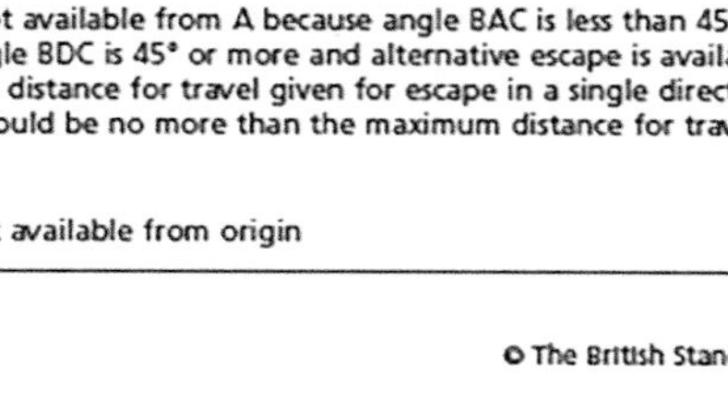

Alternative routes are not available from A because angle BAC is less than 45°. However, after reaching point D the angle BDC is 45° or more and alternative escape is available. AD should be no more than the maximum distance for travel given for escape in a single direction and AB or AC (whichever is the less) should be no more than the maximum distance for travel given for alternative routes.

b) Alternative escape not available from origin

Figure 3.4 **"Funeral of the Great Lafayette, Some Floral Tributes".** Source: Photo Postcard. Photographer unknown, May 1911. Courtesy Laurie Manton Collection. http://graveyarddetective.blogspot.com/2013/03/the-great-lafayette.html (accessed, August 24, 2021).

These dimensions, however, are likewise derived from a common formula, one that now multiplies a range of "discharge rates" by a minimum door width (two shoulders-widths), and the now-familiar constant of 2.5. It is this formula that means Scottish buildings are required to have smaller rooms, wider doors, or more stairs, for instance, than those south of the border; Scots are presumed to have wider shoulders than the English. As to whether this is on account of rude physique, or a need to wear coats indoors, is moot.[7]

3.1.3 Contingent universals

This set of compound equations creates a kind of ghostly performance – a choreography of assumed door-widths and maximum corridor-lengths, peopled by averagely broad shoulders, moving at a dignified pace. This performance is a spectral re-production of Neuberger's swan-song, a real event, fossilised into norms and coefficients, one that echoes and reverberates through every room, floor, and corridor and door in Scotland. And just like that show, this production seems to depend upon a sleight-of-hand and on our suspension of disbelief as plausible phenomena are conjured from thin air, with their back-stage mechanics protected by the stage-doors of formulae.

We could approach this performance critically, of course, and try to break its magic circle. A first place to start would be with the original newspaper report. Whether the audience really escaped in the duration of the tune is uncertain; it's reasonable to assume that accuracy was here a secondary to the value of a pithy story through which adversity is overcome by obedience. What we do know, however, thanks to the Fire Safety Committee's report, is that fire and smoke never overcame the auditorium; the blaze was trapped back-stage, and the auditorium provided a capacious smoke-reservoir. Nonetheless, that committee likewise suggested 2.5 minutes be adopted as a maximum. A third sleight comes from the Post War Building Study. This study went further, attributing the calm of the audience, not to the song itself, but to its duration, making this accidental characteristic appear essential. And this accident is further sublimated within those studies – and in those later standards that employ its formulae – being trans-substantiated into the width of a door. A final puff of smoke is added by Scottish Building Standard 2.9.3; despite recognising a clearance time as being determined by occupant capacity and exit width and understanding the effect of ceiling height on the gathering of smoke, it offered a linear transcription of 2.5 minutes, through which to limit the size of rooms and floors.

These scientific aporia are not unknown to fire-safety experts, but they elicit a variety of response. My own studies of this standard began with a moment analogous to those recalled by Leigh Star in the previous chapter: the embarrassed laughter of the head of Building Standards in Scotland in response to my asking about the origin of the 2.5-minute rule. Laughter is a strange response to a query about fire-safety standards, on that suggested an awareness of ambiguities, redundancies and deficiencies – an anomaly that prompted enquiry. For some fire-safety academics, though, this story is frustrating. It undermines their attempts to constitute a "science" of fire-safety and its engineering. Where codes and standards are based on contingent data – like anecdotal reports from a single fire more than 100 years ago – they undermine any claim to empiricism, and place unnecessary burdens on design, and as such should be scrapped.

> I think there's a need to make sure all of our regulation is based on rational thought and if we can prove that in certain cases it isn't, and that that either causes a safety risk or stifles innovation unnecessarily, we should do something about it[8]

On the other hand, some fire-safety consultants are grateful for the assumptions embedded within this code; indeed, they suggest that their discipline could not exist without them. If this "science" is to be inscribed into the built environment, and awarded the force of law, a line must be drawn somewhere, by someone. It is not unheard of for fire-safety engineers to make the pilgrimage to Piershill Cemetery and to say a few words of thanks to Sigmund and his Dog, considering their consultancy fees his greatest "trick" ever.[9]

That is, the 2.5-minute rule seems to create a problem of "sovereignty" in miniature. The line that it draws can seem arbitrary, absurd, even magical, a means of conjuring a position of authority as if from nothing. Indeed, given the specificity of this case, it might seem an example of the way that governmental thinking remains, quite literally, under the spell of monarchy. It is not hard to debunk the assumptions that underpin BS9999 or SBS 2.9.3, and this itself is a serious scientific question, one that we will return to in more depth in Chapter 6. But to focus on this particular question is to focus on matters of "fact", and to do so will only identify an epistemic aporia: the difficulty of quantifying scientifically a socially acceptable definition of "safety". In the remainder of this section I wish to shift focus away from that aporia, simply to recognise the role that certain accidental qualities of story above have had in shaping our fire-safety standards. Theatres, mesmerism, anthems and fire: these actors had a profound effect on our thinking about fire-safety; they prompted us to see certain problems, and to think certain answers. Between them, they formed the "arena" in which certain concerns about safety were first gathered.

3.1.4 Gathering in and around theatres

Theatre fires were commonplace during the period in which the UK's building standards were developed, and there is a close historic relationship between this building type and the problem of egress. The site of the Empire Palace Theatre, which now houses the Edinburgh Festival Theatre, was previously occupied by a string of other theatres: Ducrow's Circus, Pablo Fanque's Amphitheatre, Dunedin Hall, Southminster Theatre, Queen's Theatre and Newsome's Circus. The last three of these burnt down, in 1875, 1877 and 1887, respectively. That the auditorium of the Empire Palace survived, along with its occupants, did, indeed, make it a "good fire", a model to be emulated. That is, theatres are places of special fire-risk, for reasons that both are, and aren't "accidental"; theatres gather people in large numbers and dense arrangements, in unfamiliar environments, in order to suspend their disbelief through remarkable, often flammable, spectacles. They provide both the prompt, and the worst case, for the legislation of egress.

The theatre – specifically the Royal Playhouses of Drury Lane and Covent Garden – were also the arena that gave rise to Britain's national anthem. The origins of the melody of that song are unclear; attributed to Handel, it bears a close resemblance to a folk theme, as well as an earlier piece by Jean-Baptiste Lully, Grand Dieu Sauve Le Roi, written to celebrate Louis XIV's survival of an operation to remove an anal fistula. The circumstances that led to its adoption as the British national anthem, however, are well documented. The lyrics were first published on 15th October 1745, by The Gentleman's Magazine, as "A new song for two voices. As sung at both playhouses". The date is significant; this new song was first sung as a gesture of support for George II, following his defeat in Prestonpans, at the hands of the "Young Pretender", Charles Edward Stuart. With the Jacobite army gathering in Newcastle, The Gentleman launched a counter-offensive, an attempt to normalise and nationalise this metropolitan gesture, enrolling theatres across the country to adopt the cause.[10]

With this in mind, I think it is possible to see why the newspaper reports of 10 May 1911 offer such a compelling basis for legislation concerning fire-safety. Those accounts drew together the real and experienced threat of theatre fires, and a device of collective solidarity that had, by that time, been adopted even in Scotland. The "science" of the 2.5-minute rule would not, from this perspective, be located in the accuracy of that limit, but rather in its capacity for adoption; the rule succeeded in enrolling a set of pre-existing actors – the theatre, the anthem, and their associated codes of behaviour – into the construction of a broader and more distributed network which, through the standard, could be inscribed into our entire building stock, and support new governmental and technical practices. That the national anthem is used to establish this limit should not suggest its dependence on a single or localisable position of "sovereignty"; rather, in this case, what God Save the King points to is only the collective experience that it represents, that of calm, orderly behaviour. While this frame of reference makes recourse to concepts of nationalism, patriotism, religion and monarchy, these are themselves accidental predicates; the purpose of the rule is to connect that shared experience with a new situation, the moment of egress. To debunk its functionally necessary assumptions about occupant behaviour is to ignore the reflexive effect that it seeks to generates; the assumptions embedded in the 2.5 minute rule are less a record of how a population does behave, more a prescription as to how they ought to behave. Through the raft of related regulations that it underpins, its ambition is construct a population that does behave in a calm and orderly manner while in mortal peril.

3.1.5 Aesthetics of escape

Considered from this perspective, these rules raise another question, one of subjectification. If our fire-safety standards seem to sublimate and hide the assumptions they are based upon – the National Anthem – this is perhaps because they seek to replace, rather than draw on, its legitimacy. The occupants of the Empire Palace remained calm and escaped safely, we are told, because of their schooled familiarity with that tune. The stated purpose of egress regulation is that the effect of that tune be written into our architecture. Through a schooled familiarity with fire-alarms, illuminated signage, designated routes, exit doors, muster points, we too will behave calmly when faced with that situation. Should our fire alarms sound to the tune of Grand Dieu Sauve Le Roi, these two technologies of government would coincide; the familiar melody would echo and reverberate around a room whose door widths and plan arrangements, and whose number of occupants, were already its echo. But the conceit of our fire-safety standards is that that doubling is not necessary. Handel's mood music already resonates and reverberates within our legal codes, codified buildings and with us. Put in other terms, we could say that the 2.5 minute rule is an attempt to negotiate a shift between two epochs of government, one already touched on in Chapter 2. It seeks to replace an actively disciplinary mode of government – standing up for the King – with a passive, dispersed, technologically mediated one – safeguarding the population through the design of their buildings. It is part of that shift in governmental thinking that Foucault names "Governmentality": that shift in liberal governments away from spectacles of subjugation and training programmes, towards a focus on technical matters concerning the health and safety of the population. Further, we might recognise it as part of a parallel shift in architectural thinking – perhaps first made by Bentham, but discussed recently by Sven-Olov Wallenstein – in which the passive governmental potential of buildings is employed to "free" us from such active displays of subservience.[11]

But if that is the broader ambition of this rule, this case points to some of its limitations. Our fire-safety standards are based on assumptions about occupant egress, and if we are to behave as assumed, we still need to be trained. That is, this mode of governance can never be fully represented by its technical delegates, it never becomes fully "infrastructural"; a moment of subjectification is still needed. Fire-escape drills and safe egress procedures are the contemporary replacement for National Anthems and marching drills; both are the moments in which we learn to behave as expected, in which we are trained to perform everyday life. The fire-escape drill does this through a moment of "infrastructure inversion", a moment when the ready-to-hand character of the everyday environment turns against us, prompts the need for a display of obedience. As such, the problem of fire-safe design retains a stubbornly theatrical and disciplinary dimension; even as we design buildings that ensure regular fires are a thing of the past, nonetheless, we must still be a able to recognise the danger that those buildings could pose, lest we fail to see the need for such training. The architecture of fire-safety must satisfy these two ends: to negate the hazard while dramatising the risk. And this is perhaps one moment where problems of building design intersect with those of the governmentality. "Live Dangerously": that is the motto Foucault gives to life in contemporary liberal democracies.[12] He does not mean that the conditions of life in Europe and America today more dangerous than at any other time, rather that, for contemporary government, the experience of danger plays an important subjectifying role, one that here building design is clearly caught up in.

3.2 The regulatory space of Scottish Building Standards

3.2.1 *Between law and the city*

The ambition of this first case-study on fire-safety legislation is two-fold. First, it seeks to demonstrate how regulatory frameworks emerge from historically and geographically specific contexts. Second, it seeks to describe how regulatory frameworks re-shape that context, bringing to it their own materiality, texture, or techne. In the opening section above, I sought to use the 2.5-minute rule as a way into this reflection. I dwelt on difficulty of abstracting universal codes from contingent circumstances, at the same times as recognising the way that those contingencies brokered a change in governing-mentalities.

In this second section I extend that descriptive ambition from a single rule, to its broader legal framework. In doing so, I bring this reflection into relation with contemporary discourse on regulatory governance, particularly the concept of "Regulatory Space". After defining this term, and the way I wish to use it, I offer a brief genealogy of the development of Scottish fire-safety legislation. My specific focus will be to identify the way in which this framework has shaped, and been shaped by, the physical fabric of the city of Edinburgh. I recount acts of legislation, prompted by specific events and buildings, and the way that aspects of these buildings and events come to be re-inscribed into the city. Reading between these individual acts of legislation I hope to describe more fully the way the city and fire interact to shape and re-shape the way we think about governing. What follows is not a comprehensive history of Scottish fire-safety regulations, but a sketch of a series of exchanges between the City and Law, a series of moments in which govern-mentalities confront and critique each-other, in physical form.

In Capitalism, Culture and Economic Regulation[13] Leigh Hancher and Mick Moran coined the term "Regulatory Space", an analytical concept that described their approach to the study of regulation in liberal-democratic, capitalist political economies. While not readers of either Foucault or Latour,[14] their ambition in doing so will resonate with concerns already outlined. Hancher and Moran suggested that, at the close of the 20th century, the critical horizon of commentary on regulatory governance were limited by the problem of "regulatory capture", the concern that governmental initiatives, authorised by public bodies, tended to be re-directed, and re-purposed to serve the interests of private companies. While sympathising with that concern, Hancher and Moran, nonetheless, suggest that the literatures on "capture" were limited by two fundamental assumptions: that there exists a sovereign authority that reliably represents a definable public interest, and that regulation is its instrument to assert that interest against private gain. Hancher and Moran suggested that any attempt to clarify and legitimate such an aim and ambition was inadequate to the complexities of a neo-liberal context in which, for example, the most commonly adopted vehicle for the advancement of private interest is the public company, and in which governmental roles traditionally associated with the state are intentionally dismantled so as to create opportunities for entrepreneurial activity.

3.2.2 Metaphorical space, concrete poetry

They developed this concept so as to describe regulation as a space, rather than a line. As we have seen, the concept of "regulation" often returns us to problems of sovereignty, to the King. This is the etymology of the verb "to regulate"; the word comes into English from *regler* – to control, order, regulate, govern, to mark with lines drawn with a ruler; from the ruler comes the rule, and from the decision, the drawing of lines. For Hancher and Moran, these connotations are misleading; they suggest that, in language that resonates with Latour, regulatory frameworks demarcate an "arena", a set of matters of common concern, whose limits are defined less by sovereign decision, more by the concord and discord constructed between a wide range of actors. The spatial trope offered them a way to describe that arena which, like an architectural plan, operates through partitions of inclusion and exclusion, and creates uneven allotments of representation. Further, like historical cities, they recognised that regulations emerge in different historical and geographical contexts, and that their public/private divides fall along different lines from place to place, and from time to time. The formation of the EU could be described as a means to harmonise the "regulatory space" of that bloc, just as Brexit might be presented as an opportunity to create more distinction for the UK.

This trope allowed Hancher and Moran to stress the notion that regulations are there to be occupied. The lines that they draw are not simply barriers; they shape legal and governmental opportunities whose ultimate effect is steered less by intent, more by the way they are used. While offered as a way to describe the working of regulation within a neo-liberal context, the concept has supported a wide discussion, one that describes the process of regulation as a territorial struggle which constantly redraws the "frontiers, outposts, and mobile boundaries" between that which we call "public" and "private".[15]

Hancher and Moran use the term "space" here in a strictly metaphorical sense, but their government is also literally spatial. Physical space is often the object and means of governmental action, the common thing around which matters of concern emerge, the necessary vessel through which to gather and form agreement, and the tool through which that agreement is cemented in reality. In the last section I sought to demonstrate the role of the theatre in shaping our legislation on safe egress; I suggested that that building type created the "issues arena" in which that concern emerged, and was resolved. Indeed, what I sought to demonstrate through the example was a kind of poetic relationship between space and law, developed through successive processes of abstraction and transcription. More broadly, we might likewise note that the theatre is the spatial prototype of the court-room, just as the agonistic drama is the prototype of the trial. That is, while "space" offers Hancher and Moran a convenient trope though which to understand Law, in reality the two are already engaged in a complex set of exchanges between the metaphorical and the literal; Law and Space are inscribed into each other, their normativities occasionally clashing, but mostly coinciding and reinforcing. It is with a view to finding such moments of inscription or contradiction that I will now describe the "regulatory space" of Scotland's fire-safety legislation, and its relationship to the City of Edinburgh.

3.2.3 Candles, curfews and "common women"

As Alexander Reid notes in his history of the Scottish fire services, Towns and cities were late to develop in Scotland.[16] Lacking dense nucleated villages, the country was one of isolated farmsteads until David I imported the concept of the "Royal Burgh" from Newcastle. This new spatio-legal tool came with its own laws (Leges Burgorum) and was introduced as means to bring international trade under royal control. Within the Burghs, foreign merchants and cosmopolitan trades-people were granted "freedom" from baronial feu duties. These freedoms were expressed and ensured by military infrastructures, walls and gates, that the Burghs enrolled and extended.

Prior to these Burghs, there was no legislation concerning fire-safety in Scotland. Fire was a matter of personal responsibility; if your farm burnt down, it was probably your fault, but definitely your problem. The increased risk constructed by dense settlements, however, prompted a recognition that it would be "profitable" to develop forms of communal assistance and precaution. The first act of parliament to do so was the Scottish Act, passed by James I, during his third parliament, on 11 March 1426. This legislation established a punishment for arson, moved specific things and people out of the towns, and established a curfew (in these predominantly French-speaking settlements, a *couvre-feu* was to "cover the fire"): it decreed that "no stray hay, heather nor broom be put above the flame in houses with fires"; that "sellers of hay not enter their hay house with a candle"; that "that no fire be fetched from one house to another within the town except within a covered vessel"; that "common women be put to the utmost ends of the town where there is least peril of fire, and that no man make a home for them in the heart of the town"; and that "if burning happens in any town, and [the fire being] found to be deliberate, the punishment shall be forfeiture [of property, to the Crown]".[17]

3.2.4 Distant networks, vertical limits

It was not until the 17th century that such legislation was extended to consider the flammability of construction materials themselves. The Improvements Act of 1621 stated that "to prevent fire, the houses of Edinburgh shall be roofed with slate, lead, and tile... instead of straw or boards". A further Improvements bill, in 1677, extended this requirement to outlaw construction in wood. The 1621 Act also provided the first legal and physical infrastructure for fire-fighting, through measures for "the supplying of water to the city from a distance". It would take 60 years to build a damn in the Pentland hills, and lay a connecting mains to the Castle Hill reservoir, but by 1681 Edinburgh was one of the first cities to have "fire-points" – piped-water outlets – running between the 10 public wells that stretched down the Royal Mile.

Edinburgh was at the forefront of piped-water infrastructure because it had developed a reputation for frequent fires. The Improvement Acts were likewise prompted by the extreme density of 17th-century Edinburgh. Bound by the city walls, some of the tenements that lined its long, narrow "burgess plots" exceeded 10 stories in height. That height was itself facilitated by a distinctive aspect of Scotland's "regulatory space". "Flying freeholds" were not recognised in English law until the 16th century, but the owners of flats in Scotland were recognised to hold the right to property, even in the event of the building below them burning down. However, in 1674, a major fire prompted a recognition of the unintended risk constructed by this tall, constrained urbanism. The Dean of Guild's Court was tasked to draw up Scotland's first set of building standards, which, recognising the vertical nature of fire-spread, and the difficulty of escape from height, provided a rule that limited future construction within the city to 5 stories in height. This new legal framework was incentivised by a 17-year tax-break for land-owners who invested in new buildings. It would take many years to bring the Old Town into compliance with these new standards, but the 1674 Act, nonetheless, set the vertical limit of the contemporary city.

3.2.5 God and goad, providence and insurance

A particularly devastating fire occurred In 1703, one that engulfed Parliament Close, the Royal Exchange, the Bank of Scotland and part of the Advocates Library, driving over 200 families from their homes. The city responded by forming a municipal Company for Quenching Fires. The wording of the empowering Act is worth reviewing, for its tact; it suggests that while,

> ... God in his great mercy put a stop [to the recent fire], the council judges it their duty to lay down methods, and provide means, that through the blessing of God may prove effectual for preventing the like, or greater conflagrations ....

These methods and means came in the form of a company of part-time officers, provided with crowbars, axes and buckets, paid for by the common purse.

Private enterprise brigades also began to develop in Edinburgh during the 18th century, organised by insurance companies as a means to limit the financial risk of coverage. Of course, building insurance was itself another by-product of urban fire; the founder of property insurance, Nicholas If-Jesus-Christ-Had-Not-Died-For-Thee-Thou-Hadst-Been-Damned Barbon, was an English economist and speculator who worked with Wren and Hooke on the response to London's Great Fire. Barbon was influential in developing London's building standards – spatial codes for economic construction, taken from the ship-building trade – but also in setting up the first company to offer fire-insurance contracts, as a means to incentivise re-construction. In doing so, he invented a new form of financial service. During the 18th century, Edinburgh would develop its own prosperous financial services sector, the UK's biggest outside London, initially through Scottish Widows, a mutual society set up to answer the joint concerns of supporting international trade, providing soldiers with life assurance, and underwriting property speculation against the risk of fire. This sector would go on to support the most detailed urban mapping projects undertaken to date, those of fire-insurance maps. These surveys – commonly known as Goad plans – were the first maps of urban centres to include comprehensive and standardised information about the material composition of buildings – whether they were built of flammable or inflammable materials – as well as the forms of use they supported (Figure 3.5).

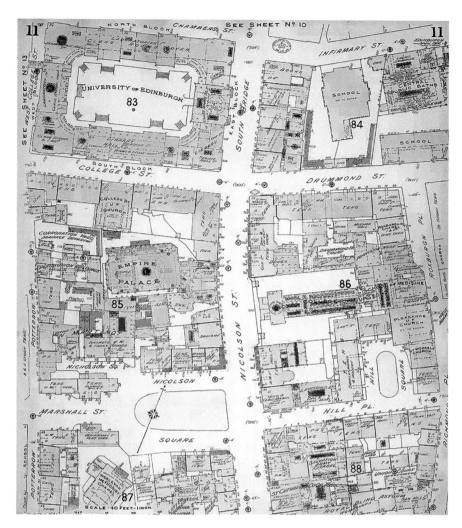

Figure 3.5 **Insurance Plan of Edinburgh, Showing Nicholson Street and the Empire Palace Theatre.** Pale tone (pink) denotes non-flammable construction material, typically stone; darker tone (yellow) denotes flammable construction materials, typically timber; darker tone (blue) denotes unprotected openings, typically skylights. Fire-points denoted on streets with a "V". Italicised text denotes building occupancy type. Source: 'Insurance Plan of Edinburgh, Sheet 11' 1906, Charles E. Goad. The British Library, Shelfmark Maps 145.b.6.(1.) Reproduced with the permission of the British Library

3.2.6 Hills and horses

This piecemeal and privatised system of fire-fighting came to be seen as limited, even counterproductive, during the 19th century. Edinburgh suffered its own "Great Fire", indeed, a year of regular and severe fires, in 1824. During this year, the sight of competing companies standing by to allow uninsured buildings, or those insured by rivals, to burn, became untenable, as did the capital flight created as those who could left, and the dwindling returns of the insurance sector. A failure to manage urban-fire was seen to reveal a municipal "confusion, inefficiency, and squabble for dignity",[18] one that prompted political and legal reform. It was in that year that the city formed the Edinburgh Fire Engine Establishment, the UK's first full-time and professional municipal fire-fighting service. This organisation was led by James Braidwood, who would then go on to found the London Fire Brigade. Braidwood shaped the fire service as we know it, authoring the first training manuals for firefighters.

Braidwood also helped to shape the physical fabric of Edinburgh, commissioning a number of stations to house the engines, horses and live-in staff of his establishment. Under his lead, the fire-services also became involved in building permits, establishing the dimensions through which fire-risk could be understood, measured and limited. Indeed, the physical fabric of these buildings – such as Edinburgh's Central Fire Station – provides an index of this new relationship between the technologies of rescue and architectural design. Its five-storey tower, used for drying five-storey hoses, and for testing five-storey ladders, sets a visible limit to the surrounding five-storey city, both representing and ensuring their safety. Likewise, its courtyard pit indexed the maximum depth from which atmospheric pressure could be used to draw water, training staff to visually gauge which rivers and ponds were suitable. And these buildings also constructed and made legible a new urban landscape of risk. Early fire-engines were heavy, hand- or horse-drawn "squirts". The difficulty of moving them reduced response-time, especially up Edinburgh's many hills. Braidwood insisted that all his stations be built on high-ground. Thus, the slow business of hauling equipment back to the station was a means of storing potential energy so as to speed later response. It is through Braidwood's success that Edinburgh can claim to be the birthplace of modern firefighting, "the first municipality to attempt to deal seriously with the constantly recurring conflagration of the time".[19]

3.2.7 The Second World War and social security

It was not until the 20th century that detailed fire-safety regulations concerning the interior arrangement of buildings were developed. We have discussed their origins already: the Empire Palace Theatre fire supported the development of a number of codes which would limit the occupant capacity of buildings, the width of doors and corridors, and the depth of floor-plates. Taken together, this history provides an outline of our contemporary standards for fire-safety: controls over the storage of hazardous material, and permitting procedures for special fire risks; controls over flammable construction materials, so as to limit surface spread of flame, and limits on the combustibility of structures; the provision of piped water supplies for fire-fighting; the financial incentivisation of fire-proof construction through insurance practices; the coordination of approval processes with the fire-services; geometric limits on buildings design to ensure adequate time for escape.

That is, the governmental rationality of fire-safety, and it attendant technologies, were already well defined before the creation of an Act that would fully coordinate them. It was only the exigency of the Second World War that would bring together the existing municipal fire-fighting forces; the National Fire Service was formed in 1941, during the Second World War, to coordinate response to bombing as part of a national war effort. And as we described in Part 2, it was post-war reconstruction that consolidated the existing array of council by-laws, voluntary schemes and trade agreements into a single, mandatory national building act. Just as the 2.5-minute rule consolidated a common experience of theatre fires, and of the national anthem, so our fire-services and fire-safety standards were amalgamated and legitimated by the common experience of war.

3.2.8 *Governmental genealogy*

I will review the above story now from two differing perspectives. First, I would like to read it as an episode within the process of governmentalisation, one which already highlights the way that this is shaped by its attendant technologies. The story begins with the ethics of personal responsibility proper to a pre-reformation Scotland, but also to a context of isolated small-holding. For fire to emerge as a matter of common concern would mean the construction of a situation within which its risk became contagious; this was first provided by the overlapping ownership patters, and public spaces, of the Royal Burgh. The problem of fire was first thought through the mechanisms of Leges Burgorum, a space of legal exceptions, constructed through selective inclusions and exclusions; in order to construct the "freedom" of the burghers, flammable materials (and inflammatory persons) must be moved outside. The anomaly that makes this mentality stand out is, no doubt, its provision concerning "common women". The logic of that measure was that uncontrolled fires occur when men become distracted from their duties. Whatever the truth of that assumption, we can see that the mentality of this era attempted to consolidate itself by overlapping two different moral codes, two differing ideas about "inflammation".

The initiatives of the 17th century, by contrast, seem to broker a more nuanced relationship between the city and its exterior. By this time the city has learned that fire cannot be excluded, but must be limited at its source, and quenched, by bringing water in. The Improvement Acts attempt, then, to both intensify and de-densify the urban infrastructure, and in doing so begin to blur its spatial and legal extents. The source of both hazard and providence is, in this period, still ultimately beyond human ken, and so our response to it is proportionately limited. But during the 18th century we see a change in attitude, one which is increasingly interested in predicting the likelihood of fire. Through the invention of private prudential communities, property owners could protect themselves from economic loss without preventing actual fires. This financialisation of risk was supported by the standardisation of material and occupancy information effected by fire-insurance maps. These maps were crucial in allowing fire-risk to be ascertained at a distance, and in the process they constructed a new means of governmental "visibility", one which would foreshadow the concerns of both planning and building control. Insurance companies would bring with them active means of preventing fires, in the form of private enterprise brigades, but also premium incentives for safe construction. To this extent, they worked as forms of economic "responsibilisation", but only for those who chose to join these volitional communities of risk-spreading.

This model, however, could not answer to the way that fire spreads. This particular problem would therefore reinforce a need for broader, municipal, responsibility bearing authority, extending its remit to coordinate the emerging fire-fighting technologies and practices. In Edinburgh, this extension was effected by the 1824 Act. And once such an organisation was in place, its logic would suggest the possibility of increasing centralisation, so as to afford a socio-technical finesse of risk-mitigation. This would be achieved through the fire-services engagement in building permission, through which fire-fighting practices came to be anticipated by the built environment itself. For this congruence to be complete – to support an integrated system of building regulations concerning fire-safety – would require an event that nationalised that risk. The Second World War and the national "war machine" would provide that event and mechanism. Through it the state expanded into a provider of social security services, national insurance, welfare and healthcare, as well as fire-services and building codes. Thought across this longue durée, then, we could see the problem of fire, and the technology of fire-safety legislation, as a key aspect in the construction of the "welfare state". That is, we can read the above story as one of a linear progression, through which fire and the city prompt an increasing imbrication of the state within logics of safety and social insurance. Concluding as we have here at the post-war moment, this tells a story of the gradual collectivisation of risk; here the history of fire-safety legislation in Scotland can be read as the gradual, accidental construction of what Francois Ewald would call a "technology of solidarity".[20]

3.2.9 Reflexive limitations

Returning to Hancher and Moran's concern, what I hope this reflection demonstrates is that it is not only under conditions of neo-liberalism that our regulatory frameworks appear warped by a wide range of public and private interest. If the immediate post-war period marks a point of clarity, through the consolidated role of Nation States, its "regulatory space" was, nonetheless, formed in an ad hoc manner, shaped by a wide range of actors and concern. Chapter 6 will return to this point in time, and reflect further on the consolidation and fragmentation of regulatory roles that occurred in the UK after the Second World War. My purpose here, though, is to highlight the role that space, or the design of the built environment, played in these shifts of govern-mentality: the city first constructs the problem of fire; then it regulates and re-designs itself to prevent future fire; but fires continue to occur, in new ways, and as they do, they offer a critique of previous modes of regulation and design. As such, the city and fire support an iterative process of re-regulation and re-design, a process through which fire-safety legislation constructs its own accidental effects, engaging in a process of reflexive self-limitation. To conclude this section I offer a final review of the above story, in order to highlight those moments of reflexivity.

The original accident in this story is the city itself – the risk of uncontrolled fire that is constructed by dense settlements, and ambiguities of responsibility and ownership. This risk is complicated, at the moment it is discovered, when James I attempts to quench the passions aroused by "common women" at the same time as the fires they are purported to cause. The regulatory space of the Scotland Act has a contemporary resonance with Edinburgh's "non-harassment zones" for sex workers. Both lump prostitutes into the same spatio-legal category as edge-of-town storage facilities. Non-harassment zones create spaces of "tolerance" within which soliciting is permitted, spaces which in Edinburgh today coincide with the peri-urban sites of big-box stores, and self-storage warehouses. This coincidence is not accidental; in both cases the problem is understood as one of proxemics; in the case of fire, prostitution, retail competition and planning objections, controversy is stoked by proximity. To limit this, dense co-habitation must define an outside, and exterior to which threatening outsiders can be banished.

The first moment of self-limitation was described between the Scotland Act and later improvement bills. Where the former depended upon a conception of Law and the City as fundamentally bounded, by the 17th century, this boundary was itself seen as the root of the problem. The prevalence of fire was growing along with the skyline, hay, or no hay. The Improvement acts, then, recognised the limits of the Scottish Act, and proposed a contrasting approach; an attempt to define the edge of the city (and so of law, and its exception) must give way to a more expansive urbanisation. As such, the distinction between Royal and Baronial jurisdictions, and between the Burgh and its surrounding landscape must be overcome, and both made subject to the same rules.

That the modes of fire-prevention developed during the 18th century were not wholly successful evidences a reflexive limitation within their mentality. Edinburgh's high level of flammability created certain benefits, supporting its growth as a centre for financial technologies, which continue today to be one of its most significant employers. That insurance does not necessarily reduce prevalence does not stop it from being "profitable", as long as premiums cover outlays. Through the logic of insurance, a fire within your building, or within a building insured by a rival company, might be advantageous. As a result, fire-brigades stood by and watched uninsured buildings burn. That arrangement reached its own limit through the events and innovations of 1824, when the need for a higher tier of authority, a "lender of last resort" became apparent.

A final set of reflexive effects can also be seen within the fire-prevention thinking of the 19th century. On the one hand, the technologies of fire-rescue reframed the physical contours of the city in terms of a gradient of risk located on top of hills more prone to catastrophic fire. However, at the same time, these gradients were enrolled within the technologies of rescue, creating a complex weave of more-or-less natural and constructed risks. Being at the top of a hill wasn't bad, as long as it was a hill with a fire-station on it (Figure 3.6).

3.2.10 *Archaeology of accidents*

What I have tried to describe through this second review of our Scottish building standards, as I did with the 2.5-minute rule, is the way that govern-mentalities are transformed as they are translated into the built environment. What I mean to highlight in doing so is the way they are shaped by "accident". Of course, those frameworks have been shaped by accidents occurring within buildings, by fire itself. They have also been shaped by accidental qualities of the built environment, the relative flammability of different modes of construction, or different types of buildings. Additionally, they have been shaped by the unintended consequences of legislation itself, by the sometimes beneficial, sometimes detrimental side-effects that occur in the course of regulating building: the moment in which dense co-location became a risk rather than a benefit; when the city walls came to exacerbate rather than mitigate risk; when loss was recognised as a kind of gain; and when a hill became an affordance as well as a hazard. I have taken the time to relate these moments, to suggest that they illustrate the way that govern-mentalities change as they are enacted, as they are confronted by the "actancy" of their technical delegates.

These reflection perhaps offer some insight into broader questions of standardisation, introduced in Chapter 2. What we don't see, in the above story, is the emergence of a coherent set of "discursive regularities" through which to understand buildings and fire. Our building standards are not a coherent "episteme". Rather, what they read like is an ever-increasing list of contingencies; straw, the location of a prostitute's house, the length of a ladder or a stretch of hose, a profit margin, the top of a hill, the length of a piece of music, the width of someone's shoulder. Over the course of history, our tools of governmental visibility increase, and our legal frameworks reach further into our buildings, and lives. Nonetheless, they don't seek to grasp "building" itself as a thing; they surround it with a halo of accidental

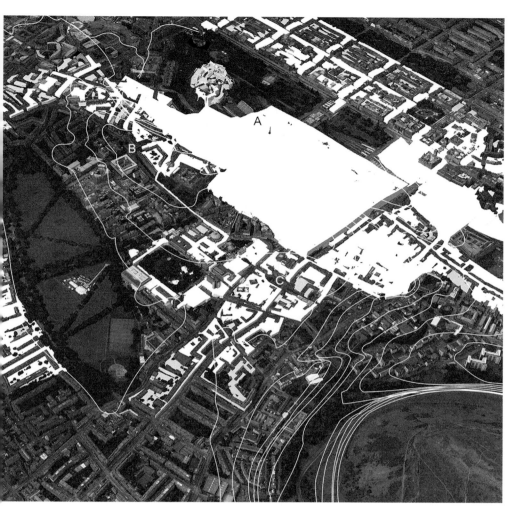

Figure 3.6 **Model of central Edinburgh showing current building heights, historic building height regulation, and topography.** The Royal Burgh, originally not limited in height, is visible in the centre as solid white. The extent to the 18th C. expansion, limited to 5 storeys in height, is visible around it. The location of the Castle Hill reservoir is noted at A. The location of Edinburgh's Central Fire Station is noted at B. The location of the Empire Palace Theatre is noted at C. Liam Ross and Cecile Perdu, 2020.

predicates. As such, we can speak of a building in 1426, or in 2017, as if we speak about the same thing, despite its having been thoroughly transformed. This combination of flexibility and stability seems to me what defined the "Boundary Object" in Susan Leigh Star's terms. Buildings are things which gather a wide range of actors, with a wide range of concerns, none of which are well known by all. Building standards define the "ill-structured" intersection of those concerns.[21] While we recognised, in Chapter 2, the architects concern that building standards leads to predictable, repetitive built environment, when studying standards themselves we might see a different, countervailing tendency. In the process of regulating buildings, the rationality of government is constantly confronted with, resisted and redirected by, the profuse, contingent and "an-essential" dimensions of things.

3.3 The texture of travel distance

3.3.1 Yin and Yang, Capitalism and Communism

To close this first case-study, this section returns to the regulation of travel distance, to consider the question of accident from another perspective. The previous sections have been retrospective in outlook, they have considered the way that regulations react to problems that emerge in particular contexts, inscribing aspects of that context within them. This section reflects briefly on what happens when standards are abstracted from that context, when they travel. It reflects on standards as projective devices, as design tools, and considers the kinds of "accidents" they create within the design process; the way they warp architectural space, but also produce of architectural concepts.

This reflection was prompted by another moment of "infrastructure inversion", one that occurred during a workshop on the sociology of fire-safety. The topic for discussion was the ways that experts in varied fields made use of fire-safety knowledge. An architect from Pelli Clarke Pelli Architects presented the design for a 400 m tall tower, part of a scheme proposed for Tianjin, China. The building would rank as one of the tallest in the world if completed, being 2 m taller than the Petronas Towers, by the same firm, which held that title until 2004. The Petronas towers are famous, in part, for their innovative fire-escape strategy; a sky-bridge on the 41st and 42nd floors allows evacuation through the adjacent twin.[22] The design of Tianjin Tower was likewise informed by egress requirements. Two circular floor-plates centred around two structural cores that converge as they rise, creating a plan the merges from a figure-of-eight at the base to a single circle at its peak. This form was presented to the client as a derivation of the Yin/Yang symbol, the convergence of the tower was intended to symbolise the happy co-existence of Communism and Capitalism. However, we were told, it was in fact determined by travel distance codes; building to the maximum permissible area allowed by BS999 created

Figure 3.7 **Xiaobailou Union Plaza Tower (Project), Pelli Clarke Pelli Associates (2009).** Source: Artist Unknown. 'Xiaobailou Union Plaza, Tower'. https://i.pinimg.com/736x/a6/8b/8d/a68b8dd8bba28df8d1e22b-b465a5d5d5.jpg (accessed, August 24, 2021).

two centroidal floor-plates centred on their means of escape (Figure 3.7). This presentation was again met with a variety of responses. The attendant fire-safety engineers took this occasion to relate the ambiguities, redundancies and deficiencies of our travel distance codes, deficiencies which frustrated the architect that had constructed an edifice around them. But at the same time, I think it's possible to suggest that this project does make an innovative contribution to fire-safety design, by discovering a distinctive "shape" to safe egress.

3.3.2 *The shape of the British National Anthem*

Limitations on travel distance, whether enforced by SBSA 2.9.3, or BS999, are suggestive of a circular plan configuration. Travel distance is measured by a line, originating at a point (the protected door), and describing a circumference. The size of that circle depends upon the occupancy profile; the presumed speed at which the people within the floor make their way to that point. This circle can never be perfect, however, because in reality a protected door is not simply a point; it must give access to a vertical circulation core, a core which itself becomes an obstacle to horizontal movement. Maximum permissible floor-plates pucker around their core, as does the cross-section of an apple. The size of the core and the location of the door within it determine the curvature and origin of that pucker. The resultant geometry achieves a baroque complexity where two directions of escape are possible. Here the circumference describes a series of inflections, which originate from the distance that an escapee can travel in one direction, prior to deciding which way to go (Figure 3.8). A building whose escape core does not stack directly, but converges or diverges, tests the dynamic range of these related parameters (Figure 3.9).

There are no diagrams within BS999 or SBS 2.9.3 that demonstrate these spatial consequences. Earlier methods of limiting travel distance (there are guidelines within the Post-War Building Studies) define X and Y vectors, presuming and reinforcing a rectilinearity of plan. However, through the looser requirements of BS999, something is discovered. Within the parametric variations permitted, one formality remains constant; the perimeter of the maximum permissible floorplate will always be perpendicular to the most direct route of escape. Or to put this experientially; for an occupant facing out of such a building, the most efficient line of escape would always be directly behind them. In this sense, Pelli did offer a compelling rationale for fire-safe design, not because it complied with the codes, but rather because it discovered within them an accidental architecture, one which suggests a form of tacit wayfinding for fire-safety. This spatial logic was in no way present within the model for the code, the Empire Palace. In that building, the risk was in the centre, and the means of escape at the perimeter. However, the "texture" of this code resonates clearly with the structural logic of a skyscraper, based as it is upon a central structural and circulation core. None of these implications were anticipated by the regulators; the way that this code intersects with other shaping concerns in the built environment only emerges through its application.

3.3.3 *Making infrastructure visible*

There is perhaps another way in which this project offers an unlikely lesson. Pelli Clarke Pelli's strategy is, at one level, a simple and familiar

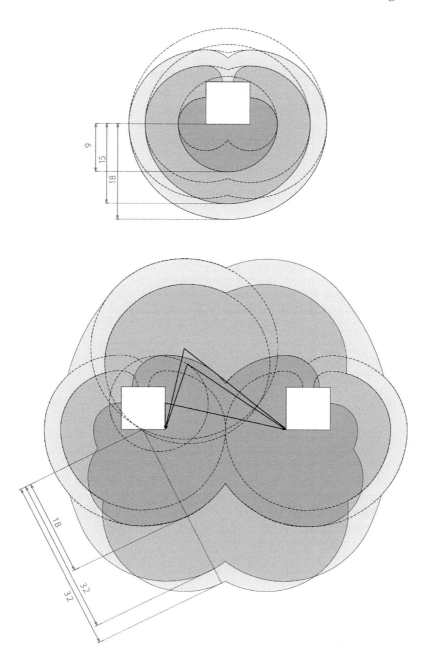

Figure 3.8 **Diagram of maximum permissible travel distance under SBS 2.9.3.** Tone identifies limits for slow, medium and fast occupant profiles. Diagrams shows limits for 1 (above) and 2 (below) means of escape. Liam Ross, 2019

one. Plot maximisation, building up to the limit allowed by the code, is something we know from the work of Hugh Ferris through to Koolhaas or MVRDV. But fire-safety standards provide an uncomfortable subject for such exercises. While they often impose constraints that become the limit-case for development density, no-one wants to think they are living or working on the very margin of safety. Pelli Clarke Pelli chose to disguise that rationale; the metaphorical meaning of the buildings form provides a cover for it technical rationale, one a puppet to the others dwarf. That the radii of permissible travel-distance traces out something like a Yin/Yang symbol and offer a ready metaphor for an Argentine-American speaking to Chinese clients; these are accidents that can only happen on an architect's drawing board. Unlikely as they might be, I do think they tell us something essential about both the architects work, and the role of standards in it.

Charles Edward Stuart, The Great Lafayette, the 1911 fire, and the length of Grand Dieu Sauve Le Roi; all these actors play a part in shaping Pelli Clarke Pelli's building, but none of them carry significance in Tianjin, indeed, the client may or may not be actively concerned about the fire-safety of the proposed tower. British Standards, if not legal requirements in China, no doubt offer some assurity, particularly for international partners. But in translating those standards, making those standards spatial, the architect gives them another, local, meaning. That is, aside from the convergence of the stair tower and its metaphorical content, another kind of "convergence" is occurring here. The design of this tower is providing that materially consistent but discursively flexible thing around which stakeholders gather. Perhaps, from an ANT perspective, this is the fundamental work of the architect; to attend to that gathering, over the course of a building project. To build something that has stabled, fixed features, but translates between and responds to a diverse range of concerns. To give that thing enough internal consistency that it is recognisably the same thing for everyone, but to make it so well-structured that any particular way of thinking is excluded. In that gathering, standards mark out the material and epistemic boundaries between actors, their points of intersection. They make clear the obligations one actor has to another, the things they need to know, but also the things they don't.

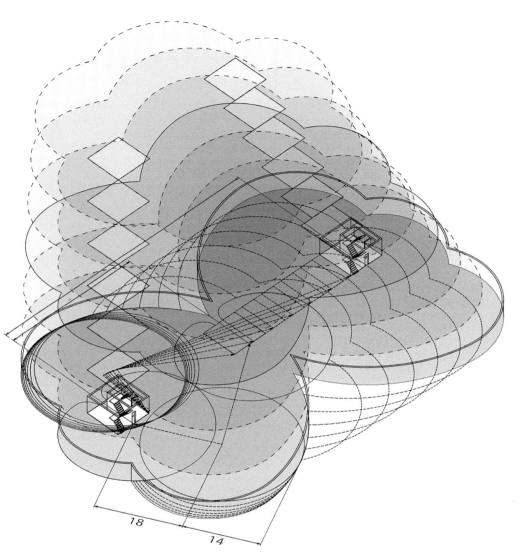

Figure 3.9 **Diagram of maximum permissible travel distance under SBS 2.9.3.** Illustration depicts how total permissible area changes in relation to location of 2 fire-exits. Liam Ross, 2019

Notes

1 British Fire Prevention Committee, *Redbooks of the British Fire Prevention Committee*, 1911.
2 My thanks to the Edinburgh Festival Theatre for discussing this even with me, and sharing their own material on this event.
3 Joint Committee on Fire Grading of Buildings, *Fire Grading of Buildings* (HMSO, 1952). p. 78.
4 Joint Committee on Fire Grading of Buildings. p. 79.
5 'BS 9999:2008 – Code of Practice for Fire Safety in the Design, Management and Use of Buildings – BSI British Standards', accessed 8 September 2015.
6 St Andrew's House Scottish Government, 'Technical Guidance', Website Section, 2 March 2009, http://www.scotland.gov.uk/Topics/Built-Environment/Building/Building-standards/publications/pubtech.
7 Personal correspondence with a variety of fire-safety experts has suggested differing explanations for this discrepancy.
8 Luke Bisby quoted in Nick Collins, 'Professor of Fire: Safety Laws "Absurd"', 22 October 2013, sec. *News*, http://www.telegraph.co.uk/news/science/science-news/10393435/Professor-of-Fire-safety-laws-absurd.html.
9 Quoting Colin Todd from an online forum discussion on the derivation of exit width standards. See 'BS 9999 Exit Flow Rates', accessed 7 November 2017, http://www.crisis-response.com/forum/index.php?topic=6578.5;wap2.
10 The *Gentleman's Magazine*, in its October 1836 edition, published the additional verse, now removed: "Lord, grant that Marshal Wade; May by thy mighty aid; Victory bring; May he sedition hush; and like a torrent rush; Rebellious Scots to crush; God save the King."
11 I refer here to the argument present in Bentham, but extended by Foucault and Wallenstein, that would posit the *Panopticon* as a tool for "liberty". Inasmuch as the building sought to act upon the will of the inmate it depends upon an irreducible but situated moment of "freedom". Discussing Foucault's lectures on Biopolitics, Wallenstein suggests that

> [i]n an important passage it also becomes clear that the famous analysis of Jeremy Bentham's Panopticon proposed in Discipline and Punish ultimately has little to do with that exclusively "repressive" model it has become among many readers of Foucault (in spite of his repeated assertions of the productive nature of power), but has to be understood as one part of a liberal governmentality. In this sense biopolitics becomes a privileged form of intervention, which is the condition of possibility for the discovery of the individual in political philosophy as a subject with all of his rights and duties (both as a *sujet* and a *citoyen*, as Rousseau said). These are the individual's new capacities, which have been produced by techniques of discipline that precede and condition political liberalism as a theory that discovers the individual as a given entity. This is why modernity for Foucault is not at all a continuous process of discipline and control, but rather a complex production of subjectivity, a "subjugation" that is also a "subjectification," in which the individual is produced in order then to discover himself as free.

Sven-Olov Wallenstein, *Bio-Politics and the Emergence of Modern Architecture*, 1st ed. (New York: Princeton Architectural Press, 2009). p. 13.
12 "The motto of Liberalism is 'Live Dangerously', that is to say, the individual is constantly exposed to danger, or rather, they are conditioned to experience their situation, their life, their present, and their future as containing danger." Foucault, *The Birth of Biopolitics*. p. 66.
13 Leigh Hancher and Michael Moran, *Capitalism, Culture, and Economic Regulation* (Oxford, New York: Oxford University Press, 1989).

14 In discussion with Mick Moran he noted that at the time of writing he was not aware of Foucault's work on governmentality, as it had not yet been translated into English. Nonetheless, he concurred that aspects of his own concerns resonate with that literature.

15 I am paraphrasing McDermont who extends the "regulatory space" literature by bringing the concept into dialogue with thinkers such as Lefevbre, Foucault and Latour Morag McDermont, 'Territorializing Regulation: A Case Study of "Social Housing" in England', *Law & Social Inquiry* 32, no. 2 (1 June 2007): 373–398. doi: 10.1111/j.1747-4469.2007.00063.x.

16 This summary of Scottish fire-safety legislation is taken primarily from the a publication developed by the Lothian & Borders Fire Rescue Services: See Alexander Reid, '*Aye Ready!': History of the Edinburgh Fire Brigade, the Oldest Municipal Brigade in Britain* (Edinburgh: South-Eastern Fire Brigade, 1974).

17 James 1, 11 March 1426, Perth, Parliament, Legislation, in 'Records of the Parliaments of Scotland', accessed 14 October 2014, http://www.rps.ac.uk/static/bottom_frame.html.

18 Shane Ewen, *Fighting Fires: Creating the British Fire Service, 1800–1978* (Springer, 2009). p. 38.

19 Quoting Blackstone in Ewen. p. 38.

20 François Ewald, *L'Etat providence* (Paris: B. Grasset, 1986).

21 I am attempting here to bring together the "object" of Susan Leigh Star's sociology with Bruno Latour's expansion of Heidegger's "Thing". In attempting to describe the distinction between Heidegger's "Object" and "Thing", Latour uses an accident – the challenger disaster – to describe the moment that technical objects demonstrate their an-essential character:

> Here, suddenly, in a stroke, an object had become a thing, a matter of fact was considered as a matter of great concern. If a thing is a gathering, as Heidegger says, how striking to see how it can suddenly disband. If the "thinging of the thing" is a gathering that always connects the "united four, earth and sky, divinities and mortals, in the simple onefold of their self-unified fourfold," how could there be a better example of this making and unmaking than this catastrophe unfolding all its thousands of folds.

Bruno Latour, 'Why Has Critique Run out of Steam? From Matters of Fact to Matters of Concern', *Critical Inquiry* 30, no. 2 (1 January 2004): 225–248.

22 This strategy is not without its own problems. By supporting the reduction of escape cores sizes within each individual towers, the bridge has made the two co-dependant, with the effect that neither function effectively if both must be evacuated at the same time. This scenario occurred during a hoax the day after the September 11 attacks in New York, and has since lead to the building needing to rely on lifts to support egress. See A. Wood, W. K. Chow, and D. McGrail, 'The Skybridge as an Evacuation Option for Tall Buildings for Highrise Cities in the Far East', *Journal of Applied Fire Science*, 13, no. 2 (2005): 113–124.

4 Lagos
The flight of a muzzle spark

4.1 The cession of Lagos, 1861

> Peaceful penetration is the uniform and unbroken course of the development of Lagos since its cession in 1861. No rising of the Natives and no punitive expeditions draw a red streak across its story of peace and trade.[1]

So begins Sir William Geary's *Nigeria Under British Rule*, though his account of the cession itself must admit to the occasional bloodstain or scorchmark. Committed to establish the British Empire as an arena of free trade, and to end slavery by either diplomacy or force, on Christmastide 1851 Lord Palmerston ordered that Lagos be reduced by bombardment from the HMS Bloodhound and HMS Teaser. After five days of fighting, during which a rocket exploding in a magazine caused a fire that left most of the town destroyed, the local ruler was driven out and replaced by a favourable alternative. From 1851 to 1861 the port remained nominally independent, under the puppet King Docemo. During these ten years the slave-trade with America was abolished, but the development of commercial relations with Britain faltered. Correspondence that Geary draws upon attributes this to a lack of "effective" government, in particular surrounding the difficulty of defining and defending "private property", a concept that was foreign to the indigenous culture.

On the 22nd of June 1861 Lagos was taken possession of as a British Dependency. "No injustice" was to be done to Docemo; he was to be provided with a generous personal pension. This offer was delivered to him by HMS Prometheus, which then took him to the British Consulate to complete the paperwork. Geary does not comment as to whether Docemo was pleased with the proposal, but according to Otonba Payne, who would go on to be Lagos's chief registrar, he did not put up a fight.

> King Docemo and chiefs stood by the flag staff in front of the consulate and went through the ceremony of touching the rope, by which the British Ensign became unfurled while simultaneously the frigate

DOI: 10.4324/9781003026297-4

thundered a Royal salute of 21 guns, while all the school children of Lagos then present sang the [British] National Anthem.[2]

Article 1 of The Treaty of Cession reads,

> I, Docemo, do, with the consent and advice of my Council, give, transfer, and by these presents grant and confirm unto the Queen of Great Britain, her heirs, and successors forever, the port and Island of Lagos with all the rights, profits, territories, and appurtenances whatsoever thereunto belonging, and as well the profits and revenue as the direct, full, and absolute dominion and sovereignty of the said port, island, and premises, with all royalties thereof, freely, fully and entirely and absolutely.[3]

Article 3 thought to add that Docemo's stamp on the treaty would be taken as proof that there were no other native claims on the land, and that Lagos was, indeed, his to give away. While Geary offers us the official story, other accounts include details he would omit. The *Anglo-African*, a Lagos newspaper, reported on September 12th 1863, Docemo proclaiming (in his native Yoruba) "Mo ofi ilu me torreh ..." ("I have not made a present of my town. Did I not in the government house ... refuse to sign? Did I not refuse on board the Prometheus? At my palace did I not also refuse to sign?")[4] This statement does not appear within the official history, though it garnered official response, by Governor Glover, who promptly declared a state of emergency:

> Gentlemen: King Docemo has this day denied that he ever gave over his town to the Queen of England, thereby defying the Queen's supremacy over this her colony of Lagos. I hereby call on all loyal subjects of her majesty to be sworn in as Special Constables for the due assertion of Her Majesty's authority and the protection of life and property within her colony of Lagos.[5]

This assertion of martial law led to the "excitement of the 13th" in which the city was once again destroyed by fire-bombing. Docemo surrendered, was stripped of his pension, and fined £50 for the bother. But absolute assertion of British Sovereignty did not end the challenges of colonisation, chief among them remaining the issue of defining and defending private property. One of the first laws passed by the newly established Town Council, Ordinance 9 of 1863, established the legal infrastructure for purchase and sale of title deeds. But the indigenous built fabric and construction practices also posed problems:

> Being essentially Yoruba, the unit of housing amongst the prosperous indigenes is the compound consisting of a group of compartments built

around a rectangular open courtyard ... The roof consists of roughly prepared palm fronds or bamboo over which a thick layer of mud was spread as a preventative against fires.[6]

This "black mud" troubled a commission of medical and engineering officers who outlawed it, declaring it injurious to health.[7] Its properties as a fire-retardant were found wanting, also. According to contemporary reports in the *Observer*, Lagos was the "veritable *fire-place*" of West Africa, suffering at least two building fires every night.[8] And moreover, the high cost of local construction materials hampered development; "the greatest impediment to building with us is the difficulty of procuring material. Bricks are made here but some are bad and all far too expensive ... badly sawn timber wood costs fully twice as much as building timber in England".[9] In 1877 a particularly destructive fire, caused by wadding discharged from a pistol, destroyed a third of the island. It prompted the Lagos Town Council to enact its first by-Law, as a means to address the complex of policing, public safety, urban planning and economic concerns it then faced: the law forbade the discharge of firearms or the letting-off of fireworks; demanded all buildings be built at a set distance from their property boundary to prevent spread of flame; granted police the power to demolish buildings that did not comply with this "setback"; outlawed the use of thatch as a building material; established corrugated iron as the mandatory fire-proof roofing material; and removed duty from the importation of this product, which was not manufactured in Nigeria.[10]

4.1.1 Reason and treason

As engrossing as the historical detail of this story is, it is important to step back from it, and to review its legal rationale, which traces out an Escher-like series of contradictions and aporia. The legal status of the treaty is the most obvious place to start. Even under British Law, the legality of sovereign cession depended upon a principle of "continuity", recognising the right of existing property owners. As was well known by the settlers, in Yoruba culture land was understood to be fundamentally inalienable, held in trust by the community through an administrative hierarchy of family, clan and royal association. To construe this land as a lawful part of the British Commonwealth thus required a number of imaginative leaps.[11] To take Docemo's signature as lawful we must first assume the alienation of land, via the administrative class of "White-Cap Chiefs", on to Docemo, of which no evidence exists. Secondly, we must choose to ignore Docemo's proclamation – more convincingly his own than that of the treaty – that he did not make Lagos a gift to the Queen. Finally we must simply accept that Lagos was *already* the Queen's, so as to take for treason, the non-gifting of what wasn't his to give. Nonetheless, this is the view that was successively upheld in court until as late as 1957; the treaty was not strictly *legal*, but as an Act of State it was rather deemed to be above the law, even those laws pertaining to the legality of cession.[12]

But ironies of logic do not end there. There is a certain flair exhibited by an assurance that "no injustice" was done to a deposed King on account of a promised pension, a pension annulled upon forced overthrow, an overthrow for which he is then charged costs. The structuring of "free" trade through legal requirements, preferential taxation and state-sponsored monopolies is its own story. But the circularities and reflexivities of legal thinking that I wish to dwell on here are the ones that this series of events and proclamations inscribe into the built fabric of Lagos. Assuming a remarkably reasonable set of concerns so soon after repeatedly fire-bombing the city, the first Lagos building regulation – the "setback" code – brings about a particularly subtle ruse. Ostensibly concerned with the health and safety of the populace, and expressing a governmental ambition that they not set their own houses on fire, this rule rendered unlawful the remaining physical fabric and construction practices of a city which had already been largely destroyed, and whose patterns of ownership had been undermined. In one set of related measures, this law strengthened the state's monopoly on violence, outlawing the use of personal fire-arms; it empowered the British authorities to demolish existing building stock where it saw fit, clearing the way for new roads; it sought to protect the new buildings – of settlers, or of prosperous locals – from the risk of accidental loss; and it established a new supply chain of imported goods, freeing British manufacturer from the need to pay tax when importing them. That is, if the cession of Lagos demonstrates some of the theoretical absurdities of discourses on Sovereign Right, this first Nigerian building regulation marks the transition to a different way of thinking. It offers us a kind of diagram – a representation in miniature – of the processes through which the direct expression of Sovereign violence comes to be governmentalised. It also reminds us that at times we need to be able to see that apparently technocratic phenomena like building codes, and the marks they leave on the city, are a "continuation of war by other means".

4.1.2 Mess trajectories of LSPPD 15

The setback code is one of the most significant factors in the development of the city's contemporary urban form. It continues to be enforced today, defined by Lagos State Physical Planning and Development Regulation 15. This rule sets out a minimum distance that any development must retain between building and the boundary (Figure 4.1). This distance ranges from 3 to 9 m in depth, circumscribing the buildable area, and development economics, of any plot. Its effect is to define Lagos as an essentially suburban settlement, making it illegal to build either up to the street, or

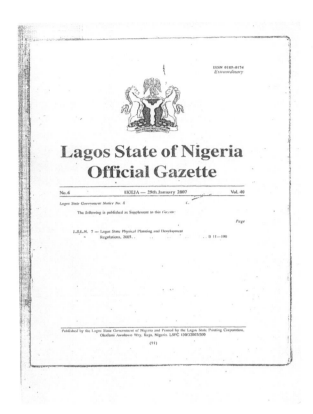

Figure 4.1 '**Lagos State Government Notice 8**'. Required setbacks are published as regulation15withinthisdocument.Source:LagosStateofNigeriaOfficialGazette40, no. 6 (2007). Photocopy by author.

up to adjacent properties. In terms of urban form, the rule effectively outlawed – indeed, inverted – the courtyard pattern that typified Yoruba settlements. It likewise made illegal the dense, Portuguese-style urbanism that had been established in downtown Lagos, arriving via re-patriated slaves (Figure 4.2). Following the paradigm of the British settlement in Ikoyi, it channelled the urban form of Lagos through the model of a house in gardens (Figure 4.3).

If its stated ambition was to improve the fire-safety of the city, its effects in practice have been somewhat different. While the code suggests no development is possible within the setback, in practice this zone is perhaps the most economically and socially active part of the city. Comprising the street frontage of every building in the city, this area is structured by two features, the "fence" and the "ditch", the city's ubiquitous infrastructures of security and drainage. Behind the fence,

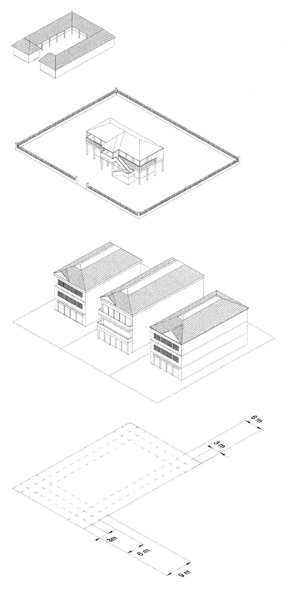

Figure 4.2 **The Urbanism of Setback.** Satellite photograph of contemporary Lagos, superimposed with urban plan c. 1960. Downtown Lagos, left, shows the dense morphology informed by Portuguese architecture and planning. The British settlement at Ikoyi, right, demonstrates a less dense urban morphology. The boundary of the British Camp is still identifiable through the location of creek and army barracks, centre. Liam Ross and Nicola Grant 2012.

the setback is used for all manner of adjunct facilities: security posts, guard houses, servants-quarters, generators, diesel storage-tanks, utility buildings, cargo-container yards, even small domestic settlements. On the street side, it accommodates a range of economic or cultural activities; the kiosks in which every-day untaxed trade occurs, the vulcanising stations of the cities famous car-mechanics, it provides a home for local "area boys", for street-side gin-distilleries, for the cities "mendicants" and for its Mosques.

That is, this part of the city is by no means undeveloped, it is not empty, rather it is developed informally. The setback code structures a space that accommodates those practices and programmes which do not have a designated place within the city. And in doing so, it becomes strictly counterproductive. Rather than creating a system of urban fire-breaks so as to protect property development from the risk of fire, it distributes people, activities, materials and buildings in such a way as to maximise the likelihood of fire-spread, creating a web of unregulated structures and activities that line the frontage boundaries of public and private space throughout the city. Emerging from an attempt to quell the streets, to bring them under governmental control, its effect today is quite different; dismantling the existing urban patterns of publicity and privacy, it developed an urban form that pre-supposed public lawlessness, retreating its architecture into compounds, leaving behind an ill-defined urban space which could be readily ceased by other actors. In the stark contrast of these intents and effects we seem to be offered an example of the way that sovereign assertions of law, codes and standards can often exist in direct and blind opposition to the realities of everyday life.

In the previous chapter I used the city of Edinburgh to reflect on a set of *congruences* between Law and the City. I sought to show how law sometimes emerges from, and is re-inscribed into our urban environment, such that the spatiality, materiality and texture of our cities has a shaping effect on the mentalities of government. In this chapter we are confronted with a different city, and a different code, one which has been violently imposed upon its social and physical context, and one that evidences an incongruity between urban fabric and legal rationale. Indeed, it was this anomaly, the "mess-trajectory" constructed by the Lagos setback code, that provided the impetus for this enquiry. But my purpose in recounting that enquiry is not to critique that code as a representation of colonial politics, nor even on account of its counter-productivity. Rather, in this chapter I wish to reflect on the political polyvalence of standards, on the difficulty of attributing a single governmental rationale to a particular governmental technology.

In this opening section I offered a way into that reflection, noting the contrast between ambitions and effects. In the second section, I reflect upon that contrast theoretically, drawing on literatures from Law and Geography studies. Specifically, I draw on the concept of "Seeing like a City", as it

Figure 4.3 **A Genealogy of the Lagos Setback.** Yoruba Compound form; British 'Government House'; Idumagbo Avenue Housing Scheme; LSPPDR 15 setbacks for Ikoyi. Liam Ross and Calum MacDonald 2012.

is developed by Warren Magnusson and Marianna Valverde. Through this concept these scholars point to a particular capacity of urban life to ignore, contest or actively defy the legal frameworks that would seem to circumscribe it. And while recognising the political polyvalence of such contestation, Magnusson will, nonetheless, suggest that we recognise its necessity, as a means through which the sovereign gesture of law is "recycled", re-incorporated into the everyday life of the city. Through this chapter I wish to use the Lagos setback as a means to study how laws, even those that are violently imposed, come to be absorbed and re-directed by a city, and to reflect on the role of building in that process of recycling.

4.2 Seeing like a state, seeing like a city

4.2.1 Domination and the city

That Law and the City sublimate violence, and define spaces of Sovereignty, should come as no surprise. In the previous chapter, we recognised the "Leges Burgorum" of Edinburgh as a means to define a set of legal exceptions, carved out of an underlying landscape of feudalism. The physical fact of the castle, and the enclosure of its city walls represented the authority that defended those exceptions, symbolising and exercising the King's capacity for violence. In his *Legal History of Cities*, Gerald Frug offers similar reflections on the relation of law and space within the European medieval town. He notes that, while these settlements offered a kind of physical and legal clearing, this did not make their inhabitants particularly "free". The medieval town was, he reminds us, filled with internal forms of hierarchy and struggle, splintering's of interest between nobility, crown and an emergent "state", new class associations and individual interests that – in his account – ultimately bring an end to this urban model. Indeed, for Krug the physical and regulatory spaces of the "modern city" emerge, less from the foundations left by the Medieval town, more from its gaps, failures and omissions, from the social forms and practices it failed to represent.[13]

Frug's account draws upon that offered by Max Weber in *Economy and Society*. Weber famously studied the sociology of European Medieval settlements, likewise noting their relative freedom from the authority of Law and the threat of Sovereign violence. However, in his analysis, this freedom was precisely what made such places an incubator for new and alternative modes of domination. Indeed, in Weber's sociology, the concept of the "City" – of densely settled, relatively bounded, impersonal and autonomous places – is synonymous with the possibility of what he calls "non-legitimate domination".[14] The intense forms of co-dependence constructed by urban environments create a circumstance in which authorities based upon Law, Tradition or Charismatic Leadership founder, being displaced by emergent modes of authority that operate in parallel, in ignorance, or in open defiance of the rules. We can't understand everything about a city by looking at its statute books; the spaces of innovation and change are often those that are ill-defined by law. Indeed, by focussing on the *congruence* between law and the city, we might blind ourselves to other questions, and walk into a methodological trap; gleaning traces of order from the mess of reality, we might construe both the city, and government, to be more organised than they actually are.

4.2.2 Reflexive error

Within the field of Law and Geography studies, this methodological risk has been given a name, that of "Seeing like a State". James C. Scott coined this term in his eponymous book, using it to explains why "certain schemes to improve the human condition have failed".[15] Scott suggests that the (often well-intentioned) ambitions of architects, planners and governments often do violence to local and established modes of organisation, precisely on account of this optical pre-disposition. Only capable of seeing within the terms of their own means of intervention, they fail to see what is actually happening "on the ground". Scott's critique would seem easy to level at Lagosian planners, both colonial and contemporary. That city seems to be organised through a by-law that imposes a utopia that first did violence to, and now appears ignorant of, existing urban practices.

But we could also see this risk operating at a different level; indeed, Scott's term has developed a wider currency, one that folds back onto questions of political theory, and research methodology. In *Seeing Like a State, Seeing Like a City,* Warren Magnusson uses it to describe a perceived state-centricity within political theory itself. Again, thanks to a tendency to assume the subject-position of architect/governor, Magnusson suggests that most political theorists are pre-disposed to assume the theoretical necessity of the State, and so to assume that defining and securing concepts of Sovereignty is their important theoretical task. Magnusson makes this argument with reference to the same imaginary relationship we have identified, via Andreas Philippopoulos-Mihalopoulos, as existing between the city and its codes and standards. The disciplines of Law and Urban Planning are engaged, he suggests, in a kind of mutual self-legitimation. Political theorists assume the necessity of something like "Sovereignty" thanks to a normative leap; The State, and so a Sovereign authority, is all around us, written in to the bricks-and-mortar of our legal frameworks, social practices and built environment, and so appears practically necessary.[16] This additional twist is likewise readily applied to our particular case. We might well say that the authors of the first Lagos Town Council by-law were engaged in a kind of reflexive self-legitimation; they "saw like a state" inasmuch as their fundamental concern was to define Sovereign Right, an end to which urban fire, constructions practices and tax arrangements were merely a means.

4.2.3 Recycling sovereignty

If we accept Magnusson's argument, we might be concerned that our current study suffers from the same optical problem; by looking at Lagos through the terms of this original governmental programme we seem to seek its legitimacy, even as we draw attention to its failures. Responding to this concern, Magnusson engages with Scott's term in order to define an alternative way of looking at the relationship between city and law. To do so he draws on Weber's account of the special sociological character of the city as a means to sketch an alternative political theory, one which abandons the subject-position of the planner, replacing it with that of the anarchist. Politics is here construed precisely as a process through which assertions of Sovereignty are *resisted*. He suggests that the practical politics of urban co-habitation – bounded, closely settled, relatively impersonal – again provides evidence of the ways in which "legitimate" modes of dominance (Law, Tradition and Charisma) find themselves ignored, contested, or actively defied, in such a way as to allow multiple overlapping and competing authority claims to co-exist side-by-side.

> To see like a state is to suppose that the most important political problems are resolved once sovereignty is established. This supposition is very much at odds with experience… Another way of achieving a kind of civil peace is when rival sovereignty-claims are moderated or held in suspense as people with radically different views work out ways of living side by side. This latter way is more akin to the other practices of urban life.[17]

That is, if the optics of political theory and of state planning seem to define a kind of blind-spot, a point of Sovereignty, in which law is effectively suspended, Magnusson points to a different kind of suspension that is constantly occurring "on the ground", as rival actors seek to employ the law for their own purposes. Magnusson cites Schmitt in order to suggest that, within this struggle, we recognise Sovereignty not as the "first mention" of politics, but rather its "McGuffin":[18]

> To use Schmittian language, sovereignty is the exception that is postponed, evaded, deflected, subverted, and ultimately transfigured… The sovereign promises to repel the invading army or to suppress the riots; the sovereign expects obedience in return. But, this bargain – which is not really a bargain, since people have no choice but to accept it – is just a moment in the re-organization of the city. Ultimately, the sovereign and the sovereign's pretensions are incorporated as another element in the life of the city. The sovereign is not the rock on which the city is built, but part of the rubble that the city transforms into reinforced concrete.[19]

4.2.4 *Ways of seeing*

Magnusson dubs his political-theoretical programme "Seeing Like a City", using it to demonstrate ways in which law comes to be shaped by the practicalities of its application, and the resistance it faces. This term has been adopted by other scholars, notably Marianna Valverde, professor of criminology and sociology at the University of Toronto. I introduced Valverde's work in Chapter 2, offering it as a means to demonstrate the utopian character of urban legislation; in studies of her native Toronto, she showed us that a majority of buildings exist within a "legal non-conforming use" category, undermining the notion of "comprehensive" zoning. Likewise, I used her work to demonstrate the political polyvalence of codes; her work on "diversity" legislation in Toronto shows us how these frameworks often disadvantage those marginalised groups they are intended to support.[20] In *Seeing Like a City: The Dialectics of Modern and Premodern Ways of Seeing in Urban Governance* Valverde brings her work into dialogue with Scott and Magnusson's terms, but in a way that complicates their oppositional logics. Taking the constitutional questions surrounding the implementation of US Zoning Law as an example, she considers the landmark case *Village of Euclid v. Rambler Reality*. This case, through which the Supreme Court found in favour of the Village of Euclid's right to impose planning restrictions – even when shown to damage the value of private property – is widely seen to have paved the way for widespread use of planning instruments within the US.[21] But reviewing the case, Valverde argues that this decision effectively worked both *for* and *against* zoning, defending the possibility of such "socialist" requirements only through incorporating a range of generous legal exceptions, "structural contingencies" that allowed them to be by-passed in specific circumstances.[22] Through this example, Valverde implies the need to recognise that governmental initiatives which might seem to "see like a state" – whether that state be Imperialist, socialist or liberal – are often designed to incorporate specific modes of suspension that accommodate alternative viewpoints. As such, the way in which laws and standards fail – the way that they create residues, others, outsiders – might, in fact, be part of their design, a mode of pre-emptive self-limitation. Nuancing Magnusson's term, then, she suggests that to "See Like a City" is to recognise that rules, through their mechanisms for non-compliance, can themselves be means to broker "civic peace" through the recognition of competing views and concerns.

If I began this chapter by "seeing like a state" – trying to understand Lagos through its rules and their rationale – here I would like to attempt to "see like a city". That is, in the section below I wish to return to the setback code, but with a focus on the way it works "on the ground". It is informed by interviews conducted with a number of architects, lawyers and planners on the way they work with and around this code, and by drawn and photographic survey of the way the setback comes to be occupied on the ground.[23] On the basis of that research it hoped to illustrate the way this code constructs a space, both legal and physical, through which the concerns of a range of state and non-state actors emerge and are gathered.

4.3 Occupying the setback

4.3.1 Gunpowder and thatch

> Let me tell you what interests me in the rule. When I travelled, when I went through to European cities, I asked myself, why do these big cities look so *expansive*? It's because they don't have fences. You can actually walk to the doorstep because they don't have fences. In Lagos you know we are all fenced in and the roads set back.[24]

The setback code is well known to local architects, lawyers and urban-planners, and it is recognised to have a formative effect of the city's urban fabric. As suggested in the above quote, from our interview with Tunji Odunlami, director of Physical Planning at The Lagos State Secretariat, the code defines Lagos as a "city of fences", one with no designed, active street-frontages. But our enquiries also prompted confusion; it was very hard to find the rule written down anywhere, and the people we interviewed were uncertain as to its purpose. The rule simply *was*; urban actor knew about it because they could see it, written into the fabric of the city. It did not take long to understand why. Although Nigeria developed a National Building Code in 2006, by 2012 this had yet to be adopted by any particular State. Building regulations in Nigeria are therefore still a matter of local by-laws. And Lagos State does not publish its by-laws online, nor through a consolidated handbook. Indeed, the very *difficulty* of approaching this particular law took on an allegorical, Kafka-esque quality. Lagos State publishes its by-laws through "Gazettes", A4 photocopied pamphlets that record the passing of new laws, organised by date. The current iteration of Physical Planning and Development Regulation 15 are published as part of the "Lagos State Physical Planning and Development Regulations", of 2005, included as a supplement within the *Lagos State of Nigeria Official Gazette*, No. 6, 2007.[25] This pamphlet, along with all the other laws of the State, is available only from the Secretariat building, a three-hour, heavily congested drive from downtown Lagos. At the secretariat they are stored in the "Cabinet Room" – a room full of cabinets – housing identical looking Xeroxed A4 documents. That room is supervised by an elderly official, with pronounced cataracts. With difficulty, the single copy of Gazette 6 was located, but a problem then presented itself. We could not be given the only remaining copy of the Law, and the Secretariat itself did not have any photocopiers. This impasse was only overcome through what seemed like a by-product of the by-law in question. Outside the Secretariat, in the "setback zone" of that building, local entrepreneurs have responded to this governmental lack, and set up informal photocopying kiosks. To stand "Before the Law" in Lagos is not to wait interminably outside its gates; it is to sneak up to its fence, huddle under its eaves, dragging a power cable out of its windows.[26]

But as to the purpose of this particular law, the gazette is of no help; in its current form, no rationale is stated. To understand its governmental ambition, then, requires a personal interview. And even for Tunji Odunlami, the most senior figure concerned with the States building regulations, the answer is not entirely clear:

> Gunpowder and thatched roofs, they are not friends you know. They go up in flames. Yes, the setback rule evolved from British regulations, from colonial times, as a means of stopping spread of flame. However, I don't *think* that is what it is about today. The setback, for all terms and purpose, does not belong to you. Before the setback, that bit of property does not really belong to you. It is an easement, the government can take it back at any time, for road widening for instance. It doesn't say this in any laws, but I make a deduction. That's why you can't build your main building there, but also why there is a relaxation on the kind of structures that can be built in this space. You can put up temporary structures there, and we don't hound you.[27]

That is, its contemporary governmental rationale today has nothing to do with fire; the urban problem that it now seems to address is that of infrastructure expansion. Lagos lacks a sewage system, a storm-water drainage system – indeed, much of the fixed physical infrastructure associated with a city of its size. Its notorious "Go-Slows" (areas of perpetual gridlock) are understood to threaten the city's function as the commercial hub of Nigeria, and therefore road and infrastructure expansion are key areas for governmental action. It is in this context that "the retention of the provision for setback zones in the statute is critical to maintaining the stability of the State's economy".[28] The temporary settlement of this zone is not seen as a governmental problem, rather it is a "meanwhile use" that holds the space open for future appropriation.

4.3.2 Regulatory space of LSPPD 15

But if that is what the code means today, this has not always been the case. Indeed, its purpose and requirements have been re-conceived and re-articulated numerous times. This is not unusual within Nigerian legislation, much of which was imported by the British. Until 1960, when Nigeria claimed independence, all Nigerian planning laws and building regulations were based on British models. Even today, the primary legislation remains that of the *1932 Town and Country Planning Act*, introduced to Nigeria in 1946, and retained post-independence. Initially drawing on the same putative authority, and retaining the same legal architecture, these rules have nevertheless been edited and re-purposed to the local environmental and political exigencies. In the case of the setback code, for instance, by the early 20th century this had already been re-conceived as an instrument of public health. When the Lagos Executive Development Board (LEBD) was set up to respond to an outbreak of bubonic plague, they recognised the potential within the setback to define a "cordon sanitaire" around dwellings. They re-purposed the code to establish restrictions on the density and height of buildings, expressed through the requirement that no part of the building – with the exception of balconies, deemed beneficial for health – should extend in front of an imaginary line at 60 degrees to the boundary. While legitimating clearance and reconstruction in the slums, this change reduced the amount of required setback – disease was seen as less mobile than fire – also permitting a general densification, with schemes such as Idumagbo Avenue (Figure 4.3) acting as models.[29]

The setback code was reconceived again in 1946 when, carried by the Town and Country Planning Act, Ebenezer Howard's Garden City movement arrived in Lagos. The suburban spatiality of Ikoyi, the original British settlement, was rediscovered as a nascent Garden Suburb.[30] Its plan, seen as a native equivalent of Welwyn, informed Lagos planning from the 1940s–1960s. In this period, the LEDB density rules were re-written, re-establishing a minimum setback, and reinforcing the house in garden pattern; they required that "not more than 50% of the site should be covered for residential purposes, or 70% for other uses, and that an air space of 5'6" be left round a single storey building other than a 3'-6" boundary wall in front of the building line".[31] Today, in the context of ambitions to establish a national building code, the setback offers other potentialities. Lagos State requires all rooms to be provided with cross- or adjacent-ventilation – an environmental requirement that would be both unthinkable and unpractical in cities that developed from the European medieval city – something that is achievable because all buildings are already provided with air-space to all sides. That is, it is difficult to attribute a single rationale to the Lagos setback code. This statute has created an opportunity for legal re-appropriation on the part of the town's planners. Originally rationalised as a means to limit fire, it has since been construed to have a range of other governmental values; as a public health measure, as an environmental asset and as an easement for fixed infrastructure.

4.3.3 Materiality of law

To see the code in terms of its original urban ambition, the best place to look is the British Council headquarters. These are located in Ikoyi, the former British settlement. Here we see the setback as an instrument of security, in the face of a presumed urban lawlessness. Outside that building's compound, a disruptive surface of raised beds has been planted up to the road-side, prohibiting informal commercial activity. The fence here takes the form of a white stucco wall, with chunky Iroko-clad steel verticals. Stepping over the ditch, access is gained by way of a single-story security

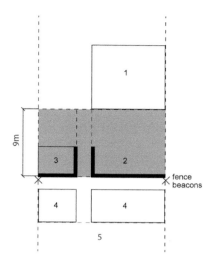

Figure 4.4 **Occupying the Setback: Disruptive planting.** 1. British Council Headquarters. 2. Protective fencing. 3. Security booth. 4. Disruptive planting. 5. Road. Liam Ross with Maria Esteban Castenas, 2012.

building; the kind of adjunct facility that, in practice, are allowed within this zone. Inside the wall, a ramped, landscaped garden provides the regulation 9 m setback to a second round of Iroko members, here screening a curtain-wall of anti-ballistic glazing (Figure 4.4). But this clear architectural expression of the law is unusual, even exceptional; only across the road, a more relaxed scene exists. Here the setback has been occupied by a vulcaniser's workshop, who use the 9 m space as a workshop; behind the fence, in the garden of an abandoned colonial mansion, shipping containers support this informal street-side commerce (Figure 4.5). Heading west through Ikoyi this arrangement repeats itself; next door is a gin distillery, a garden centre, a ceramics shop.

Reaching Obalende, we find ourselves at the edge of the former British settlement, where the army barracks once stood, in an area still characterised by institutions of State. Here the required setbacks are deeper, and within them we find more organised settlements. At the Lagos State Police Barracks, a "mammy market" occupies the zone (Figure 4.6); rows of commercial stalls, with living spaces above, provide accommodation and employment for the wives and mothers of the poorly paid policemen who work in the building. At the Lagos Motor Boat Club, the space is convenient for storing boats; at City Mall, for car-parking. And at the monumental Tafawa Balewa Square we see the opportunities for infrastructural expansion provided by this rule. Here a new bus station occupies the space between the street and this modernist arcade and parade ground, where Nigeria's independence was declared and celebrated (Figure 4.7). Indeed, a number of new bus stations have been built across the city through the compulsory requisition of such land.

In downtown Lagos, we see the effect that this code has had on precolonial architecture, and the way it has shaped future development. Residential buildings that pre-date cession exist in a dilapidated state, rendered illegal by the code (Figure 4.8), where those built more recently continue to exist in compliance. In early 20th-century development, supported by the revised codes of the LEBD, we find a denser, more urban arrangement, with apartment buildings separated by reduced setbacks, the space between them again filled with single-story adjunct facilities: a street kiosk, a taxi mechanic's workshop (Figure 4.9), a mosque. And in the commercial centre of Lagos Island, banks stand back from the street, with isolated ATMs placed in the fence, or headquarters of international companies overhang this space, making room for small scale entrepreneurs on the street below. Only the historic Broad Street is exempt from this requirement, and as such offers a moment of that "expansive" urban environment, one where the street extents to the doorstep, of which Tunji spoke (Figure 4.10).

4.3.4 Authority in suspense

The *legal* space of the setback, then, has created an opportunity for spatial occupation. The relaxed enforcement of this law – that Tunji "won't hound you" – means that, in practice, it carves out an opportunity for

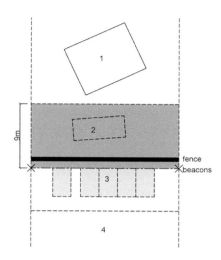

Figure 4.5 **Occupying the Setback: Ikoyi, Vulcanisers.** 1. Dutch Colonial House (derelict). 2. Cargo Storage. 3. Vulcanisers. 4. Road. Liam Ross with Maria Esteban Castenas, 2012.

informal settlement. Indeed, we could say that, precisely because nothing is technically permitted within this zone, anything appears possible. As such, it seems to create a space for those who – having no land, and not being officially accommodated by the state – might otherwise have nowhere to go. At the same time, the *physical* space of the setback creates an opportunity for legal occupation. The continued existence of this space within the city, void of legally-visible structures, has allowed successive governments to claim and re-claim it, be that for safety, public health, environmental or economic concerns. Viewed from the perspective of its original rationale, these two forms of occupation contradict each other; the informal settlement creates a fire-risk, as opposed to a fire-break. But viewed in terms of it practical application, a kind of *entente* seems to exist between these two kinds of opportunities. It doesn't say this in any laws, but we can make our own deduction. On the one hand, the code permits informal development as a means to hold open the potential for future state cession; it is a means through which the State sustains a capacity for future action, but also recognises that which, at present, it can't do. That is, in the setback code we see something like the impotentiality of the state, its limited capacity for intervention, but also its self-conscious recognition, its employment, of that limitation.[32]

Returning to Magnusson's argument, what I want to suggest is that, in the lax enforcement of the Lagos setback zone we are offered an example of the suspension of law, of a space carved out from one set of authority claims, in which others compete. And this moment of suspension, we might conclude, does seem to create a kind of "civic peace", in which difference lives side by side. But can we say, of this example, that sovereignty is here postponed, evaded, deflected, subverted and ultimately transfigured? I don't think so, at least, not yet. What seems "anarchic" about the Lagos setback is, at another level, the representation of an absolute authority. This ostensibly governmental measure, based on the distance a spark might fly and set light to thatch, is today – as it was to begin with – as a means of legitimating the state cession of land. The civic peace that it brokers is therefore fragile; it allows the dispossessed a foothold on land outside the conventional channels of legal and economic investment, but only on the condition of their future dispossession. That is, where in Edinburgh, fire seemed to support the governmental transfiguration of sovereignty, in Lagos, that process seems stalled. And I would like to suggest that it is this state of suspension – which is both anarchic and absolutist – that prohibits anything really changing. The physical space of setback zone offers a space of possibility for government, an opportunity to constantly re-define the law; but that legal space never recognises anything that happens physically within that space. That is, the structures and uses that come to occupy this physical space never really become inscribed within it, they never become legally visible. They therefore cannot

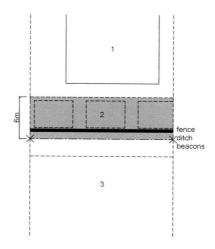

Figure 4.6 **Occupying the Setback: Obalende, Mammy Market.** 1. Lagos State Police Barracks. 2. Mammy Market. 3. Road. Liam Ross with Maria Esteban Castenas, 2012.

assist in the "re-cycling" of authority claims; there is here no "cycle", no materio-semiotic exchange. As such, the authority of the setback code never really becomes governmentalised; the rationalities and technicalities of this rule never quite interact – they remain mutually invisible – and so never open themselves up to exchange.

4.3.5 Practical politics of visibility

If the street fronts of Lagos are in a state of suspense, I would like to conclude this chapter by looking for some hints of denouement. That is, if the governmental value of the space is at present as a reserve, a kind of "fleet in being", I would like to cast forward to think about the circumstances in which that might change. By doing so, I think it is possible to see how the legal and spatial character of this zone might steer the future trajectory of the city. The code *is* connected, for instance, to the construction of a specific identity, that of the "public". The state's capacity to revoke ownership is enabled by the 1978 *Land Use Act*, which requires that such land to be designated to a specific "public purpose". At present, this concept appears ill-defined; the Land Use Act has empowered the state to cease land for almost any conceivable purpose, including the purpose of gifting it to other private individuals or companies. Attempts to contest this in courts – as in *Oviawe v. Integrated Rubber Products LTD* – have so far failed.[33] Nonetheless, should such requisitions become more regular, the setback zone might offer a "boundary object" through which the definition of this identity becomes more well-structured.

The most obvious "public" purpose, as we have seen, is that of infrastructure expansion. Through the requisition of this land for street-widening and bus-interchanges, this code is already facilitating a slow, ad hoc morphological transformation, from a town of dense courtyards settlements, to a metropolis of wide avenues, through which the colonial house-in-garden was only a disappearing mediator. Through this process, more streets within the city will come to assume that "expansive" character which Tunji found wanting in the city. And relationships between public and private, and between formal and informal trade, will shift, both becoming more architecturally mediated. That is, if Lagos is to develop an urbanism of the active street-frontage, one where you can "actually walk right up to the front door", it will need to resolve through built structures those things that are accommodated spatially by the setback; that urbanism will need to think of new approaches to security, and to fire-safety, but it will also need to accommodate people and uses that currently have no place, formalising aspects of the city's economy. And transport is not the only infrastructural concern; flooding, for instance, is a major problem in Lagos. 50% of the city is less than 6 feet above sea level, in a city which lacks either sewage system, or a storm-water infrastructure.

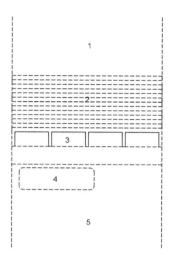

Figure 4.7 **Occupying the Setback: Lagos Island, Bus Station.** 1. Tafawa Balewa
Square (Military Parade Ground). 2. Stalls. 3. Shops. 4. Bus Station.
Liam Ross with Maria Esteban Castenas, 2012.

The setback zone creates an easement along which a conventional drainage infrastructure might be installed, but perhaps also the combined footprint required for an urban-scale "soak away".

But will the current spatial occupation of the setback shape the way it is developed in future? We have seen that, at present, the setback operates as a kind of "othering" device, gathering a wide variety of peoples and practices with nowhere else to go. This gathering offers, in some sense, its own definition of the "public"; everything that occurs within the zone is open to view by all, and is not "private", in the sense that it cannot be owned. While this diverse array of actors has no current legal claim to the space, might they find ways of forming networks with other governmental concerns, so as to find a place within a new, legal definition of the "public"? Or alternatively, might they assert their own "principle of continuity", making claims to private ownership? Nigerian law does recognise "squatters rights" for instance; it is conceivable that, through settling and occupying the zone, some of its tenants might become recognised as "legitimate" owners. That is, this mechanism of state-cession, cutting through both tribal and private ownership, might create a path towards direct occupation.

There is pressure from the other side of the fence, too. Limits to foreign investment for Naira-based development funds have led to a sharp rise in local land and property development. The development ceiling for plots in Lagos is set by a combination of planning factors; maximum eaves heights, car-parking provision and the setback code. Given that the *proportion* of a site given over to setback reduces with plot *size*, the code is leading to a phenomenon of plot bundling, and leaving small plots undevelopable. After outlawing indigenous patterns, imposing its own imported model, and retuning this to afford subdivision, the code is once again reshaping the city, steering development towards super-plots. But the reducing margins of development might support changes to the legislation. If developers could contribute to infrastructure-expansion in other, more spatially economic ways, might they broker new spatial codes, allowing them to build hard up to the street, or their neighbours?

And while we have recognised fire was the McGuffin to this story, might it return to haunt it? The risk of urban fire constructed by the code is real; a fire spreading within this space might lead to regulatory reform. Alternatively, a simple recognition of the mess that the code is creating, the way it channels informal development to the most visible parts of the city, might be an impetus to change. In whatever configuration these issues come together, however, the practical political question they raise seems to be one of visibility. That is, to what degree might the peoples and the practices who currently occupy this space be better off "in the dark"? The current non-enforcement of this code might well be considered "tolerant", even "cosmopolitan". Even for the wealthiest Lagosian, the poor are only on the

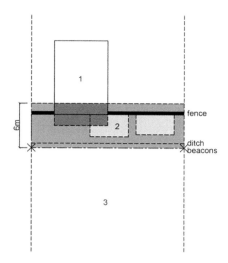

Figure 4.8 **Occupying the Setback: Lagos Island, Veranda.** 1. Pre-colonial House. 2. Veranda. 3. Road. Liam Ross with Maria Esteban Castenas, 2012.

other side of a fence. And in a country in which 80% of taxable individuals remain outside the tax net, the "impotentiality" of the State is an important practical consideration. If the dividing lines between public and private in Lagos are to be redrawn – through a revised strategy to mitigate fire-spread, a widened street, an improved public-transport infrastructure, a sustainable urban drainage scheme, a more profitable or attractive pattern of settlement – what of the peoples, activities and functions which currently occupy this legal shadow? At what moment will it be seen as beneficial for them to take shape, legally and spatially?

Notes

1 William Geary, *Nigeria Under British Rule*, 1st ed. (London: Routledge, 1965). p. 24.
2 Otunba Payne provided this report in a letter to the editor, published in The Weekly Record, cited here in Michael J. C. Echeruo, *Victorian Lagos: Aspects of Nineteenth Century Lagos Life* (London: Macmillan, 1977). p.17.
3 Article 1, The Treaty of Cession, 6 August 1861, cited in Taslim Olawale Elias and Nigeria, *Nigerian Land Law and Custom* (London: Routledge & K. Paul, 1951). p. 7.
4 King Docemo, speaking at 9pm, on September 12th 1863, as reported by the Anglo-African on September 19th, cited in Michael J. C. Echeruo, *Victorian Lagos: Aspects of Nineteenth Century Lagos Life* (London: Macmillan, 1977). p. 17.
5 A statement released by Governor Glover at 6am, September 13th (6 hours after Docemo's denial) cited in Eceruo, Victorian Lagos. p. 18.
6 Kunle Akinsemoyin and Alan Vaughan-Richards, Building Lagos, 1976 Prestige. p. 7.
7 Echeruo, Victorian Lagos. p. 20.
8 *The Observer*, November 5th and 26th, 1887, cited in Echeruo. p. 19.
9 *The Anglo-African*, May 1st, 1863, cited in Echeruo, Victorian Lagos. p. 19.
10 Kunle Akinsemoyin and Alan Vaughan-Richards, Building Lagos, 1976 Prestige. pp. 35–38.
11 For an outline of contrasting contemporary interpretations, see Elias and Nigeria, *Nigerian Land Law and Custom*.
12 Mieke van der Linden, *The Acquisition of Africa (1870–1914): The Nature of International Law* (Leiden: Brill Nijhoff, 2016). pp. 120–136.
13 See "Legal History of Cities" in Gerald E. *Frug, City Making Building Communities without Building Walls* (Princeton: Princeton University Press, 1999). pp. 27–32. The section on "the Medieval City draws particularly on Weber's account.
14 Chapter 16 of Economy and Society is titled "The City (Non-Legitimate Domination)". Within that chapter, Weber never actually uses the term "non-legitimate" directly. Nonetheless, in his sociological account of numerous city types – from "The Patrician City in the Middle Ages" to "The Plebian City" – he describes the way that particular forms of authority and "domination" emerge, that are particular to cities, but operate as exceptions to wider, rural patterns of domination; for example – resonating with our study of the Dean of Guild courts in Edinburgh – he discusses the rise of medieval craft association, located within cities, as a means of opposition to ancient territorial units. Likewise, he describes the importance of the "freedmen", craftspeople and labourers freed from bondages of slavery of serfdom, as an important and specifically urban pre-cursor to the bourgeoisie. See Max Weber, *Economy and*

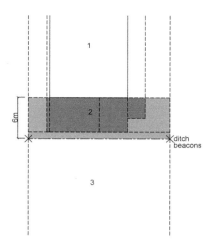

Figure 4.9 **Occupying the Setback: Idumagbo, Auto Garage.** 1. Flats. 2. Auto Garage. 3. Road. Liam Ross with Maria Esteban Castenas, 2012.

Society: An Outline of Interpretive Sociology (Oakland: University of California Press, 1978). pp. 1212–1374.

15 James C. Scott, *Seeing like a State : How Certain Schemes to Improve the Human Condition Have Failed / James C. Scott, Yale Agrarian Studies* (New Haven; London: Yale University Press, 1998).

16 Warren Magnusson, *Seeing Like a State, Seeing Like a City* (Annual Meeting of the Canadian Political Science Association, Vancouver, 2008), http://www.cpsa-acsp.ca/papers-2008/Magnusson.pdf.

17 Magnusson. p. 8.

18 A MacGuffin is a Hitchcockian motif, an empty pretext with which to begin a story:

> Two gentlemen meet on a train, and the one is struck by the extraordinary package being carried by the other. He asks his companion, 'What is in that unusual package you are carrying there?' The other man replies, 'That is a MacGuffin.' 'What is a MacGuffin?' asks the first. The second says, 'A MacGuffin is a device used for killing leopards in the Scottish highlands.' Naturally the first man says, 'But there are no leopards in the Scottish highlands.' 'Well,' says the second, 'then that's not a MacGuffin, is it?'.

See Slavoj Žižek's, *The Iraqi MacGuffin, and Everything You Always Wanted to Know about Lacan: (But Were Afraid to Ask Hitchcock)* (London: Verso, 1992).

19 Magnusson, 'Seeing Like a State, Seeing Like a City'. p. 8.

20 Mariana Valverde, *Everyday Law on the Street: City Governance in an Age of Diversity* (Chicago: University of Chicago Press, 2012).

21 Planning instruments that designate use categories to areas of land are called, in the US, as a result of this case, "Euclidean Zoning". The strange coincidence created by this term – between a place name, a legal precedent, and a mathematical theory – is further ramified by the concept of "non-Euclidean zoning". This term refers to any planning mechanism that does not operate through land-use designations (i.e. through 2-dimensional, flat, or geometrically "Euclidean" means). For further details see Russell Reno, 'Non-Euclidean Zoning: The Use of the Floating Zone', *Maryland Law Review* 23, no. 2 (1 January 1963): 105.

22 Mariana Valverde, 'Seeing Like a City: The Dialectic of Modern and Premodern Ways of Seeing in Urban Governance', *Law & Society Review* 45, no. 2 (1 June 2011): 277–312.

23 The *Venice Takeway* project for the British Pavilion at the Venice Architecture Bienale, 2012. I would like a acknowledge the support of the British Council is facilitating this research visit, and Tolulope Onabolu for his intellectual contribution to it.

24 Tunji Odunlami speaking during an interview with the author, concerning the origin of LSPPD15. Tunji Odunlami, Liam Ross, and Tolulope, Interview, Ministry of Physical Planning and Development, Lagos State Secretariat, 2012.

25 Lagos State Government of Nigeria, 'Lagos State Government Notice 8', *Lagos State of Nigeria Official Gazette* 40, no. 6 (2007).

26 In Kafka's existential parable *Before the Law*, first published as a short story then included as a story within *The Trial*, a man stands before closed doors which block his access to the Law, which he is, nonetheless, told has been written exclusively for him. See Franz Kafka, *The Trial, trans. Idris Parry, New edition* (London: Penguin Classics, 2000).

27 Odunlami, Ross, and Onabolu, *Interview, Ministry of Physical Planning and Development*, Lagos State Secretariat, 2012.

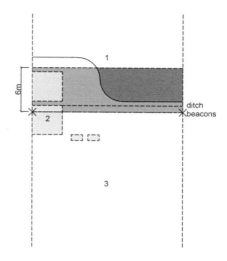

Figure 4.10 **Occupying the Setback: Lagos Island, Kiosk.** 1. Commercial Building. 2. Street Kiosk. 3. Road. Liam Ross with Maria Esteban Castenas, 2012

28 I am quoting here from an unpublished report prepared at the request of the author by Akeem Kolawole of Oluwakemi Balogun and Co., Legal Practitioners and Notaries Public, Lagos. My thanks to Akeem, Kemi and Ola Oduku, for their assistance here.

29 Kunle Akinsemoyin and Alan Vaughan-Richards, *Building Lagos* (Prestige Books, 1977).

30 Akinsemoyin and Vaughan-Richards.

31 LEBD guidelines cited in Kunle Akinsemoyin and Alan Vaughan-Richards, Building Lagos, 1976 Prestige. p. 59.

32 In this phrase I'm again paraphrasing here Prozorov's reading of Schmidt and Agamben. "The paradox of sovereignty is thus the uncanny identity of the foundational and the transgressive" Linking Schmidt's definition of Sovereignty to Agamben's definition of "potentiality", he suggests that "as a foundational transgression that remains inscribed in the existence of the diagram as its constitutive outside, sovereignty is nothing other than the potentiality for order not to be, its being capable of its own impotentiality". See Sergei Prozorov, *Foucault, Freedom and Sovereignty* (London: Routledge, 2016). p. 86. Prozorov.

33 I base this observation on the above-mentioned report provided by Oluwakemi Balogan and Co. A report on this specific case is available in Bamgbose John Olatokunbo, *Digest of Judgements of the Supreme Court of Nigeria: Vols 1 and 2* (Ibadan: Safari Books Ltd., 2013). pp. 221, 227, 235.

5 Tokyo

Spectres of Edo Castle

5.1 Great fires of Edo/Tokyo, 1657, 1923 and 1943

5.1.1 Cursed Kimono

> Well now, at the hour of the dragon, on the 18th day of the first month
> of the year of the cock, the third year of Meireki, a wind blew up from
> the north-west and then became a gale. Dust was blown up into the air
> and trailed through the sky. It wasn't clear what it was: was it a cloud or
> not, was it whirls of smoke, or was it a spring mist hanging in the sky?
> Throughout Edo, rich and poor alike were unable to open their doors;
> although the day was dawning it was still dark and there was nobody
> in the streets. Eventually at the hour of the sheep flames suddenly shot
> up from the Honmyōji, a temple of the Nichiren sect at the western end
> of Hongō yonchōme and black smoke raced across the heavens.[1]

So begins the *Musashi Abumi*, an account of the Great Fire of Meireki, seen
through the eyes of the haberdasher Rakusaibo as he tries to save his family
and possessions from the blaze. The fire took place in 1657 and lasted for
three days, destroying two-thirds of Edo and claiming over 100,000 lives.
Popularly known as the *Furisode,* or "Young-girls-kimono", the blaze is
said to have been started by a priest who was cremating a cursed kimono
(it had been owned in succession by three teenage girls who all died before
ever being able to wear it). As the garment was being burned, a large gust
of wind fanned the flames causing the wooden temple to ignite. Few written
records of the event exist, mostly in the form of journals kept by European
visitors to the city at the time, and the *Musashi* is the only Japanese account
(Figure 5.1). Its historical accuracy is limited, though. Written as a parody
of Buddhist disaster parables, the comic plot reveals less about the event,
more about a contemporary cultural attitude towards it. According to the
story, Rakusaibo survived the first day of the fire, returning to his house
in the evening to search for his mother. Having identified what he took
to be her corpse among the crushed and charred remains he gathered his

DOI: 10.4324/9781003026297-5

Figure 5.1 **Great Fire of Meireki, Asai Ryōi, Musashi Abumi (1661).** Illustration from the image shown depicts Asakusa Gate during the Great Fire of Meireki. The architecture of fire-defence, gates, ramparts and moats, can here be seen turning against the inhabitants of the city, who are trapped by them. Source: Musashi Abumi, Asai Ryōi, 1661, (Manji 4) Acquisition 584, Tokyo Metro Library.

family to mourn, only to be surprised when his mother walked by, very much alive. First the family took her for a ghost; next they cursed her for wasting their time in prayer, then they all got drunk. Rakusaibo awoke the next morning, hung over, inside a coffin. He climbed out into a blackened city, engulfed once more in flames, concluding that he must be in hell. But finding the remains of his family around him, he realises that he is alive, and all is lost; he decides to become a monk.

5.1.2 Cook-pots and char

The rumbling sound of apocalyptic fires added further terror to it. Screams and shrieks were everywhere, fire burned into an inferno – it was hell …. The big city of Tokyo, the largest in the Orient, at the zenith of its prosperity, burned down and melted away in two days and three nights.[2]

The Great Fire of Meireki was only the first of three events which, over the course of Edo/Tokyo's history, saw the city completely razed by fire. The second was the Great Kanto Earthquake, of 1923, described above by Takashima Beiho. That quake began at 11:58 in the morning, caused by the subduction of the Philippine Sea plate at the Sagami Trough, under the mouth of Tokyo Bay. Accounts of this event are plentiful and detailed; 9,000 miles away at the Vienna Institute of Meteorology seismographers confirmed the quake as the most powerful on record, at 8.3 on the Richter scale. The quake generated a 12 m high tsunami, which inundated the port of Yokohama, leaving buildings destroyed, and infrastructure severed. But the most deadly and destructive aspect of the event was the fire which broke out in its aftermath. Striking at lunchtime the quake overturned cook-pots and spilt char, starting over a hundred recorded fires within 30 minutes. Fuelled by broken service mains and combustible debris, these individual house fires merged into three distinct fire-storms which engulfed most of eastern Tokyo. An estimated 140,000 people died in the following three days, as the infrastructure of the city turned against them. Generating its own winds, the storm moved around the city, consuming what fuel was available; inhabitants burnt to death or were asphyxiated as their homes became infernos. They were trapped in the streets by molten tarmac; blocked by canals and rivers as bridges burnt down; crushed to death by crowds swelling into squares and open spaces; or drowned in waterways leaping to extinguish burning hair and clothes. The greatest tragedy befell those who made it to the city's largest designated refuge space, the Military Clothing Depot. An estimated 44,000 people died in this location alone, as the storm passed through, bringing an "an enormous wall of fire, like a tidal wave" with air "as hot as melting rock", lifting people from the ground, then depositing their bodies in charred heaps.[3]

5.1.3 Napalm and Broomsticks

It was March 10, Army Day. It had been rumored that the enemy was planning a huge air raid to coincide with this special day. As if to confirm those fears, a fierce northwesterly wind had been blowing since the previous evening ... I went outside to look. In every direction – east, west, south and north – the dark sky was scorched with crimson flames. The steady roar of the B-29s' engines overhead was punctuated by piercing screeches followed by cascading sounds like sudden showers. With each explosion, a flash of light darted behind my eyelids. The ground shook. Flames appeared one after another. As our neighbors looked outside their air raid shelters defiantly holding their bamboo fire brooms, they cursed when they saw how fiercely the fires were burning. They were helpless against the raging flames. Fire trucks, sirens wailing, were already speeding toward the fires, but what could they do in this gusting wind and intensive bombardment?[4]

Twenty-two years later, memories of the post-Kanto fires returned to haunt Tokyo. In the closing years of the Second World War, with the completion of the US airbase in Saipan, American B-29 Superfortress bombers began aerial bombardment of Japanese cities. On March 10, 1945, in a single run code-named Operation Meetinghouse, 165,000 tons of napalm was dropped on Tokyo. This event – referred to in Japan as the Great Tokyo Air Raid – is the single most destructive air-raid in history, with acute effects greater than the allied bombing of Dresden, or the nuclear bombardment of Hiroshima and Nagasaki combined. As described above by the verbal testimony of Saotome Katsumoto, wind spread the fire through the dense residential districts of eastern Tokyo, destroying 16 square miles of largely working-class housing, again killing around 100,000 people, and leaving over a million homeless. This time, the principal cause of death was not burning, asphyxiation or the crush of escape. The population took refuge in air-raid shelters, where they suffocated, as the fire-storm consumed all available oxygen.

5.1.4 Disaster by design

The story of Edo/Tokyo is often told through this sequence of superlative catastrophes – The Great Fire of Meireki, The Great Kanto Earthquake, The Great Tokyo Air Raid – in which the Feudal, Imperial and proto-modern cities were destroyed so as to be built again. In the mythology of the city they are, perhaps, a source of uncanny vitality; Tokyo is the world's largest and most populous city, but also one of its most frequently destroyed, excessive both in life and death. Of course, Tokyo doesn't hold a monopoly on such tragedies; Japan as a whole is closely associated with disaster. Situated on the Pacific "Ring of Fire", the island is susceptible to volcanic activity, seismic risk and tsunami; a mountainous country prone to heavy seasonal rainfall, the shape and settlement of its landscape is scarred by frequent and destructive landslides; synonymous with the nuclear risk, both as the first and only target for the military use of atomic weaponry, but also one of the worst civilian nuclear catastrophes; marked by strong currents of social and political unrest, through the "era of popular violence", to acts of cult-inspired terror, such as the Akihabara massacre, or the Sarin Gas attacks. But whether the result of urban accidents, "natural" disasters, or military attacks, fire has consistently proved the deadliest aspect of Japan's most significant catastrophes, and those catastrophes have struck Tokyo disproportionately often. Indeed, beyond and between these three historic fires, countless uncontrolled fires have formed part of the everyday pulse of that city. During the Edo period, from 1601 to 1867, there were a total of 1,798 major recorded fires in the city, compared to the 184 in Japan's second city, Osaka, explaining the popular saying that *Kaji to kenka ha Edo no hana* (fires and fights are the "blossoms of Edo").[5]

Why has Tokyo suffered from fire more than other Japanese cities? At first glance there appear some simple reasons; Japan is a country in which almost all houses – from the peasant hut to the shogun's palace – were traditionally made of wood and paper, providing ready sources of combustion. Built on an exposed and windy plain and subject to long dry winters Tokyo is the country's largest tinder-keg, in which sparks spread most rapidly. But such a physical explanation would fail to account for the fact that, despite the frequency and severity of fires within the city, Edo/Tokyo is famous for having continued to rebuild itself in largely flammable materials. Indeed, during the 17th century, when the use of fire-resistant construction materials such as plaster wall coverings and ceramic roof tiles were common in other Japanese cities, such practices were explicitly outlawed in Edo.

5.1.5 *The repeated failure to build an unburnable Tokyo*

Despite repeated reconstruction in flammable materials, the frequency of fire in Edo/Tokyo has often been interpreted through a religious and moral lens. Earthquake, tsunami and fire were often understood as acts of divine punishment. This idea was the subject of parody as early as the *Musashi Abumi*, but persisted until the modern era. Takashima Beiho, quoted above, interpreted the Great Kanto Earthquake in this way, calling upon the city to see reconstruction an opportunity for moral, as well as physical, reform.[6] Indeed, contemporary popular accounts of fire in Japan often draw on a similar logic, linking an apparent acceptance of cyclical destruction with a fatalism perceived as inherent to Buddhism.[7] Following that logic, the repeated reconstruction of Tokyo might be seen as an accidental and secular equivalent to the ritualised and religious reconstruction of the *Grand Ise Shrine*.

Scholarly accounts have offered more material interpretations. While economist Lionel Frost and urban historian Greg Bankoff do identify a distinctly Asian "Fire-Regime", concerned less with the protection of property, more with mobile valuables, they explain this culture in relation to local material and construction practices.[8] Historian Charles Schenking recognises how events like the Kanto Earthquake were used as focussing devices through which to justify programmes of political reform, but would interpret this as part of a governmental strategy he refers to as a "Culture of Catastrophe".[9] And in their study of building and property law in Edo, Japan scholars Jordan Sands and Steve Wills show that urban fires were often beneficial for occupants, as well as by government, and that many were not accidents, but rather choreographed events. This chapter builds upon the work of the above scholars, but also extends it. As in previous chapters, it seeks to understand how fire has shaped the legal and physical fabric of Edo/Tokyo. In this chapter the focus is less on one historical moment, more on why fire as a repeated and persistent problem for that city, one that remains today. It reflects on the *historical imagination* fire in Edo/Tokyo; it considers the way the experience of past fires has been drawn upon and become enmeshed within broader political-economic equations, so sustaining a particular attitude towards fire.

After this introduction, the next section studies the political-economy of fire in feudal Edo. Following Sand and Wills, it considers the economic and governmental benefits of fire for Shogunal rule, so complicating a simple physical explanation for the frequency of fire during that period. In the Shogun's response to the Great Fire of Meireki, it finds the origin of Tokyo's contemporary fire-safety legislation: practices of "land-readjustment" and subsidised fire-safe construction. It suggests that the limited effect of these practices – their failure to prevent repeated city-wide fires – was in some sense calculated, a means to sustain beneficial aspects of urban fire. The third section reflects upon this limitation theoretically through the work of Ulrich Beck. In his theory of "reflexive modernisations" Beck likewise considers how past tragedies motivate historical change. However, he also suggests a set of reasons as to why policies and technologies of risk mitigation often *sustain* the hazards they are intended to guard against, condemning the future to repeat past mistakes. With Beck's schema in mind, a fourth section returns to Tokyo, offering a brief genealogy of that city's fire-safety legislation from the Meiji Restoration to the present day. This section shows how, as Tokyo opens to the West, and urbanises, the problem of urban fire-safety – previously structured by class struggle – comes to be understand through a cultural opposition between the European and Japanese values in urban design. The final section illustrates the way that this cultural conflict is written into the urban fabric of Tokyo today. However, it also suggests means by which it is being overcome. The chapter concludes by suggesting the fire is effecting a kind of "enforced cosmopolitanism" in Tokyo, changing patterns of construction and ownership that have remained stable since the feudal era.

5.2   The political-economy of fire in Edo

5.2.1   Consumption city

Edo was formed in 1457 by the Samurai-poet-monk Ōta Dōkan with the construction of Chiyoda Castle (Figure 5.2). It came to national prominence only a century-and-a-half later, though, when made the seat of power by the Tokugawa Shogunate, the feudal rulers of Japan from 1603 to 1868. At the beginning of this period, preceding the Great Fire of Meireki, the city was essentially a fortress and encampment. The castle sat at the mouth of a river (Edo means "estuary") on an elevated area of land 2 km^2, defined by a series of concentric ramparts and surrounding moats. The citadel inside was divided into numerous wards (*maru*) by further walls and canals. It housed the Shogun, his *bakufu* (his military government, literally his "tent"), and the local *Daimyo* (the nobility, literally meaning the "big land owners"). Surrounding the castle to the north and west – on dry, hilly land – were

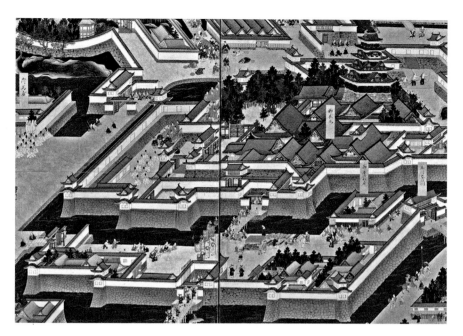

Figure 5.2 **"View of Edo"** (**Edo zu**). Pair of six-panel folding screens (17c.) illustrating Edo Castle. Note concentric moats (black), stone ramparts and plaster walls (white), defining concentric wards, or maru. The Donjon is located in the upper-right panel. Source: https://en.wikipedia.org/wiki/Edo_Castle (accessed, July 29, 2020).

the verdant mansion complexes of Japan's other Daimyo. To the south and east, on islands made from sludge dredged from the castle-moats was the "floating city" of merchants and tradespeople, a dense settlement of cheap and poorly constructed buildings.

As architectural historian Morton Schmorleitz describes, the physical disposition of Edo was, from its inception, a political-economic diagram whose purpose was,

> not only to build a capital and castle fitting for the shogun but also to reduce the wealth of the daimyo by making them supply labour, materials, and money for the construction, thereby lessening their ability to overthrow the Tokagawa Dynasty.[10]

The *Sankin Kotai* policy was an important part of this diagram. It fuelled the cities physical and economic growth by demanding that regional nobility build seasonal residences in the city, throwing lavish annual receptions for the Shogun. This policy established Edo as the nations "consumption city", while impoverishing rival nobility and the regions. The physical mass of the castle was also part of this diagram; the castle ramparts, 20 m high and 16 km in circumference, were not just part of a military strategy, but also an economic one. The stones for their construction,

> came mostly from Izu and were transported by ship to Edo, the 3,000 ships required being provided by other Daimyo. For each 100,000 koku of income, the daimyo were to furnish 1,120 stones of a size that took 100 men each to handle.

"[I]t is said that there were some 300,000 workers employed during this phase of the building".[11] Thus, the construction of the castle ramparts was a system of need-generation and of taxation which necessitated, funded and organised a nationalised workforce.

Fire also played an important role in this governmental diagram, which worked not only through the cities construction but its perpetual reconstruction. While everyone from the Shogun to the tradesperson lived in wooden buildings, these buildings differed significantly in terms of fire-resilience. The tenements of the urban poor, for instance, were known as *yakiya*, literally meaning "burnable buildings".[12] In an era without piped water, and in which fire-fighting was conducted through preventative demolition, the *yakiya* were built cheaply and simply so as to be quick to demolish, without great financial loss. By contrast, the architecture of the Shogun's palace – the *Donjon* – was rich with symbols, icons and indices of fire-security. Its ridges were capped with *Shachikoko* – a Vedic sea monster, a carp with a tigers head – who was seen to provide symbolic protection against fire; its many roofs were covered with ceramic tile, whose wave form and raised eaves made iconic allusions both to the fishes tail, and to waves; its exposed beam-ends were literally and symbolically protected by ceramic caps featuring a wave motif peculiar to Edo; its walls were plastered externally, their interiors often papered with repetitive patterns that continued the double allusion to scale and wave. Earthquake being the most common cause of fire, the Donjon also featured a number of devices for seismic resilience; its timber structure was isolated from its masonry base, allowing it to slip and bounce in the event of earthquake; its un-braced members were able to sway, reducing the lateral force transmitted upward; its decorative eaves-brackets were also isolated one floor from the next, creating two-dimensional slip-planes which further dampened and delayed the transmission of lateral force; its heavy ceramic roof acted as an early form of "tuned mass dampener", whose inertia limited the movement of the upper storeys; and a central suspended column further dampened this movement, rattling against its adjacent structure. Like Japan's celebrated Pagodas – the prototypes of contemporary seismic design in Japan – these devices allowed the building to perform a "snake dance" in the event of an earthquake, whose irregular rhythm interrupted and absorbed seismic force.[13]

Figure 5.3 **Urban Paradigms: Chiyoda Castle**. Imperial palace and inner moat of the former Chiyoda Castle. Note fire-safety paradigms of moat (black), rampart (white) and fire-resistant planting (grey). Max Ochel and Liam Ross, 2020.

5.2.2 Castle as urban paradigm

The most important instrument of fire-security for the Shogun, though, was the castle itself (Figure 5.3). Never subject to military assault, its real defensive value was to ward against the spread of fire from the surrounding encampment. Moats formed a wide watery fire-break, ramparts a high non-combustible fire wall; gardens were planted with fire-resistant trees; the *maru* formed effective internal fire compartments; the soldiers who patrolled its walls were armed not with spears, but with fire-brooms. For the emergent Japanese State and its administration, ensconced within the castle, fire was an external problem, something to be held at bay like an invading enemy. As Historian's Jordan Sand and Steven Wills show, the Shogunate did not lack laws on urban fire-safety; it had a range of fire-related initiatives, but these were not concerned with *preventing* fire per se. The Shogun sought to develop individual responsibility through criminalisation; Arson was illegal during the period, as was the accidental creation of fire, and even of the failure to put out a fire as it passed through one's property. Indeed, Sand and Wills suggest a number of ways in which fire was politically expedient, offering the Shogun an opportunity to demonstrate his sovereignty: public executions of convicted arsonists or failed fire-marshals offered a spectacle of his power over life and death, just as financial aid in post-fire reconstruction was also an opportunity to demonstrate compassion and largesse, and so justify feu duties and target economic stimulus. But perhaps most importantly, the aftermath of a large fire allowed him to re-partition landownership, and so to re-design the city, reminding townspeople and nobility alike of their feudal dependence upon him. And fire was also an ambivalent phenomenon for the townspeople, too. Arson was widespread; for a destitute tenant, with rent in arrears, burning down the house was a way to write off debt.[14] That is, following Sand and Wills argument, we could say that fire was an important actant within the drama of feudal Edo. Like the *Sankin Kotai* policy, it provided the Shogun with a means to reinforce differentials of wealth and security; for the urban poor it was a means to escape debt in circumstances of extreme precarity.

From this perspective I think we can understand something of the significance of the Great Fire of Meireki (Figure 5.4). That fire, a kind of non-human assailant, overcame the castle's physical defences for the first time; sparks and embers were carried over its moat and walls, beyond the reach of the soldier's fire-brooms, igniting the timber buildings within. It marked the end of Chiyoda as a military base proper; fire engulfed the whole of the castle complex, destroying the palace, its temples and the central keep, which was never to be rebuilt. But the event also overwhelmed the Shogun economically. The scale of property loss within the town was such that it exceeded his capacity to fund reconstruction, and so weakened his position as opposed to strengthening it. That is, the Meireki fire demanded a change in governmental approach to fire. Fire was no longer external to government, a threat to be defended against; it was something to be approached "on a war footing", addressed at source. The Shogun's response was led by

Figure 5.4 **The Great Kanto Earthquake.** Extent of destruction, superimposed over Google Earth plan. Note that Chiyoda Castle is not destroyed in the fire. Max Ochel and Liam Ross, 2020

Rōjū Matsudaira Nobutsuna, one of the Shogun's leading *Daimyo*, and its effect can still be read on the city today. Nobutsuna used the event to radically extend and de-densify the footprint of the city, relocating townspeople and nobility alike. The remaining *daimyo* were moved out of the castle, allocated new estates forming a ring to the north and west of castle, beyond the outer moat. The encampment of tradespeople was moved to the east, creating a large clearing between the Castle and the Town. The canals of this area were used to break-up this accommodation, and Nobutsuna also proposed a series of fire-breaks, in the form of walls and clearings, dividing the eastern part of the city into Wards. That is, in this first attempt to re-plan Edo so as to limit the spread of flame, Nobutsuna re-deployed a set of spatial strategies that were essentially military in nature. The canals, walls, clearings and fire-districts he proposed effectively reproduced the castles architectural features at the level of urban design. So, while the fire undermined the fortress castle in one sense, spelling the end of its governmental and physical autonomy, it also gave it an uncanny afterlife, with the city as a whole being reconceived through a network of moats, ramparts, clearings and wards (Figure 5.5).

5.2.3 Indulgence and poverty

No efforts were made to enforce the use of fire-proof materials in the reconstruction of the town, however, which remained illegal. To understand the logic of this proscription *against* fire-proof construction it is important to understand something of sumptuary law in feudal Japan. Japanologist Donald Shively suggests that the legislation of "indulgence" was the key governmental rationale of this era.[15] Sumptuary laws limited expenditure on "luxuries", allowing the *Daimyo* to indulge more expensive tastes than tradespeople, for instance. Ostensibly safeguarding individuals from unaffordable loss, these laws enforced and made legible a rigid social order. Some of the fire-safety features already discussed – from ridge ornaments, to specific modes of detailing eaves – were themselves considered "luxuries", and so played a part in this symbolic ordering of wealth and status.[16] Sumptuary laws often responded directly to fire; the immediate aftermath of fires provided the opportunity and perceived necessity to re-regulate. For instance, in the immediate aftermath of the Meireki fire, tile roofing was temporarily banned, even for the *Daimyo*, whose wealth was considerably reduced.[17] But these laws also effected a particular approach to fire-safety; in a context of frequent fires, where preventative demolition was the only available mode of fire-fighting, sumptuary laws limited economic obstacles to demolition. But this attempt to limit the loss entailed by future fires also structured the likelihood and severity of those fires. As such, the fire-safety of Edo's built environment was enrolled not just in the representation of class distinctions, but also in their sustenance.

At the time of the Meireki fire, then, we could characterise Edo's built fabric through to starkly opposed approaches to fire-safety. The

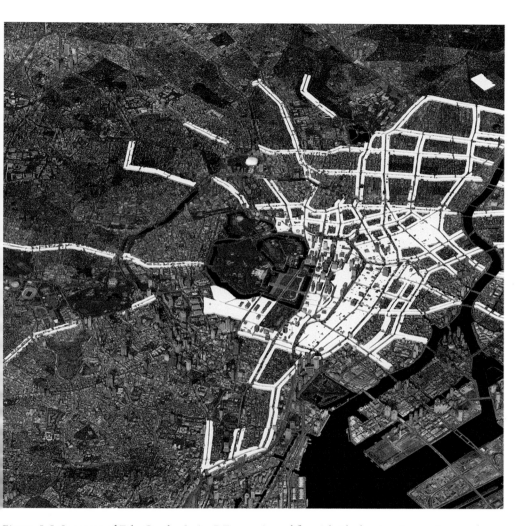

Figure 5.5 **Spectres of Edo Castle.** Swiss RE mapping of fire risk (darker tone) superimposed over "City of Tokyo Fire Prevention Districts" (white). After the Kanto earthquake, major routes were planned to be lined with fire-safe construction, dividing the city into fire-prevention "wards." White volume depicts designed height and depth of the urban fire wall. Note that contemporary fire risk reads as the inverse of the Kanto fire map; note also that areas of greatest fire risk are areas beyond the reach of planned fire-prevention construction. Max Ochel and Liam Ross, 2020.

architecture of the castle made use of fire-safe technologies and materials to maximise durability in the event of fire. By contrast, the architecture of the *Yakiya* sought to minimise the difficulty of demolition, building with materials that were cheap, but also susceptible to fire. As Jordan Sands describes, these two distinct "fire-regimes" also structured attitudes to property in Edo at this time. The defensive architectures of the castle supported the accumulation of fixed capital, where the architecture of town had to be thought of as a disposable commodity. The Shogun advised speculative builders and landlords to calculate for a return on investment within six years, assuming their buildings would be lost to fire after that time.[18] As such, Edo's construction industry was focussed on ensuring the minimum use of material, the maximum speed of supply-chain, ease of construction and ease of demolition. Tokyo's *Yakiya* came to be built of timber post-and-lintel construction, secured without metal fasteners, based around standardised component sizes determined by Tatami – the celebrated modularity of Japanese architecture. Structural members and modular fixtures could be dismantled and used in other locations as and when was required.[19] The profitability of building and leasing were, in this model, based upon volume and turnover, and while fire limited return on investment it, nonetheless, guaranteed continuity of demand.[20] That is, like supplies for the Shogun's seasonal parties, buildings were another disposable commodity which Tokyo needed a constant supply of. Indeed, it might be accurate to say that fire, rather than the Shogun, was the real *consumer* of Edo, the real appetite that sustained its continued construction and reconstruction.

5.2.4 *Phenomenology of law*

When Rōjū Matsudaira Nobutsuna sought to replan Edo, compartmentalising the town with urban elements drawn from castle architecture, he was attempting to bring together two starkly opposed fire and property regimes. That ambition was to be fraught with difficulties. The scale of his proposed interventions was beyond the scope of the Shogun to realise or enforce autocratically, walls and canals being expensive to construct. In their place, he sought to create simple clearings, through compulsory re-partitioning of land. These clearing – like the Lagos setback today – were quickly filled in by illegal settlements, so undermining their function.[21] By the turn of the 18th century, the continued failure to secure these fire-breaks led Tokugawa Yoshimune to overrule the edict banning fire-proof materials, and to begin what would be the first of many attempts to convince Edo's townspeople to re-build their homes in fire-proof materials. Yoshimune offered to subsidise the costs of plaster and tile, but his initiatives were of limited effect, for apparently paradoxical reasons. Economic historian Lionel Frost demonstrates that contemporary landlords and tenants complained that they could not afford to invest in expensive, fire-safe construction on account of the losses they had accrued through previous fires. That is, they re-stated the logic of sumptuary law from their own perspective. Edo's political-economy of indulgence had constructed something like a "prisoner's dilemma", which neither individual nor government appeared able to escape.[22]

This dilemma was worsened by the way fire-regimes sedimented legally. Land and property were legally distinct in Edo, seldom owned by the same people, and often overlapping; it was possible to have legal rights to the use of a building that sat on land owned by others, or straddled multiple land-ownership boundaries, just as it was possible to own land without having any rights over the buildings standing upon it.[23] This division of ownership worked against Yoshimune's attempts to incentivise fire-safe construction. Tiles, masonry and plaster, and excavated basements: these materials are phenomenologically grounded; they are in the ground, or made of the ground; and they are heavy, fixed, immoveable. They not only posed a danger during demolition, but also worked against mobility of building as capital. Investment in such construction practices therefore required changed practices of property ownership and investment, changes that would not originate out of a concern for public safety, or the preservation of property value.

Developments in fire-safety practices in the remainder of the Edo period were led by a coalition of interests that developed between the Shogun, an emerging merchant class, and the urban precariat, over the question of how to secure high-value items of mobile capital against fire-risk. The poverty of Edo's working class was such that it could not afford the risk of owning basic commodities – futons or mosquito nets – while they were not in use, and so almost all belongings were leased or pawned seasonally. This created the need for storehouses in which these goods could be secured from fire-risk. Likewise, merchants required shops and storage facilities in which stock was kept safe from fire. A new building typology emerged to service the needs of these constituencies, the *dozu zukuri*, or storehouse.[24] These were the first buildings to feature significant fire-safety features; their walls were made of plaster and mud, their doors and windows were designed to be sealed seasonally with plaster, and their foundations included cellars (indeed, these buildings were known colloquially as "godowns"). These buildings were not simply a physical innovation, but also a new legal vehicle. The Shogunal registers of land and buildings made no mention of moveable timber buildings, but the *dozu zukuri* were noted, being understood less as buildings, more as an "improvement of the land". Thus, without undermining an economy based upon rapid consumption of moveable capital, a different urban order began to emerge within the *Yakiya*. The urban pattern of Edo began to develop – as demonstrated by reconstructions at the Edo-Tokyo museum – in the form of wide commercial streets, fronted by fire-resistant shops, pawnbrokers and storehouses, creating lines of defence within an otherwise perishable, timber city.

5.2.5 Reflexive limitation

I have dwelt here at length here on Edo's Tokugawa-era fire regime for a number of reasons. Firstly, because through the architectural, economic and legal histories offered I think it is possible to demonstrate that Edo did not continue to rebuild itself in flammable construction materials because of a *lack* of urban fire-safety regulations; indeed, I think we can see – particularly from Sand and Wills work – that Edo was profoundly shaped by legal frameworks concerning fire. Without invoking a religious rationale or perceived fatalism, we have seen the economic rationale of reconstruction in flammable materials, as a means to limit potential losses for the townspeople, and to maintain sovereign control of land-use for the Shogun. We have also see how – as they sediment legally, economically and in terms of construction practices – how practices of flammable reconstruction become hard to change, by either individual or government. The final observation I wish to make, though, is to suggest a constitutive limit within Nobutsuna and Yoshimune's attempts to incentivise fire-safe construction practices within certain parts of the city. Drawing on the sources cited here, I think it is possible to make a novel argument, and to suggest that Edo-era practices of land-readjustment and fire-safety promotion necessarily *sustained*, rather than overcame, the continued threat of fire.

The first part of this argument is geometric: when futons and mosquito nets are distributed in houses across the city they cover a lot of ground. When they are gathered together in store-rooms, they cover much less. It is not possible for buildings that store futons to *surround* the buildings those futons will occupy when re-distributed. That is, it is not possible for the *dozu-zukuri* to protect the *Yakiya*. This geometric fact also has an economic dimension. The pawn-shops and store-houses of feudal Edo could not provide an infrastructure of fire-safety because, if the physical mass and disposition of these buildings were to overcome the problem of urban fire, they would also undermine their commercial base; the urban poor would be able to keep their futons and mosquito nets, having no need to pawn them. Putting that another way, we might say that fire-safety was the condition of impossibility for Edo's govern-mentality; fire was the risk that it sought to outlaw, but nonetheless had to sustain.

5.2.6 *Fortified village*

For anyone familiar with contemporary Tokyo, this description of feudal Edo may sound uncannily familiar; to close this historical section on Edo and its fire-regime, I would like to cast forward briefly to present-day Tokyo, noting some surprising similarities that exist between the two cities. One of the most distinctive features of Tokyo, for instance, is that unlike most Western cities, density does not cluster towards the centre, but is distributed along arterial roads, surrounding and defining large urban precincts known as "superblocks" (Figure 5.6). These large urban areas comprise the cities fire-safety "wards". They are defined by tall, reinforced concrete buildings, housing commercial programmes, intended to act as urban scale fire-breaks. However, despite its image as a contemporary, even futuristic city, the majority of Tokyo continues to be made up of the low-rise,

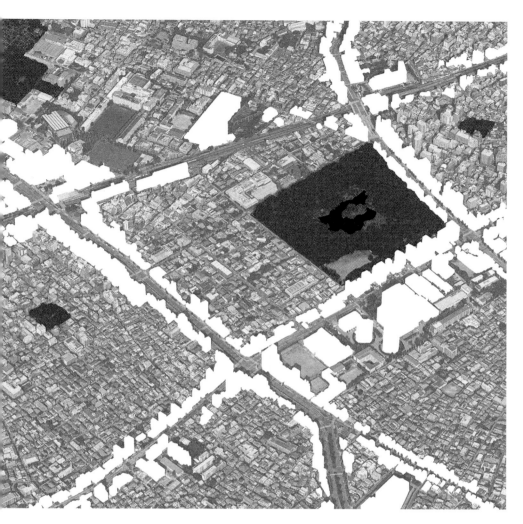

Figure 5.6 **Urban Paradigms: Sengoku Superblock.** Example of a well-formed "hard shell / soft yolk" morphology. Note fire-safety features of roads and waterways (black), firebreak buildings (white) and fire-resistant planting for urban muster zones (grey). Max Ochel and Liam Ross, 2020.

closely settled and cheaply built timber buildings that fill the interior of these contemporary *Maru*. And those timber buildings are still remarkably short-lived. Where the Shogun offered a 6-year estimate, the Japanese Land Ministry today recommends that investors anticipate a 30-year life-cycle for new construction.[25] That is, this global megalopolis still understand itself as a series of "fortified villages", surrounded and separated by castle-like ramparts, moats and parks.[26]

This morphological continuity is not carried by any physical trace; little survives of old Edo, the city having been destroyed and re-built many times in the intervening period. If contemporary Tokyo resembles its predecessor, it is due to the persistence of its fire-regime, not its built fabric. But just as fires were common to Edo, so they continue to pose a problem for Tokyo; indeed, later sections in this chapter will show Tokyo to be one of the most fire-prone cities in the world. Nonetheless, as will be argued, the cities spatial continuity sustains a reflexive limit in its approach to fire-safety. Just as the *Dozu-zukuri* only lined a small proportion of streets, so Tokyo's "superblock" morphology only becomes legible where land-value and commercial activity justify high-rise corporate buildings. In the majority of the city – the peri-urban sprawl where residential development reaches its greatest density – there are no urban fire-safety measures. That is, like feudal Edo, Tokyo continues to re-build itself in a highly flammable arrangement, one justified governmentally by mitigation measures that are geometrically inadequate to the problem they address.[27] It is to reflect on how the governmental problems of feudal Edo might sustain themselves across such a long historical period that the next chapter turns to reflect on theoretically on why governmental programmes might sustain the risks they seek to mitigate, through a close review of Ulrich Beck's *Risk Society* analytic.

5.3 Risk, regulation and reflexivity

5.3.1 Tragedy and farce

That history tends to repeat itself is something both Hegel and Marx prepare us for, Marx through his famous quip in the *Eighteenth Brumaire*. In part of a reflection on the way the past is called upon by those who imagine the future, he states,

> The traditions of all dead generations weighs like a nightmare on the brain of the living ... in creating something that has never yet existed they anxiously conjur up the spirits of the past to their service and borrow from them the names, battle-cries and costumes in order to present this new scene of world-history in this time-honoured disguise and this borrowed language.[28]

In Marx's schema, properly *tragic* events can only occur once; these can be distinguished as moments in which historical contradictions and oppositions surface and unfold in all their necessity, novelty and unavoidability. We might see the Great Fire of Meireki as "tragic" in this sense. It was a moment in which the precarity of Edo's urban poor, constructed by the Shogun's economic policy and building regulations, overwhelmed and undermined his authority. From this historical-materialist perspective, that fire might be seen as part of an enlightenment process, through which social inequalities intensify, become unsustainable, and so prompt political or economic change. Tragedy changes to farce, however, when events repeat themselves, stripped of either novelty or necessity; when historical actors call upon past tragedies to dramatise contemporary struggles, trapping thought within outdated horizons. The Shogun's attempt to re-build his capital to the plan of a failed castle, and the towns-persons' decision to rebuild his house in timber, again, might be seen as "farcical" in this specific sense. Stumbling backward into the future, these actors fail to guard against predictable catastrophes, their thought and action trapped by precedent.[29]

In Chapter 2 I outlined a series of methodological prompts, drawn from Susan Leigh Star's work, that structure this book. One of those prompts reminded us that infrastructures are never built de novo, but always depend upon inherited structures, both material and discursive. That inheritance exerts a pressure on future action; indeed, it might trap us within "mess-trajectories" we wish to escape. As such, Leigh Star suggested that designers need a kind of "historical imagination", an ability to re-tell stories of the past in ways that suit contemporary circumstances. Marx's observations above speak to the same problem, but it is Ulrich Beck's treatment that this chapter suggests offers particular insight. In his "Risk Society" analysis, Beck outlines a number of reasons as to why governmental initiatives often sustain or repeat past tragedies, but also suggests how we might escape from such vicious circularities.

5.3.2 Risk society, reflexive modernity

In his seminal engagement with the subject – *Risk Society: Towards a New Modernity* – the sociologist Ulrich Beck argues that "risk" is the most important conceptual tool through which to understand contemporary processes of historical change. This argument might be read as a descendent of, indeed, a replacement for, Marxist problematics and analyses. Beck suggests that while the problems and conflicts of earlier societies might have been caused by unequal distributions of *wealth*, and understood through concepts of class solidarity and struggle, the ontological base of such issues – that of material scarcity – has since been overcome. In advanced industrialised societies he suggests that political problems increasingly originate through unequal distributions of *risk*, and come to be understood through rationalities and technologies of "safety". Like Marx above, Beck makes his analysis in response to a specific historical moments; the *Risk Society* was written with a range of late 20th and early 21st century concerns in mind – from the nuclear risk and environmental crisis to terrorism – suggesting that questions of hazard and safety have come to play a particularly dominant role in the governing-mentalities of advanced industrialised societies. However, as others have suggested, we might be circumspect about Beck's generalisations and his periodisation.[30] In this section I suggest that aspects of the *Risk Society* hold in quite different times and places, offering this case study as contribution to the more plural history of "risk".[31]

Beck suggests that a consciousness of "risk" brings about a new historical dynamic, one which can be characterised through its through *reflexivity*. At its first level of iteration, this reflexive dynamic is quite simple: Just as Marx suggested that the emergence of industrial capital was a means to work through inequalities and contradictions created by feudalism, so Beck invites us to see a "risk-society" working through inequalities and contradictions created by industrial capital. The problems we encounter in developed capitalist economies – from environmental degradation, to concerns over the health and safety of the population – are not "external" or "natural" problems, but rather the manufactured side-effects and unintended consequences *of* industrialisation, which now return to haunt us. When our governmental focus shifts to concentrate on manufactured risks, processes of "modernisation" enter a new phase – industry no longer acting as a motor of "rationalisation", but rather as a thing which, in turn, needs to be rationalised. Whether we recognise Beck's description of "modernity" or not, we can, nonetheless, see how a consciousness of risk creates a reflexive loop within any govern-mentality, introducing the need for feedback and self-limitation.

In Beck's analysis, though, the term "reflexivity" does not connote an increased self-awareness. Indeed, Beck uses the term "reflex" in its biological sense, as an action performed without conscious thought: the patellar reaction of a knee struck by a mallet, the start of a person startled. Beck uses this metaphor to describe, at a sociological level, the "involuntary" nature of contemporary historical change: he suggests that the governmental problems of "reflexive modernity" are seldom defined by a coherent progressive agenda, but rather appear as ad hoc responses to emergent crises. Governmental programmes organised around the mitigation of pollution – combating inequality, abolishing nuclear proliferation or compensating for work-place accidents – only seek to limit the negative side-effects of an industrial production system that itself remains unquestioned. That is, in Beck's analysis, contemporary crises and their governmental responses never lead to "revolution" because our problems and solutions have become so co-dependent.

> The basic insight lying behind [the Risk Society analysis] is as simple as possible: everything which threatens life on this Earth also threatens

the property and commercial interests of those who live from the commodification of life and its requisites. In this way a genuine and systematically intensifying contradiction arises between the profit and property interests that advance the industrialization process and its frequently threatening consequences, which endanger and expropriate possessions and profits.[32]

Organised around the management of manufactured risks, Beck suggests that history itself takes on an accidental dynamic, lurching involuntarily from discovered problems to failed mitigations. Accidents and side-effects takes on a central role, becoming something like the "motor" of history; they define the political programmes of their time, as well as the material condition of the future. As he puts it, in what is this time a quip at Marx,

> Industrial society exits the stage of world history on the tiptoes of normality, via the back stairs of side effects, not in the manner predicted by the picture books of social theory.[33]

Abstracted from its intended periodisation, this Risk-analytic can be used to reflect on Edo's fire-regime. Edo's sumptuary laws clearly symbolise and make legible unequal distribution of wealth, but they were most consequential – they sustained that inequality – on account of the different "risk positions" they constructed. And while the risk of fire may well have been significant in making space for a newly emergent merchant class, this did not lead to revolution, even at the local level of fire-safety policy. By aligning urban fire-safety with the profit and property interests of that merchant class, a genuinely and systematically intensifying contradiction was created between those concerns.

5.3.3 Conjured demand

That historical change appears accidental does not mean it is entirely beyond governmental control. Tragedy or no, that urban fire reinforced the Shogun's position can only have come as a surprise once. If we follow Sand and Wills's argument, Tokugawa era legislation was precisely a means to structure the likelihood and effect of future accidents. Likewise, as we learned from Edo's arsonists, "accidents" and their side-effects are not always negative; if burning down your house means a relief from debt, you might set that fire yourself. This particular risk is one that is well understood within the insurance industry. Arson was not only a problem in feudal Edo; it creates a reflexive problem for building insurers today. If I own a structure that I cannot sell, there is risk I might burn it down myself, and claim the insurance. Likewise, but more subtly, if I ensure my smartphone against loss, I become statistically more likely to lose it. That is, Insurers recognise that coverage against a specific hazard often increases its probable frequency or severity. This reflexive phenomenon is known as "Moral Hazard", and it creates a problem for self-governance; why should I expect myself to act responsibly, when the calculus of risk already charges me for the likelihood that I will not? But if Moral Hazard seems like a problem for the individual, it might be seen as a boon for the insurer; if the provision of cover increases risk, insurance creates a feedback loop of accidental need-generation, through which supply *increases* demand.

Analogous phenomena might be seen to exist at the level of government. Beck's *Risk Society* analysis reflects on the same problems and period addressed by Foucault through his studies of governmentality. And as both Foucault and Ewald have suggested, the transformations in the role of government in post-war Europe and America – whereby the state came to take an increased role as social insurer and care-taker of the populations health and well-being – can be described as an engagement, by government, in actuarial rationalities.[34] Where this began through projects of nationalised risk-spreading ("technologies of solidarity", in Ewald's terms) supported by the experience of industry and mechanised warfare, this governmental project soon encountered its own forms of "moral-hazard": that an increased scope of governmental action might construct an increased dependency. This reflexive logic underlies, for instance, can be seen in populist concern over welfare dependency but also in criticism of neo-liberal privatisation, where a dependency on rhetorically "free" markets are seen to be structured through state-mandated but privately provided services.[35]

I suggest that the case studied here can be considered through the same framework. The "prisoners dilemma" that Lionel Frost suggested was trapping Edo's urban poor is itself a variant of "Moral Hazard"; assuming that no-one else would take the risk of rebuilding in fire-proof material, it was economically safer to re-build with flammable materials. Cheap flammable construction was an insurance-policy that created a self-generating and inexhaustible need. If we understand Edo's fire-regime, like the *Sankin Kotai* policy, as a means of need-generation, its limited success is perhaps not surprising; indeed, it is its purpose. As Beck puts it,

> Risk production and its cognitive agents – critique of civilization, critique of technology, critique of the environment, risk dramatization and risk research in the mass media – are a system-immanent normal form of the revolutionizing of needs. With risks the economy becomes self-referential, independent of its context of satisfying human needs…in this way, the risks must grow, they must not actually be eliminated as causes or sources. Everything must take place in the context of a cosmetics of risk, packaging, reducing the symptoms of pollutants, installing filters while retaining the source of the filth. Hence, we have not a preventive but a symbolic industry and policy of eliminating the increase in risks. The 'as if' must win and become programmatic.[36]

5.3.4 Spectres of risk

As a final analogy, Beck's analysis also offers a means to reflect on the metaphysical dimension of discourses on fire risk in Japan. Risk is, of course, fundamentally virtual: it is not the reef upon which our hopes are dashed, but the *likelihood* of ship-wreck[37] – not the catastrophe itself, but our *"anticipation* of catastrophe".[38] Organising themselves around such virtual foes, Beck suggests that govern-mentalities of Risk necessarily take on a metaphysical dimension. They learn something from the sooth-sayer and confidence trickster, developing something like a cult of the supernatural. In the Risk Society:

> The role of the spirits would be taken over by invisible but omnipresent pollutants and toxins... even where they approach us silently, clad in numbers and formulas, risks must be believed, that is, they cannot be experienced as such... New communities and alternative communities arise, whose world views, norms and certainties are grouped around the centre of invisible threats.[39]

The conjuration of an invisible threat – be it fire, pollutants or jihadists – is a powerful tool for governmental dramatisation.[40] The construction of power and authority in the risk society, Beck suggests, has little to do with *reducing* the hazards, but rather with *representing* them, dramatising them, submitting them to calculation. What the term "Risk" names, properly speaking, is neither the hazard, nor our uncertainty, but only the mechanisms through which both can be submitted to probabilistic accountancy – whatever cannot be calculated, cannot therefore be speculated on and cannot therefore be a "risk". It is perhaps at this level that we might understand the frequent association between Japan's approach to fire-safety and Buddhism. Technologies of risk mitigation – from procedures to exorcise cursed kimonos to policies for fire-proof construction – always have a magical dimension; they are attempts to transfigure absolute uncertainty, materialise it, use it as a means to conduct.

5.3.5 Homeopathic irony

In this section I have sought to introduce a number of concepts drawn from Beck's analysis, and use them to describe our particular case. I have suggested that we can understand the political-economy of feudal Edo through fire "risk-positions": that its sumptuary law can be seen to sustain those positions reflexively; that flammable construction was a mode of insurance, and the action of its townspeople defined by a kind of "moral hazard"; and that fire, and fire-safety measures, functioned as a form of need-generation that sustained, rather than overcame, particular governmental problems. In the next section I will go on to consider fire in modern Tokyo through the same concerns. Before doing that, though, I wish to outline how, in Beck's analysis, these accidental and reflexive problems might nonetheless be seen to contribute to something like an "enlightenment process".

The over-arching irony that Beck associates within the Risk discourse is that our technologies of risk mitigation tend to focus on those hazards that most readily submit to calculation, typically those that have happened in the past. As such, they often direct our attention away from uncertainty as such, away from real threats, but also real opportunities away from the aleatory character of the future per se. Echoing concerns outlined by Marx to open this section, then, the fundamental reflexivity that Beck describes is one of being captivated by past tragedies, which as opposed to preventing, we develop means to profitably sustain:

> The narrative of risk is a narrative of irony. This narrative deals with the involuntary satire, the optimistic futility, with which the highly developed institutions of modern society – science, state, business and military – attempt to anticipate what cannot be anticipated.[41]

But in Beck's analysis Irony is a double-edged sword, a solution as much as a problem: "[our] knowledge of the Irony of risk suggests that the omni-presence of risk in everyday life should also be treated with sceptical irony. If irony were at least the homeopathic, practical antidote to world risk society ...".[42] Echoing Latour, Beck associates a rise in risk-consciousness with a process of democratising science and technology, rendering science accessible to social and political concerns. While advocating a scepticism towards both scientific assertions and populist fear-mongering, Beck, none-theless, champions the emergence of a global public discourse on risk, one that recognises the negative consequences of technology. He describes this discourse as a process of "involuntary enlightenment", one through which we come to learn about things we didn't really want to know, that are forced upon us by accident.[43] Through that process, Beck suggests that the Risk Society is typified by a kind of "enforced cosmopolitanism".[44] Through risk, we witness the return of externalities and "others" excluded from the calculus of capital – those populations endangered by climate change, inspired to terrorism, and the troubling persistence of toxins, or nuclear isotopes. As industrial culture adapts to recognise those "others", it achieves an impure but actual form of cosmopolitanism.

> The experience of global risks is an occurrence of abrupt and fully conscious confrontation with the apparently excluded other .... The distant other is becoming the inclusive other – not through mobility but through risk. Everyday life is becoming cosmopolitan: human beings must find the meaning of life in the exchange with others and no longer in the encounter with like.[45]

Through Beck's framework, I suggest it is possible to understand the changing attitudes to urban fire-safety in Edo/Tokyo as learning process that concerns a range of "others": the material properties of wood, paper and fire; the environmental character of the place, but also the self-governing capacity of the urban population, particularly its poor. Like Beck, I suggest this is a process not characterised by revolutionary or emancipatory breaks, but rather a conjoined process of intensification and mitigation. Nonetheless, I suggest this affects political processes – in the period discussed so far, the emergence of a merchant class as spatial and economic intermediary between Shogun and the urban poor. The next section offers a brief history of fire-safety in modern Tokyo, attempting to follow this learning process up to the present day. In so doing, it pays particular attention to the way that Edo's infrastructures of fire-safety come to be re-imagined in relation to another "other": The West. Through its close relation to questions of foreign capital investment, this section demonstrates how, in this period, urban fire-safety comes to be seen explicitly as a front of "enforced cosmopolitanism".

5.4 Fire and historical imagination in Tokyo

5.4.1 Haussmann and the village

The Edo period came to an end with the Meiji restoration of 1868, when Shogunal rule was overthrown, and Imperial administration began. Edo the city also ceased at this moment, becoming Tokyo, the Imperial Capital. That change brought with it a set of concerns that would link the problem of fire, and those of fixed capital investment, to the question of internationalism. The prevalence of urban fire in Japan was recognised as a barrier to foreign investment, and through plans to re-design Tokyo as an Imperial capital, fire-safety became a rhetorical, and consciously Western-facing ambition.[46] Perhaps the most spectacular example of these plans was again prompted by fire. In 1872, a major fire destroyed Ginza, the mercantile centre of the new capital. The Imperial administration commissioned an English architect, Thomas Waters, to re-design this district, connecting the commercial port to the castle, in a consciously Western style. Ginza's "Bricktown" was acted as gateway and advertisement for foreign visitors and investors. It generated mixed feelings among the local, however; "everyone wanted to look at it, but not many wanted to live in it", as the cramped building were considered stuffy and damp, ill-suited to a monsoon climate.[47]

Ginza was to offer a model through which to develop wider plans. Consequential to these was a state visit to Europe, during which the administration saw Haussmann's city of broad boulevards, and regulated facades. In 1886 they invited Wilhelm Bockman and Herman Ende to Tokyo, and commissioned them to prepare a design for the capital, one of ceremonial, axial boulevards. But this first "grand design" for Tokyo came to an abrupt halt;

the scheme was abandoned as too costly, due to resistance from landowners, and through an emerging cultural backlash against imported concepts.[48] It was replaced by the "First Plan for Urban Improvements of Tokyo". Like Bricktown, and Bockman and Ende's plan, this imagined a network of new, fire-safe streets, carving through the dense, flammable fabric, if more modest in extent. It likewise looked to Haussmann, from whom it took an urban law, facilitating the state expropriation of land along the edges of newly created streets (Figure 5.7). However, despite being adopted into Japanese law – as the Tokyo Urban Improvement Ordinance of 1888 – the urban plan was likewise never enacted. Where redevelopment did occur during the Meiji period, it happened in a piecemeal fashion, prompted by urban fires, and with quite different results. Following the feudal logic of plot re-distribution after city-wide fires, practices of "land readjustment" continued during this period. Without compulsory purchase by the state or organised capital, agreements were brokered with individual landowners to accept a reduction in plot-size so as to facilitate new or widened access infrastructure. However, since fire struck mostly within the dense centre of urban wards, this form of development did not support the creation of wide urban axes, but rather the further subdivision of the already dense "village".[49] The failure of this first plan was such that, while Tokyo's planners were looking to the West, Tokyo remained

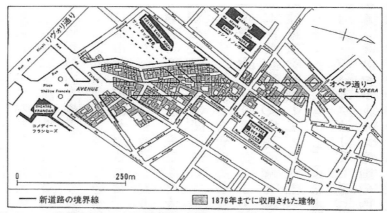

図 4・7　超過収用による直線的大通りの建設（オペラ通り）
出所：レオナルド・ベネーヴォロ著　佐野敬彦・林寛治訳(1983)『図説・都市の世界史 4』60頁

Figure 5.7 **Japanese annotation of George Haussmann's plan for urban reform in Paris.** Source: Author of annotations unknown. Included in Ai Sekizawa, History of Urban Disaster Preparedness since Meiji-Era 1868 to the 1923 Kato Earthquake, Tokyo Graduate School of Global Fire Science and Technology, Tokyo University of Science, October 21, 2016.

more village than were still a long way apart. Indeed, in the eyes of Paul Claudell, French ambassador at the time of the Great Kanto Earthquake,

> Tokyo and Yokohama were not cities but huge villages, indefinite areas of dry wooden shacks separated by narrow paths. Those two cities burnt like a construction site or a forest burns. Nothing was planned to prevent the fire propagation.[50]

5.4.2 New Tokyo, ad hoc Tokyo

That earthquake undermined Meiji-era thinking on pyro-seismic design, destroying the district of Ginza again in its entirety. It's Western looking, masonry architecture was not only damp, but also brittle. But the Kanto earthquake did lend support to other euro-philic ambitions. As described by Carola Hein, professor of history of architecture and urban planning at TU Delft, the Kanto Earthquake and reconstruction suggests that this event was seen as a "golden opportunity" to import planning principles that had been developed in Europe and the US. The quake struck only four years after the enactment of the 1919 *City Planning Law*, and it allowed Shinpei Goto, the leading urban planner, Mayor of Tokyo and then minister for the interior, to develop his *New Tokyo Plan*. That document embraced a range of ambitions then common to Western planning discourse: the combination of urban and economic planning, speculation on population increase, ambitions for de-centralisation, social housing, increased public spaces and amenities, as well as coordinated visual control of the streetscape. But this comprehensive plan was again abandoned, in favour of the *Ad Hoc Town Planning Law* of 1923. The two principal vehicles that this law supported were the *Imperial Capital Reconstruction Plan for Tokyo City*, of 1923, and the *Earthquake Reconstruction Land Readjustment Project*, of 1927. Again, both cited the risk of fire, and the need to develop a fire-resilient urban pattern, as the key concern for the reconstruction of the city (Figure 5.8). However, neither suggested the widespread use of fire-proof construction materials, nor planned construction projects, instead formalising already established practices of plot adjustment to facilitate the creation of broader street networks.[51]

That is, the *Imperial Capital Reconstruction Plan* worked within the rationale and physical remains of Edo's fire-regime; the garden residences of the former *daimyo* that had been seized by Meiji governmental offices were now re-conceived as a fire-protecting green-belt flanking the west of the city. In the dense working-class housing where the chief fire-risk remained, the plan suggested a further widening of key streets, re-trenching the spectral castle-wards. Requirements for fire-proof construction were still limited to a specific area of subsidised construction within the district of Ginza, the mercantile quarter, which now formed a fire-safety blockade between the Castle and working-class residential district. Re-enacting

流火ト点地火發

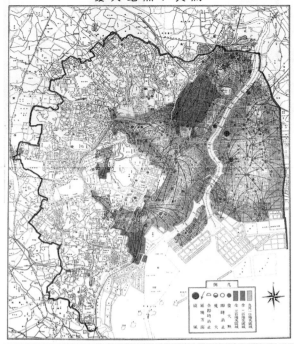

東京防火地區圖

Figure 5.8 **City of Tokyo fire prevention district plans**. Map illustrating fire-prevention districts proposed in the aftermath of the Great Kanto Earthquake. This scheme, similar in nature to the Imperial Capital Reconstruction Plan for Tokyo City, shows the mercantile centre to the east of the castle, including Ginza, rebuilt in fireproof building materials. New arterial roads to the north and east are proposed, facilitated by "land readjustment" practices, inspired by Haussmann. These are to be wide and lined with fireproof buildings. Author unknown: Images 11 & 24, http://greatkantoearth-quake.com/map_archive.html (accessed, August 24, 2021).

Nobutsana's plan, the city officials re-drew the cadastral map of 33 million m² of the city, reducing individual plot sizes and increasing orthogonality of the street layout, in order to create the expanded infrastructure of fire-prevention (Figure 5.9). The approach set out by this plan was to prove

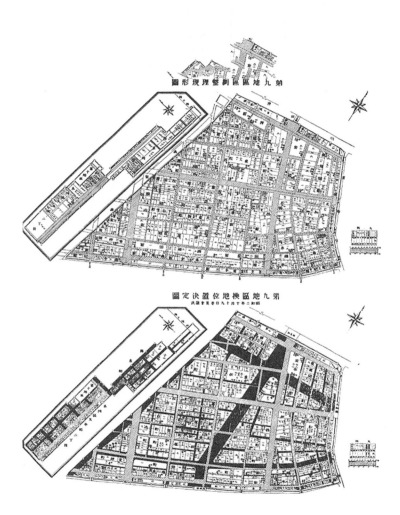

Figure 5.9 **Land readjustment used to create the intersecting Showa- dôri and Yasukuni- dôri Streets in 1927 left the surrounding areas largely untouched, creating numerous irregular and tiny sites.** Source: Carola Hein, "Shaping Tokyo: Land Development and Planning Practice in the Early Modern Japanese Metropolis", *Journal of Urban History* 36, no. 4 (January Jan. 7, 2010), 459.

nationally influential, lending its name to the prominent urban design journal of the time; it is during this period that "Land Readjustment" came be to be recognised as the "mother of urban planning" in Japan.[52]

5.4.3 Modernology and the Barrakku

Like those of Nobutsana, Tokyo's post-Kanto plans were never fully realised, due to a lack of funds required for compulsory purchase, and meeting resistance on the ground from local landowners. The limits of reconstruction at this time are perhaps most evident in relation to the question of emergency housing. In 1924, in the context of acute and extensive homelessness, the Japanese Government drew up plans for an innovative social-housing enterprise, the *Dōjunkai*, or "mutual benefit society". This organisation proposed the first concrete multi-family housing projects in Tokyo, which would provide fire-safe accommodation for refugees from the earthquake.[53] But these housing projects – again received as politically and architecturally "western" – were met with hostility, considered unsuitable for Japanese family life, and the scale of the intervention was dwarfed by the need. The majority of emergency housing needs were satisfied, not by the state, but through self-built *Barakku*. Destitute and homeless survivors of the earthquake picked up the remains of their broken homes, carried them to the edge of the city, and rebuilt them. Taking advantage of the mobile character of their building components, and by loose legal ties to landownership, the urban poor built informal settlements of temporary "barracks" around the perimeter of the city.

Records of these *Barakku* remain, surveyed by the architect and educator Kon Wajiro. Wajiro is famous for the coining the term "Modernology", which he used to describe the forms of urban and social change that Tokyo was undergoing during this period.[54] Offering a kind of mythic counterpoint to Shinpei Goto, Wajiro saw the earthquake as stimulus and opportunity to transform Edo into a Westernised, technocratic capital. He celebrated the *barakku* as a form of political resistance. Far from simply satisfying the existential needs of survival, he suggested we read these buildings as an attempt to recreate familiar aspects of everyday life; in particular he noted the reconstruction of decorative features – traditions of embellishment dating back to feudal sumptuary law – that were shunned by modernist city planners and the architects of the Dōjunkai. Indeed, he formed his own "Barrack Decoration Company" as a means to use this practice to launch a critique against modernist re-planning of the city.

5.4.4 Unburnable city

The association of European urbanism with fire-safety would take on a more urgent significance in the build-up to the Second World War. During the 1930s the Japanese Home Ministry prepared a number of educational films intended to prepare the population for war on the home front. One of these films, *Moenai Toshi* (the Unburnable City), concerned the "absolute inevitability" of aerial bombardment, and sought to habituate citizens to the fact that "many Japanese cities, overnight, will be completely destroyed". The purpose of these films – like the incentives of the Shogun – was to compel individuals to fire-proof their homes, this time on the basis of national solidarity. These films, and associated leaflets and posters, drew on memories and images of the Kanto earthquake to conjure an image of the Japanese city in ruins, contrasting these with aerial photography of the European city. Emblazoned over images of broad streets and masonry buildings was the slogan "Air Defence is Fire defence!"[55]

But again, the effect of these campaigns was limited. As Kari Shepherdson-Scott suggests in her work on their reception, it was well known that despite their predominantly masonry construction, European cities remained vulnerable to incendiary bombing, and the drive did little to cement fire-proof construction as a norm. She suggests that the films effect was limited to accelerating the preventative demolition of fire-breaks outlined in the reconstruction plan, providing clearings around key pieces of infrastructure. Needless to say, the intensity of bombing – like Godzilla ripping through power cables – would overwhelm this defensive measures, leaving Tokyo in ruins for a third time.

5.4.5 The metabolism of cheap wooden apartments

The way Japanese architects have wrestled with European precedents, tailoring them to their local context, is perhaps best known through the work of the Metabolist architects. In their 1960 group show, these architects and urban designers exhibited a range of projects that engaged with modernist ambitions – particularly the use of in-situ cast concrete, and the development of megastructural projects – bringing them in to dialogue with specifically Japanese concerns. The elevated infrastructures of Kisho Kurakawa's *Agricultural City* were intended to lift inhabitants above flood and tsunami, while allowing for flexible infill accommodation. In Kenzo Tange's *Tokyo Bay Plan* a similar structure is lifted free from land altogether, as if in doing so its inhabitants would escape all imperialist ambition.[56] Common to these and many other Metabolist schemes of the period is a perceived need for resilient fixed infrastructures, typically of reinforced-concrete, that support flexible and replaceable living accommodation – the castle-town diagram of medieval Tokyo taking Modernist architectural form.[57] Indeed, Kurokawa's *Wall City* – which proposed a network of elevated and inhabited highways, dividing up a city which remained otherwise low-rise and piecemeal in its arrangement (Figure 5.10) – faithfully renders Nobutsuna's vision in a modernist idiom. But this now familiar ambition contrasted absolutely with the adopted plan. Ostensibly favouring a policy of national de-centralisation, the Tokyo Metropolitan

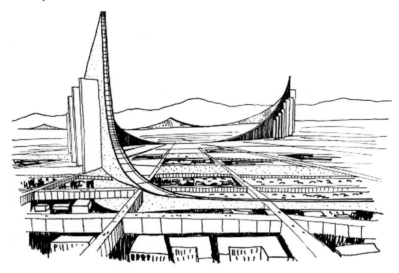

Figure 5.10 **Wall City, Kisho Kurokawa (1959).** The resilient infrastructures of Wall City (1959), which proposes a network of raised arterial road subdividing the existing city, bears a striking resemblance to previous plans for urban fire-safety in Tokyo, from the Tokugawa era onward. Source: Kisho Kurokawa, Metabolism in Architecture (London: Studio Vista, 1977).

Government had failed to prepare for the massive population increase that would occur in the immediate post-war context, its reconstruction plans essentially re-iterating the Imperial Reconstruction Plan. Again, some 20,000 hectares of land were scheduled for re-adjustment, so as to facilitate infrastructure widening as preventative fire-breaks. But by 1983, when the post-war reconstruction plan was officially considered complete, only 1,600 hectares had been re-planned.[58]

While there were continued plans for reinforced concrete refugee housing, organised through a new Housing Management Foundation, due to the exigency of demand, most were completed in timber. Post-war reconstruction in Tokyo therefore failed to eradicate dense cheaply built timber buildings; indeed, it increased their concentration. Government sponsored timber refugee housing jostled for space at the perimeter of the city, overwriting the informal *Barakku*. And as Tokyo's population increased – doubling between 1945 and 1950 alone – the majority of this population found itself accommodated in cheap timber tenement buildings constructed by the private sector. This confluence of self-built, state-subsidised and private sector construction created what came to be known as the "Cheap Wooden Apartment Belt", a halo of high-density low-rise timber housing that surrounds Tokyo's city centre, marking the extent of its historic fires.[59]

5.4.6 Escape from Tokyo

Fears about massive urban fires became widespread again in the late 1970s, prompting the then governor of Mukojima ward – a poor district situated in the Cheap Wooden Apartment belt – to use this concern as a platform for a Mayoral bid.[60] His proposed means to improve urban fire resilience was as a single project, the Shirahige-Higashi complex. This building would return the question of fire-safety to a Japanese idiom, explicitly invoking the Chiyoda castle as its urban and architectural precedent. In its initial plans, the scheme was conceived as a series of defensive ramparts surrounding a protected bailey, with staggered and overlapping entrance sequences reminiscent of the traditional Japanese "maru", or citadel, typology.[61] As constructed, its 18 interconnected apartment blocks, each 15 stories high, form an urban fire-wall that running along the banks of the Sumida River. The elevation of the city-side of this building, which looms over a district of 2–3 story timber buildings, is equipped with steel shutters that, in the event of fire, create an unbroken fire-wall over a kilometre in length (Figure 5.11). Beneath the building, underground trenches connect it to the cities fire-fighting command centre. And along the river-side of the building, lined with open access galleries, are fire-cannons. The orientation of these canons is telling: the purpose of the scheme is not to defend Mukojima, or even the inhabitants of the complex. The fire canons are aimed at a strip of land that runs along the edge of the river. The scenario that this building anticipates is of an uncontrollable urban fire-storm, during which its purpose is to maintain a means of evacuation for the entire population of the city. Fire-safety experts in Tokyo suggest that while the Shirahige-Higashi complex with is considered a technical success – an example of the forms of urban and architectural resilience the city needs – it was a political failure, coming to be seen as an extravagance the city could not afford.[62] Thirty years on it still sits in the midst of 2–3 storey timber buildings, despite the fact that this district has been entirely demolished and rebuilt during this period.

5.4.7 Risk imaginaries

From this summary account we can see continuities and differences between the fire-regimed of Edo and Tokyo. At one level, a line of continuity seems to lead from the Shirahige Higashi complex, through the work of the Metabolists, wartime air-defence measures, the *Imperial Capital Reconstruction Plan* and the *First Plan for Urban Improvements of Tokyo*, back to Yoshimune and Nobutsuna's urban plans. All have proposed grand urban plans for widened streets and resilient structures, facilitated by the re-zoning of landownership patterns. And all those plans failed to deliver the scale of infrastructure proposed, while supporting – directly or indirectly – a continued densification of less resilient, more flexible structures. What seems novel in this modern story, though, is that the problem of fire-safety is imagined

Figure 5.11 **Urban Paradigms: Shirahige Higashi.** Complex of 15-story, interconnected, housing units of reinforced concrete, creating a firebreak protecting the urban egress route beyond. Urban egress route follows the waterway (black), protected by firebreak buildings (darker tone) and fire-resistant planting (grey). Max Ochel and Liam Ross, 2020.

through different terms, with reference to "Western" practices of urban and architectural design, not native precedents of castle architecture. That is, Edo and Tokyo seem to have different risk imaginaries; in one fire it seems like an agent of class struggle, in the other of warring nations. That the Shirahige-Higashi project and the work of the Metabolist architects draw on native precedents does not, I think, undermine this general trend. Rather, these designs make sense as examples of the imaginative work needed to shift how infrastructure projects are understood.

Reflecting on why Tokyo's many visionary plans have failed, Carola Hein recognises this narrative. She suggests that Tokyo's planners consistently rejected comprehensive urban plans, empowered and supported by detailed regulatory frameworks, considering such measures too "western", favouring instead loose zoning codes.[63] Tokyo's limited success in disaster resilience planning might therefore be explained as part of a more general failure of Western-style planning to take root in Japan. Such an argument would seem to dovetail with Lionel Frost analysis, identifying a particularly Asiatic "fire-regime", one which seems to accept regular loss of property, explaining this through the different historical significance of fixed capital assets in those cultures. But Hein's analysis also recognises that opposition to urban planning measures also related to questions of landownership and national economic productivity. In her analysis of reconstruction following the Kanto earthquake and Second World War, she notes that unitary plans were specifically resisted by both the government finance departments and the land-owning lobby.[64] That is, Hein shows that concerns over "westernisation" coincided with the interests of a land-owning class not keen to cede its autonomy, and with national economic calculations, issues familiar from feudal Edo.

Looking for enlightenment or cosmopolitanism, we might be disappointed to discover nationalism and repeated mistakes. Further, we might be concerned that, by coming to be understood through a narrative of cultural opposition the practical problem of urban fire-safety in Tokyo has become all the more intractable. If this chapter has sought to trace that problem back to Edo, it has been precisely to avoid becoming trapped in this particular imaginary, and to try to focus on what appear to be the underlying material and economic issues. In the concluding section of this chapter I will outline the urban fire-safety measures of contemporary Tokyo, and the way fire-risk patterns in that city today. In doing so I will try to show how tensions between the East and West, questions of economic productivity and ambitions for landowner autonomy coincide in such a way as to sustain and indeed escalate that risk. Nonetheless, I also hope to suggest that those interests are, in the contemporary city, reaching their limits of possibility, and that due to particular material and spatial phenomena, the problem of urban fire-safety seems to be solving itself, as if by accident.

5.5 Petrified governmentality

5.5.1 The programmatic "as if"

Tokyo no longer burns down every six years. The severity and frequency of fire in the city has reduced, but not on account of the urban or architectural innovations discussed thus far; historical analysis shows that the introduction of piped-water infrastructures, and a professional fire-corps both led to radical reductions in loss of life and property.[65] No longer part of the everyday pulse of the city, the spectre of catastrophic fire, nonetheless, hangs over the city. Japan is a global centre for fire-science, and its state-of-the-art concern is the real-time computational modelling of urban fire-dynamics, used to coordinate fire-fighter activity. The scenario that this science studies is that of multiple, post-earthquake fires. Its findings are that, within dense timber fabric, such fires are unfightable; the goal of fire-fighting policy in these situations is not to extinguish the fires, but to coordinate efforts so as to secure arterial routes, and maximise available time for urban egress.[66] Through this technology we might say that fire in Tokyo is transforming from something of everyday experience, becoming something that needs to be imagined, calculated; it is becoming virtual, becoming "risk". Earthquakes are relatively susceptible to prediction; seismologists suggest a 70% chance of a factor 7 quake striking the Tokyo Metropolitan region within the next four years, increasing to 98% over the next 30 years. And while the infrastructures of fire-fighting have improved, the combustible mass of the city is growing all the time. A "big-one" in Japan is likely to kill tens, or hundreds of thousands of people, and lead to property damage worth hundreds of trillions of yen, with fire playing a major role in both losses.[67] It is for these reasons that the global re-insurance Agency Swiss RE rates Tokyo the world's most risky city within which to invest in property.[68] Swiss Re's mapping shows how risk patterns in the contemporary city; along the major circulation axis, pyro-seismic hazards are considered well-managed, through the use of reinforced concrete construction. Fire risk concentrates in the dense interior of the "superblocks", and the peri-urban sprawl of the Cheap Wooden Apartment Belt (Figure 5.5).

Despite the fact that there have been no major urban conflagrations since the Second World War, Tokyo continues to behave as if it were constantly being destroyed. The city is in its "third generation" of development since the Great Tokyo Air Raid; on average, every plot has been demolished and rebuilt three times during this period. Since 1957, a total of 1 million m^2 of Tokyo real-estate has been destroyed by fire and earthquake, while 87 million have been intentionally demolished, and almost 500 million constructed. And though the rapid rate of reconstruction in the city is no longer a direct material consequence of fire, it is, nonetheless, shaped by fire *risk*. As we have already noted, the Japanese Land Ministry suggests that developers anticipate their buildings being demolished within 30 years, providing two reasons as to why this is beneficial.[69] Rapid reconstruction is seen to facilitate improvements in seismic and fire-resistant construction, and land-use flexibility. This guidance broadly reflects reality; buildings are notoriously short-lived in Tokyo. In contrast to European cities, there is little market for second-hand buildings in Tokyo, which are often considered unsafe. This trend – which might be considered a consumer preference – is nonetheless formalised through standardisation; the three generations of post-war development in Tokyo can be defined broadly through policy changes in urban fire-prevention (in 1943, 1973 and 1996), with each new code rendering the existing fabric as non-compliant.[70] Further evidence that Tokyo rebuilds itself due to the fear of fire is offered by charting the rate of construction against time. Spikes in demolition and reconstruction occur like echoes and reverberations of real catastrophes elsewhere; when earthquake and fire strike in Kobe, Tokyo demolishes and rebuilds itself. That is, today as before, earthquake and fire offer both the need and the opportunity to ensure Tokyo's constant reconstruction.

5.5.2 Vicious circle

We have already seen that at least part of the above logic is false; Tokyo still rebuilds from the same quick, cheap flammable fabric it always has. Nonetheless, that process of reconstruction does facilitate the frequent and rapid change of landownership and use, allowing Tokyo to be re-zoned for different programmes as commercial needs dictate.[71] This flexibility is important for another governmental reasons, that of taxation. Inheritance tax is very high in Japan, reaching a peak of 70% during the asset-price bubble, and now standing at around 40%. That tax burden often means that inherited property is sold off, or subdivided. Indeed, inheritance tax is perhaps the most powerful regulatory lever for stimulating or limiting property speculation; it necessitates a continuous increase in development density to realise this generational yield. From the Second World War to the present day, average plot-sizes have reduced every generation, from 240 m^2 to around 80 m^2.[72] At the same time, this rate of inflation devalues Tokyo's building stock, which must be regularly demolished so as to liquidate and release the potentially limitless inflation of land-value. This explains why during the height of the asset-bubble, the land on which Chiyoda Castle sits could be valued more highly than all of the real-estate in the state of California while at the same time, the aggregate value of all buildings in Tokyo was effectively nothing. Buildings within the city tend become worthless after around 15 years, about half their lifespan, when their potential rental return dwindles in relation to forecast demolition cost, turning what was an asset into a liability.[73]

That is, the two logics provided by the Land Ministry interact to create a vicious circle, one that reproduces the "prisoners dilemma" of feudal Edo. Individual Tokyoites cannot afford to invest in fire-resistant technologies, because they cannot afford to lose them. Tokyo's individual property developers keep building in cheap, flammable building materials to safeguard themselves against trans-generational debt-liability, a risk which is more certain than that of fire. But in so doing, they reproduce the circumstances of their precarity. That is, after Beck, we could identify a kind of reflexive irony within the "risk" of fire. Tokyo's urban legislative frameworks undermine their own stated aims; reinforcing the cultures of rapid reconstruction which provide their ontological base, the city *makes itself fear*. Whether this state of affairs is intentional is not the concern here; the fact that programmes of building standardisation have been consistently resisted by both landowners and the finance ministry, though, suggests that it is well understood. Rather, my point is to suggest that the "non-subjective intentionality" of the legal frameworks here considered is to sustain the risk of catastrophic fire, not to negate it.

5.5.3 Piecemeal castle

The current legislation for fire-safe construction in the city is defined by the *Fire Resistance Promotion Areas* included in the Tokyo Metropolitan Government's Urban Planning guidance.[74] This document defines its famous "Hard-Shell, Soft-Yolk" morphology, incentivising fire and seismic resilient construction through relaxations to building height limits along major arterial roads. This document again seeks to carve the city up into fire-protection wards, defined by wide clearings and reinforced concrete ramparts. Indeed, through this ordinance, the shape of the city becomes a direct index of future catastrophe; the heights and depths of its buildings, and the width of its roads, are defined in relation to the anticipated height of fire within neighbouring wards (Figure 5.12). Beyond the Hard Shell, the next layer of streets is dedicated to emergency vehicle access, and is lined with "semi-fire-protected" buildings, of a lower height. In the Soft-Yolk, buildings heights are limited further still, but there are no restrictions on the use of flammable materials. This gradient of fire-protection also implies a gradient of locality; the major arteries are called "Global" roads, and the interior roads "Local", while the fire-service access streets are given the Jinglish portmanteau "Glocal".[75] That is, the structures of urban fire-safety are still associated with a gradient of internationalisation; the regulated facades of broad streets are identified as "western" in character, and the dense, impermanent, imperfect interior an expression of "Japaneseness" or "Wabi-Sabi".

In reality, however, this plan remains far from complete, it's realisation again subject to a kind of reflexive limitation. The construction of today's defensive, fire-safe ramparts requires large-scale corporate clients in need of big buildings, who can identify large plots of land, and are willing to engage in real-estate speculation beyond the generational life-cycle of most buildings. As such, this new "castle" is not evenly distributed. Even within the commercial centre defensive walls are incomplete, and so ineffective; plots redevelop according to the vagaries of the market, and the local

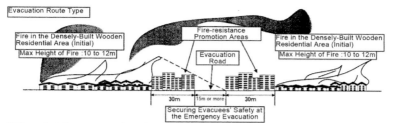

○ To protect the evacuees from the radiant heat of neighboring massive fire by making the area fire-resistant within approx. 30m from the evacuation roads designated in the Community Disaster Prevention Plan.

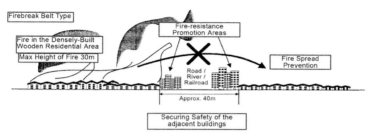

○ To prevent the fire spread to the adjacent blocks and secure the safety against urban area massive fire by making the area fire-resistant within approx. 45m combined with the width of the principle roads which are the framework of the Firebreak Belts designated in the Regional Disaster Prevention Plan.

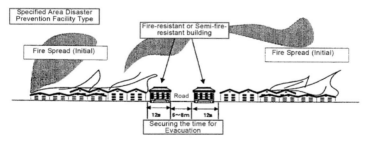

○To prevent fire spread in a few hours against initial fire and secure the evacuation time, by making the area fire-resistant within approx. 12m (a space of one unit) surrounding the Specified Area Disaster Prevention Facility under the Act on Promotion of Improvement of Disaster Control Districts in Populated Urban Districts.

Figure 5.12 **Fire Resistance Promotion Areas, Tokyo Metropolitan Government.** Illustration describing extent of Fire Resistance Promotion areas around evacuation routes, sites, firebreak belts and disaster prevention facilities. Note that no degree of fire resistance is required within "Densely Built Wooden Residential Districts", and that the scale of the required fire resistance promotion zone relates to the time of evacuation required from those districts; these regulatory mechanisms are not anticipated either to stop the outbreak of massive urban fires nor to prevent those fires from ultimately overcoming the whole of the urban fabric, but only to delay this presumed inevitability. Source: Outline of Urban Planning, Section 5, "Urban Disaster Resilience", 119–120. Bureau of Urban Development, Tokyo Metropolitan Government.

context, leaving some empty, or others not built to the design height, or depth (Figure 5.13). And these commercial pressures fail to extend to the Cheap Wooden Apartment Belt at all, where the risks are greatest. That is, far from resembling the kind of coordinated authority embodied by Chiyoda Castle's ramparts, the "Hard-Shell" of contemporary Tokyo has more in common with Kafka's "Great Wall of China"; their state of incompletion seems less a momentary condition, more an end in itself, a rhetorical gesture intended to announce the impossible scale of the task.[76]

5.5.4 Horizon of the subdivurban

Meanwhile in the village, domestic plots halve their size generationally through a process referred to as the *subdivurbanism*.[77] The resultant low-rise hyper-density has spawned a kind of accidental architecture, described by Atelier Bow-Wow as "pet-architecture": miniaturised buildings – sushi-bars, micro-residences, shops and shacks – that squeeze into left over urban spaces.[78] Associated with this micro-architecture is a micro-urbanism. Plot coverage in the village is approaching 100%,[79] the only remaining space being the by-product of another law – this time a civil code – which requires a 700 mm boundary be left around the perimeter of all buildings (Figure 5.14). This rule – intended to allow maintenance access and facilitate demolitions – is creating new patterns of urban infrastructure. As land-locked plots are created, these small gaps become the only means of access. These spaces have been celebrated by photographers, film-makers, novelists and architects. Ryue Nishizawa, in his Moriyami house, intentionally subdivides a generous lot into 5 micro-dwelling in order shift the focus of design from the object of architecture, to the "accidental" spaces created between buildings, and to enjoy the quasi-public sociability of these alleys. And Koh Kitayama, in an explicit critique of the "Haussmannian" character of "Global" streets, would see in them a model for social "resilience":

> Large Scale buildings erected with huge amounts of capital stand along arterial roads in Tokyo, part of an urban planning project to introduce a fire-belt to the area. As business efficiency is low in this crowded inner-city neighbourhood, there has been little in the way of large-capital development ... [Here] the shop workers and residents are generally familiar with each other's faces. In this densely populated area of wooden houses, people exchange glances and have some idea about each other's lifestyles. This type of environment, imbued with a sense of community, helps to create a rich and fulfilling life.[80]

Figure 5.13 **Incomplete Castles: Sumida Ward.** Contemporary fire risk in Sumida ward (darker tone) superimposed with contemporary fire-safety promotion zones (white). White volume depicts desired height and depth of urban fire wall; wherever this is visible, existing buildings fail to reach this height or depth. Note that fire-risk patterns within dense low-rise areas where the fire-wall is most incomplete. Max Ochel and Liam Ross, 2020.

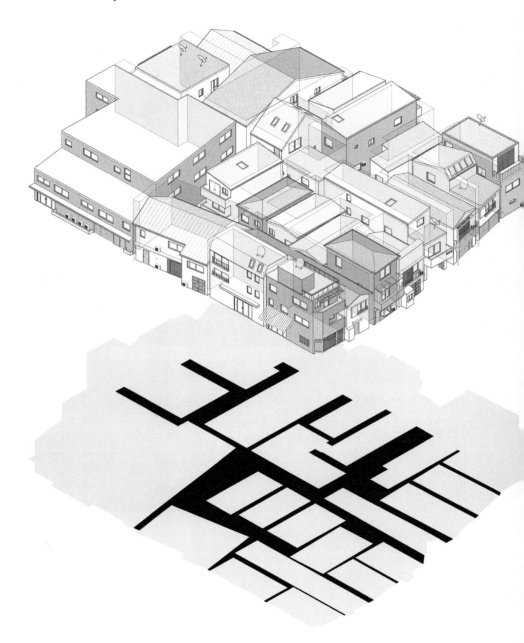

Figure 5.14 **Accidental Urbanism: Ojima Roji.** Survey of dense wooden housing and narro roads in Ojima ward. Note that building coverage approaches 100%, and that mar properties have no street address, only being accessible through informal alleys, roji (black), created by the regulated gaps between buildings. Yida Zhou, 2020.

The small lanes created by this civil law are known as Roji, and they present the city with a significant pyro-seismic risk. Not recognised as pieces of designed infrastructure, they are not subject to planning ordinance.[81] Punctuated internally by unprotected openings – windows and extract grilles – they provide a space for the spread of flame both between adjacent buildings, and between superblocks, and a major risk for urban egress. Likewise, they concentrate seismic movement within a small distance, creating the phenomenon of seismic "pounding", preventing buildings taking support from their neighbours. Nonetheless, despite – or perhaps because – of the dangers associated with this micro-urbanism, it is identified as being quintessentially "Japanese".

5.5.5 Petrified metabolism

If the above suggests that Tokyo is still trapped in the fire – regime of old Edo, there are some signs of change. In the "4th generation" village, plot sizes are too small for further subdivision. *Subdivurbanism* has reached its horizon of possibility; the only remaining direction for growth is up. That is, if we have considered the fire-regime constructed between durable, corporate slab-buildings and low-rise, disposable domestic timber dwellings, one further Tokyo typology demands consideration, that of the mixed-use high-rise tower. Tall buildings in Tokyo typically make use of reinforced concrete cores for structural as well as fire-safety purposes; the higher yields offered by high-rise buildings both necessitate and justify more resilient construction practices, and longer life-cycles. That is, if the problems of fire, land-value and a timber building stock seem to create a viscous circle, that circle breaks when land reaches a certain value. The problem of urban fire-safety seems to solve itself as soon as concrete construction becomes the norm for residential architecture. Indeed, the experts I spoke to in Tokyo suggested that this view – that the fire-safety problems created by land-value escalation would likewise be solved by land-value escalation – has supported a tacitly laissez-faire attitude by urban regulators since the 1980s.

But this shift from mediating fire and property through timber, to concrete, is not a simple one. Indeed, what I wish to suggest by way of a conclusion, is that it changes the nature of the perceived problem. This change is demonstrated by the ironic fate of Kisho Kurakawa's Nagakin Capsule Tower. The Capsule Tower responds to a design challenge we are now well briefed to understand – how to increase the density of the city, and improve its urban resilience, while retaining patterns of individual ownership, and cultures of cyclical replacement; and how to learn from European Modernism, while respecting and continuing a particularly Japanese architectural culture. Kurakawa's project attempts to address these concerns through a design that seems to synthesise aspects of both *Donjon* and *Yakiya*. This residential tower sits on a durable, concrete base, raised above the city. It is organised around a central column, this time of a robust, reinforced concrete structural and access core. Around this core, individual dwellings are organised, made from modular, off-site manufactured "capsules". That is, in this project we see an attempt to bring the architectonics, and the metabolic rates, of the "castle" and the "village" into close relation; Kurakawa famously proclaimed that, while the capsules would be replaced every generation, its core would last for 200 years.[82]

So far, only one of these claims has been proven false. Like those it inspired elsewhere – as in the Lloyds Headquarters, a building we will consider in the next chapter – the capsules of this tower have never been replaced. The reasons for this are perhaps obvious; the high costs of construction and installation make it inconceivable for an individual tenant to replace a single unit. What is not inconceivable is that the core of this building might last another 155 years. Built in 1972, the Capsule Tower has become an unusually static feature of Tokyo's built environment. It has not survived because it is liked by its occupants, who recently voted to demolish it.[83] And despite a public campaign supported by the Japan Institute of Architects and Kurokawa himself, no action has been taken to actively conserve it. Rather, the building remains because there is no economic incentive to replace all, or part of it. The individual capsules at Nagakin can neither expand, nor be made smaller, and the high cost of demolition means that replacement of the building as a whole is not yet economically attractive. The irony of Nagakin is that it broke what it sought to celebrate; what it reveals about the "metabolism" of Tokyo is that this city replaces itself to grow, and to subdivide. Concrete construction slows down these processes. Where timber buildings last on average only 27 years, reinforced concrete buildings in Tokyo today last an average of 37 years, despite being less common and relatively more recent.[84]

5.5.6 Governmental Skeuomorph

Adrian Forty has suggested that, in their use of fine carpentry for formwork, the Metabolist architects sought to safeguard a traditionally Japanese skill, offering it a place within a modern form of construction.[85] I think it is possible to suggest that the work of this group also attempts something analogous at the level of urban fire-safety. By attempting to find a place for periodic replacement within a city of resilient infrastructures, they sought to sustain a traditional aspect of Tokyo in its modernised form. The failed replace-ability of the Nagakin Capsule suggests a problem with that ambition, though. The Nagakin Tower seeks to sustain a particular culture at the same time as undermining their ontological base. Those capsules offers us a kind of governmental "skeuomorph", a govern-mentality of timber that has become *petrified*.[86]

What I have sought to describe in this chapter is the way that Tokyo's approach to urban fire-safety and its culture of rapid reconstruction co-produce each other. I have sought to identify economic and governmental reasons as to why a susceptibility to fire might, for some actors, be seen of continued value to the city. I have tried to show how certain practices of urban fire-safety – particularly land-readjustment and subsidised fire-proof construction – might continue to be used, despite their limited effect. More specifically, I have sought to show how attitudes to urban fire-safety can become entangled with broader cultural concerns, such as the openness of Japan to the importation of people, money and concepts from "The West", and the definition of a properly "Japanese" architecture and urban design. However, what I have resisted is an attempt to offer a cultural explanation for Tokyo's continued susceptibility to catastrophic urban fire – to suggest that the city rebuilds itself in an ad hoc and dangerous manner because of an aesthetic or architectural preference. I avoid this argument not because it is untrue – I have recounted many instances in which this is directly stated by architects and planners – but because such an argument would seem to consolidate the status quo. Indeed, I have sought to deconstruct this cultural argument, by demonstrating how Tokyo's fire-regime has struggled with analogous problems both before and after the Meiji Revolution. Chiyoda Castle is just as "Japanese" as the Yakiya. Rather, I have sought out what appear to be the material, economic and governmental concerns that underpin this cultural interpretation, and to demonstrate their contingency, their capacity for change.

I use the Nagakin Tower as a means to draw this reflection to a close for two reasons. The building seems to illustrate the limits of a cultural explanation, demonstrating that Tokyoites do not replace their dwelling due to a simple aesthetic preference. But the very stasis of that Tower, I suggest, illustrates the potential for a certain kind of historical change, one that occurs via the "back stair of side-effects". Tokyo's fire-regime has depended upon practices of Land Readjustment made possible by the frequent replacement of building stock since the Great Fire of Meireki. But that govern-mentality depends upon timber as a default building material; it stops making sense as soon as it is translated into concrete. As Tokyo builds higher, and in concrete, its urban fabric will become more durable. As a result, the city will need to learn to think about fire in new ways, through buildings that are both more durable, but also more valuable. This will have broader political and economic effects, changing patterns of capital accumulation, and the role of building as an economic stimulus. These are changes that the Capsule Tower anticipates. Through its gesture of an aestheticised and redundant replacement cycle it seems to ask, if earthquake, fire and building are what fuel the metabolism of this "consumption city", how will Tokyo sustain itself once land-value and safety concerns petrify it into a fixed form?

Notes

1 The *Musashi Abumi*, Asai Ryōi, 1612–1691, quoted in Peter Kornicki, 'Narrative of a Catastrophe: Musashi Abumi and the Meireki Fire', *Japan Forum* 21, no. 3 (24 May 2010): 351.

2 Takashima Beiho, quoted in J. Charles Schenking, *The Great Kanto Earthquake and the Chimera of National Reconstruction in Japan* (New York: Columbia University Press, 2013). p. 13.

3 In this paragraph I draw on the historical account of this event provided by Schenking.

4 The verbal testimony of Saotome Katsumoto, recorded in Richard Sams, 'Saotome Katsumoto and the Firebombing of Tokyo: Introducing The Great Tokyo Air Raid', *The Asia-Pacific Journal* 13, no. 10 (2015): 1–30.

5 This phrase, and statistics on the frequency of fires in Edo, are introduced in Matsukata Fuyuko, 'Fires and Recoveries Witnessed by the Dutch in Edo and Nagasaki: The Great Fire of Meireki in 1657 and the Great Fire of Kanbun in 1663', *Itinerario* 37, no. 03 (December 2013): 172–187. doi:10.1017/S0165115313000892.

6 See Schenking, *The Great Kanto Earthquake and the Chimera of National Reconstruction in Japan*. pp. 121–122.

7 Innumerable popular accounts of the rapid replacement of Japan's building stock seek to ground this phenomenon within Japanese spiritual practices, particularly the Ise Shrine replacement practices. The following article in the *Economist* is indicative: 'Why Japanese Houses Have Such Limited Lifespans – Nobody's Home', accessed 20 August 2018, https://www.economist.com/finance-and-economics/2018/03/15/why-japanese-houses-have-such-limited-lifespans. Within academic literatures on property and fire, Jordan Sand cites the work of Lafcadio Hearn and Lionel Frost as supporting this same cultural explanation, one he finds ahistorical. See Jordan Sand, 'Property in Two Fire Regimes: From Edo to Tokyo', in *Investing in the Early Modern Built Environment*, 2012. p. 36.

8 See Lionel Frost, 'Coping in Their Own Way: Asian Cities and the Problem of Fires', *Urban History* 24, no. 01 (May 1997): 5–16. Greg Bankoff, 'A Tale of Two Cities: The Pyro-seismic Morphology of Nineteenth-Century Manila', in *Flammable Cities: Urban Conflagration and the Making of the Modern World* (Madison: University of Wisconsin Press, 2012). pp. 170–189.

9 See J. Charles Schencking, 'The Great Kanto Earthquake and the Culture of Catastrophe and Reconstruction in 1920s Japan', *Journal of Japanese Studies* 34, no. 2 (2008): 295–331.

10 Morton S. Schmorleitz, *Castles in Japan* (Rutland, VT: CETuttle Co, 1974). p. 30.

11 Morton S. Schmorleitz. p. 30.

12 Richard L. Wilson, ed., *The Archaeology of Edo, Premodern Tokyo* (Tokyo: International Christian University, 1997). p. 15.

13 My thanks to four students, Euan Miller, Damien Theron, Yannick Scott and Rachel Smilie, for drawing my attention to the relationship between decorative orders and seismic performance at the Edo Donjon.

14 Stephen Pyne, 'Fire on the Fringe', in Bankoff, Greg, Uwe Lübken, and Jordan Sand. *Flammable Cities: Urban Conflagration and the Making of the Modern World*, vol. 390–396 (Madison: University of Wisconsin Press, 2012).

15 The impoverishing effect of sumptuary law, and the way the Bakafu used fire as an opportunity to impose new regulations, are recognised by Shivley in Donald H. Shively, 'Sumptuary Regulation and Status in Early Tokugawa Japan', *Harvard Journal of Asiatic Studies* 25 (1964): 123–164.

16 A detailed review of the way sumptuary law affected architectural style is offered in Laurell Cornell, 'House Architecture and Family Form: On the Origin of Vernacular Traditions Early Modern Japan', *Traditional Dwellings and Settlements Review* 8, no. 2 (1997): 21–31.

17 Wilson, *The Archaeology of Edo, Premodern Tokyo*. p. 14.

18 Sand, 'Property in Two Fire Regimes'. p. 57.

19 The status of buildings within a hierarchy of mobile property is reflected on in Sand. pp. 47, 53.

20 Pyne, 'Fire on the Fringe'. p. 59.

21 In his account, Sand notes an ironic aspect of the legality of informal settlements in these clearings which turned on issues of fire in more ways than one. Drawing on 18th C. legal testimonies, James McClain describes how the legal right of the Shogun to banish a landlord for renting a house to tenants in a firebreak turned on the question of whether the tenants – four Sumo wrestlers – kept a fire in the property. The presence of a fireplace was, in the period, what qualified a building as a "normal residence". Fire provided the material base through which laws of property and eviction were organised, and subverted, with a fire-place-less settlement being hard to remove from the fire-break.

22 Frost, 'Coping in Their Own Way'. p. 12.

23 See Pyne, 'Fire on the Fringe'. p. 46. Also Carola Hein, 'Shaping Tokyo: Land Development and Planning Practice in the Early Modern Japanese Metropolis', *Journal of Urban History* 36, no. 4 (1 July 2010): p. 451.

24 Sand, 'Property in Two Fire Regimes'. p. 42.

25 'Understanding the Lifespan of a Japanese Home or Apartment', 6 February 2014, http://japanpropertycentral.com/2014/02/understanding-the-lifespan-of-a-japanese-home-or-apartment/.

26 I borrow this term from Yoshiharu Tsukamoto of Atelier Bow-Wow. See 'Atelier Bow-Wow: Tokyo Anatomy', Archinect, accessed 17 August 2018, https://archinect.com/features/article/56468/atelier-bow-wow-tokyo-anatomy.

27 I presented this argument to two professors at the Tokyo Graduate School of Global fire, who by way of personal correspondence support this conclusion. Sekizawa Ai, Nishida Yukio, and Ross Liam, Fire Regimes of Edo-Tokyo, Graduate School of Global Fire Science and Technology, Tokyo University of Science, 21 October 2016.

28 Published as the first issue of the magazine *Die Revolution*, New York, 1852, this contains Marx's most quoted passage:

> Men make their own history, but they do not make it just as they please; they do not make it under circumstance chosen by themselves, but under circumstances directly encountered, given and transmitted by the past. The traditions of all dead generations weighs like a nightmare on the brain of the living... in creating something that has never yet existed they anxiously conjur up the spirits of the past to their service and borrow from them the names, battle-cries and costumes in order to present this new scene of world-history in this time-honoured disguise and this borrowed language.

See Karl Marx, *The Eighteenth Brumaire of Louis Bonaparte* (Chicago: Charles H. Kerr, 1907).

29 Marx's "farce" bears a close relationship to Benjamin's "Angel of History",
as presented in the *Theses on the Philosophy of History*. There Benjamin
speaks of,

> A Klee painting named Angelus Novus shows an angel looking as though he
> is about to move away from something he is fixedly contemplating. His eyes
> are staring, his mouth is open, his wings are spread. This is how one pictures
> the angel of history. His face is turned toward the past. Where we perceive a
> chain of events, he sees one single catastrophe which keeps piling wreckage
> upon wreckage and hurls it in front of his feet. The angel would like to stay,
> awaken the dead, and make whole what has been smashed. But a storm is
> blowing from Paradise; it has got caught in his wings with such violence that
> the angel can no longer close them. The storm irresistibly propels him into
> the future to which his back is turned, while the pile of debris before him
> grows skyward. This storm is what we call progress.

The following account is informed by that image, which resonates likewise
with the Beck's account of the 'Risk Society', characterised by horror, by a
transfixed gaze, by backward-looking, and the counterproductivity of the
means of historical development. See the Theses on the Philosophy of History
Walter Benjamin, *Illuminations* (Houghton Mifflin Harcourt, 1968).

30 Beck's Risk Society analytic is not without its detractors, some of whose commentary we have already touched upon. Pat O'Malley, whose work we will
engage with in the next chapter, would caution against generalising as to the
social effects of this specific concept. See Pat O'Malley, *Risk, Uncertainty and
Government* (London: Taylor & Francis, 2004). Latour has also commented
on Beck's work, expressing a concern that – while offering a powerful meta-
narrative to the contemporary critique of technology – its periodization rein-
forces a false opposition between "modern" and "pre-modern" world-views.
See Bruno Latour, 'Is Re-Modernization Occurring – And If So, How to Prove
It? A Commentary on Ulrich Beck', *Theory, Culture & Society* 20, no. 2 (1
April 2003): 35–48.

31 The work of the Aggregate Architectural History scholars, and their project
"Archiving Risk", likewise speaks to the plurality of rationalities and technologies to which this term has been attached. See 'UCLA AUD : News & Events
SYMPOSIUM: ARCHIVING RISK', accessed 29 July 2016, http://www.aud.
ucla.edu/index.php/news/symposium_archiving_risk_398.html.

32 Ulrich Beck, *Risk Society: Towards a New Modernity* (London: SAGE, 1992).
p. 39.

33 Beck. p. 11.

34 Michel Foucault, *The Birth of Biopolitics: Lectures at the Collège de France,
1978–1979: Lectures at the College De France, 1978–1979*, trans. Mr. Graham Burchell (New York: Palgrave Macmillan, 2010). François Ewald, *L'Etat
providence* (Paris: B. Grasset, 1986).

35 Chapter 6 reflects on such a reflexive process; in the deregulation of UK fire-
safety standards I suggest we see a process through which discourse on this
topic becomes caught up with a concern for its own side-effects. Ambitions
to "free" design practices from prescriptive codification come to depend upon
those codes, at the same time as introducing additional layers of regulation that
depend upon them.

36 Beck, *Risk Society*. p. 56.

37 The material origins of both the concept of risk, and practices of risk-spreading,
are nautical. The etymological root of the English word "risk" is the Latin *riscus*
(cliff), which came to mean, by extension, "reef", "difficulty to avoid in sea"

and the likelihood of shipwreck. The first risk-spreaders were traders taking our insurance against shipwrecking, as they waited for their "ship to come in".

38 Ulrich Beck, 'Living in the World Risk Society', *Economy and Society* 35, no. 3 (1 August 2006): 329–345.

39 Beck, *Risk Society*. p. 71.

40 This is the fundamental diagram of liberalism as Foucault describes it, whereby the individual is subjectified both through the apprehension of danger, and the subscription to practices of safety. "The motto of Liberalism is 'Live Danger-ously', that is to say, the individual is constantly exposed to danger, or rather, they are conditioned to experience their situation, their life, their present, and their future as containing danger." Foucault, *The Birth of Biopolitics*. p. 66.

41 Beck, 'Living in the World Risk Society'. p. 329.

42 Beck. p. 345.

43 Beck. p. 338.

44 Beck. p. 340.

45 Beck. p. 331.

46 For Jordon Sands, it is the Meiji restoration that brings a significant shift in governing-mentality, at which point – due to the ambition for fixed capital accumulation – fire becomes an enemy of that state. See Sand, 'Property in Two Fire Regimes'. pp. 64–65.

47 Edward Seidensticker, *Tokyo from Edo to Showa 1867–1989: The Emergence of the World's Greatest City* (North Clarendon: Tuttle Publishing, 2011).

48 Charles Emmerson, *1913: The World Before the Great War* (New York: Random House, 2013). pp. 416–417.

49 Carola Hein, 'Visionary Plans and Planners', in *Japanese Capitals in Historical Perspective: Place, Power and Memory in Kyoto, Edo and Tokyo*, edited by Nicolas Fieve and Paul Waley (London: Routledge, 2013). p. 313.

50 This translation is offered by Marie Sagnières. Original source Paul Claudell, 1923. "A travers les villes en flames" published in Ebisu (1999): *le Japon des séismes*, 21, pp. 35–47, translated and cited in Marie Sagnières, 'The Impact of Earthquakes on Japanese Cities: An Urban History of Tokyo', accessed 9 August 2018, https://www.academia.edu/11414299/The_impact_of_earthquakes_on_Japanese_cities_An_urban_history_of_Tokyo.

51 In this chronology I am drawing from Hein's detailed account of changing land practices and urban regulation in the aftermath of the Kanto Earthquake, see Hein, 'Shaping Tokyo'. pp. 450–461.

52 Carola Hein, 'Visionary Plans and Planners', in Fieve, Nicolas, and Paul Waley *Japanese Capitals in Historical Perspective* (New York: Routledge, n.d.), p. 315.

53 Gennifer Weisenfeld, *Imaging Disaster: Tokyo and the Visual Culture of Japan's Great Earthquake of 1923* (Oakland: University of California Press, 2012). p. 329.

54 Wajiro Kon and Izumi Kuroishi, 'Selected Writings on Design and Modernology, 1924–47', *West 86th: A Journal of Decorative Arts, Design History, and Material Culture* 22, no. 2 (1 September 2015): 190–216.

55 Kari Shepherdson-Scott, 'Toward an "Unburnable City" Reimagining the Urban Landscape in 1930s Japanese Media', Volume 42, issue 3, page(s): 582–603 *Journal of Urban History* (17 March 2016).

56 Rem Koolhaas, *Project Japan: Metabolism Talks…* (Köln: Taschen GmbH, 2011). pp. 284–292.

57 This aspect of the Metabolist legacy in explored in Meike Schalk, 'The Architecture of Metabolism. Inventing a Culture of Resilience', *Arts* 3, no. 2 (13 June 2014): 279–297.

58 Carola Hein, *Visionary Plans and Planners* (New York: Routledge, n.d.), pp. 312–316.

59 In *The Making of Urban Japan* Sorensen describes the emergence of the "cheap wooden apartment belt", its recognition as a specific fire risk, and its leading to a new planning principle of *machizukuri*, or "community building" through incremental change. André Sorensen, *The Making of Urban Japan: Cities and Planning from Edo to the Twenty First Century* (London: Routledge, 2005). pp. 269–271.

60 I was directed to the Shirahige-Higashi project through a personal correspondence with Prof. Sekizawa and Nishida, whose verbal account of the political background of this project I draw upon here. Ai, Yukio, and Liam, Fire Regimes of Edo-Tokyo, Graduate School of Global Fire Science and Technology, Tokyo University of Science. 2016.

61 Initial plans for the complex illustrate the urban and architectural lineage it shares with Edo castle, conceived as an urban "maru", with a long defensive wall, and ceremonial protective gates. See Murao, 'Case Study of Architecture and Urban Design on the Disaster Life Cycle in Japan' (14th World Conference on Earthquake Engineering, Beijing, China, 2008), https://www.iitk.ac.in/nicee/wcee/article/14_S08-032.PDF.

62 Personal correspondence with Prof. Sekizawa and Nishida revealed this ambivalent legacy of the project; they noted that the public and academic are split as to the merits of that scheme, some seeing it as a prototype to be repeated, others a costly mistake. Ai, Yukio, and Liam, Fire Regimes of Edo-Tokyo, Graduate School of Global Fire Science and Technology, Tokyo University of Science. 2016

63 Hein, 'Shaping Tokyo'. p. 450.

64 Hein. p. 480.

65 Ai, Yukio, and Liam, Fire Regimes of Edo-Tokyo, Graduate School of Global Fire Science and Technology, Tokyo University of Science. 2016.

66 Ai Sekizawa's work for the National Research Institute of Fire and Disaster, and the School of Global Fire Science and Technology Tokyo University of Science, are exemplary. Indicative papers include A. Sekizawa, K. Sagae, and H. Sasaki, 'A Systemic Approach For Optimum Firefighting Operation Against Multiple Fire Following A Big Earthquake', *Fire Safety Science* 2 (1989): 423–432, and 'Post-Earthquake Fires and Performance of Firefighting Activity in the Early Stage in the 1995 Great Hanshin Earthquake' Yuji Hasemi, ed., *Fire Safety Science: Proceedings of the Fifth International Symposium* (Amsterdam: Elsevier, International Association for Fire Safety Science, 1997).

67 Elizabeth Yuan CNN, 'Tokyo Sees High Quake Probability, Scientists Warn', *CNN*, accessed 8 December 2017, http://www.cnn.com/2012/01/24/world/asia/tokyo-quake-forecast/index.html.

68 The global reinsurance agency claims that Tokyo is,

> the most earthquake-threatened in Swiss Re's Mind the risk, a global survey of cities under threat from natural disasters. In addition, the Tokyo-Yokohama region is on the coast and close to waterways, which means the area is also exposed to river flood. If an event comparable to Tokuhu were to happen closer to Tokyo-Yokohama, the results could be devastating.

See 'Mind the Risk: Cities under Threat from Natural Disasters', accessed 13 March 2018, http://institute.swissre.com/research/collaborations/in_focus/Mind_the_risk_cities_under_threat_from_natural_disasters.Html.

69 Masako Tsubuku, 'Japan's 30-Year Building Shelf-Life Is Not Quite True | The Japan Times', accessed 8 February 2017, http://www.japantimes.co.jp/community/2014/03/31/how-tos/japans-30-year-building-shelf-life-is-not-quite-true/.

70 For a review of significant changes to pyroseismic codes see 'Earthquake Building Codes in Japan', JAPAN PROPERTY CENTRAL (blog), 28 May 2011, http://japanpropertycentral.com/real-estate-faq/earthquake-building-codes-in-japan/. Also Atelier Bow-Wow, *The Architectures of Atelier Bow-Wow: Behaviorology*, 01 edition (New York: Rizzoli International Publications, 2010).

71 'Harvard Design Magazine: What Goes Up, Must Come Down', accessed 20 August 2018, http://www.harvarddesignmagazine.org/issues/3/what-goes-up-must-come-down.

72 Yoshiharu Tsukamoto, 'Void Metabolism', *Architectural Design* 82, no. 5 (1 September 2012): 88–93.

73 Richards Koo and Masaya Sasaki, 'Obstacles to Affluence: Thoughts on Japanese Housing', *NRI Papers*, No. 137 (12 January 2008), https://www.nri.com/global/opinion/papers/2008/np2008137.html.

74 See *Outline of Urban Planning*, Section 5, "Urban Disaster Resilience", pp. 119–120, 'Bureau of Urban Development Tokyo Metropolitan Government', accessed 2 September 2016, http://www.toshiseibi.metro.tokyo.jp/eng/.

75 A description of the morphology of the typical "superblock" is offered by Shelton in his description of Gokisu, see Barrie Shelton, *Learning from the Japanese City: Looking East in Urban Design* (London: Routledge, 2012). pp. 138–168.

76 In the story, the "Great Wall of China", Kafka's mason struggles to understand the construction logic of his imperial commissioners. Work proceeds in a piecemeal fashion – with work crews completing isolated fragments of wall within the vastness of the steppe – appearing to defer any possible military advantage. The mason concludes, though, that the purpose of the wall is not, in fact, to keep out the "invaders from the north", but rather to create a subjectifying experience in which the scale of the individual labourer's accomplishment is rendered insignificant with respect to the scale of the empire. See Franz Kafka, *The Great Wall of China, Stories and Reflections* (New York: Schocken Books, 1970).

77 Atelier Bow-Wow's Yoshiharu Tsukamoto defines this term in his essay "Escaping the Spiral of Intolerance: Fourth Generation Houses and Void Metabolism", in *Tokyo Metabolizing: Koh Kitayama, Yoshiharu Tsukamoto, Ryue Nishizawa* (Toto, 2010).

78 *Pet Architecture Guide Book* (World Photo Press, 2002).

79 This is another phrase introduced by Tsukamoto in his essay "Escaping the Spiral of Intolerance: Fourth Generation Houses and Void Metabolism" in *Tokyo Metabolizing*.

80 *Tokyo Metabolizing*. p. 119.

81 My understanding of the fire-risk posed by *Roji* is again informed by personal correspondence with Ai Sekizawa. Ai, Yukio, and Liam, Fire Regimes of Edo-Tokyo, Graduate School of Global Fire Science and Technology, Tokyo University of Science. 2016.

82 Kurokawa introduces his concept for the "metabolism" of this tower, at the same time as calling for its preservation in Tokyo Art Beat, *Kisho Kurokawa Pt. 2: Nakagin Capsule Tower*, 2007, https://www.youtube.com/watch?v=9roy5mbz5fk.

83 'Tokyo's Tiny Capsules of Architectural Flair | The Japan Times', accessed 20 August 2018, http://cached.newslookup.com/cached.php?ref_id=263&siteid=2 203&id=8628700&t=1412499065#.W3rECy-ZMdV.

84 Japan Property Central. 'Understanding the Lifespan of a Japanese Home or Apartment', 6 February 2014. http://japanpropertycentral.com/2014/02/understanding-the-lifespan-of-a-japanese-home-or-apartment/.

85 Adrian made this argument in a lecture entitled *On Nations and Materials: a nineteenth-century question revisited in the 21st century*, presented at the 2015–2016 cycle of the ESALA Research Seminar series. See 'ESALA Research Seminar Series | Edinburgh College of Art', accessed 20 August 2018, https://www.eca.ed.ac.uk/esala-research-seminar-series.

86 A Skeuomorph is an object that imitates features or characteristics of another, usually in a nostalgic form: a digital camera that makes a "click" sound when taking photographs, or an online PDF viewer that animates the "turning" of pages.

6 London

Engineering uncertainty

6.1 Arup Associates and the meta-engineering of governance

6.1.1 Post-modern engineering

They're the people you go to when you're tendering for the structural steel package on the CCTV building. You're worried about the construction sequence of the bridge section. Prior to their connection, the asymmetrically canted towers are subject to differential sagging and expansion due to self-weight and sunlight exposure. They'll simulate this deflection, design the towers to be self-supporting while incomplete, and confirm that they can only be connected at dawn, when they're both equally cool.[1] They're also the people to talk to when you want to know why the World Trade Center Towers *really* collapsed, and what regulators should learn from the event. By developing software to simulate structural deflection through heat, they'll argue that the buildings would have collapsed due to the fire alone, regardless of the airplane impact.[2] Their Extreme Events Mitigation Taskforce will use this analysis to contradict the National Institute of Standards and Technologies, and call for a review of fireproofing codes for tall building.[3]

While such simulations and calculations are the stock-in-trade for engineers at Arup Associates, one of the world's largest building design consultancies, according to Rem Koolhaas they are also indicative of the "post-modernity" of contemporary engineering.[4] Through their fastidious devotion to the empirical – always enabled and mediated by the "hypnotic window" of computational analysis – the work of Arup Associates seems to transcend a dependence on universalising structural principles or their didactic architectural expression. If Ove Arup's "Total Design" once stood for the (somewhat preachy) ambition to integrate architectural and structural rationalities, it now seems to have taken on a simpler yet more expansive meaning; that anything and everything can be designed:[5]

DOI: 10.4324/9781003026297-6

[O]nce avid supporters of High Tech, modernism's moment of deca-
dence, [Arup are], – in a form of emancipation – now exploring a kind
of science fiction, meta-engineering as a total answer to everything.[6]

6.1.2 Architecture after thrift

These journalistic assertions are given more academic depth by Arindam
Dutta's essay, "Marginality and Meta-engineering: Keynes and Arup".[7]
Dutta charts the firm's contribution to the "signature" architectural projects
of nineties and noughties London, likewise noting an apparent loss of faith
with modernist concerns for the expression of structural logic. If there is a
meta-narrative to Arup's diverse projects of this period – on the South-Bank
alone we can think of the Millennium Bridge, the Tate Modern, the London
Eye, the GLA, or Anish Kapoor's Marsyas, not to mention the Gherkin, or
the ArcelorMittal Orbit Gallery – it seems to be to stretch the envelope of
what is technically do-able. Drawing upon Keynesian economic principles,
Dutta situates these projects in related governmental thinking. He suggests,
for instance, that we should understand the Modernist concern for structural and material efficiency as an instance of the classical economic concern
for "thrift". Keynes specifically argued, in the context of Britain's post-war
re-construction, against this govern-mentality; the architectures of thrift –
while answering to the immediate exigency of the housing need – threatened
to undermine the long-term value of construction as a mode of economic
stimuli (and from a Keynesian perspective, the UK's post-2008 "austerity"
politics could be subjected to a similar critique). By contrast, the govern-
mentalities of Blairite Britain appear, to Dutta, like a late realisation of
Keynesian economic principles. Here building design seems to forego thrift,
adopting instead a kind of calculated "irrationality" visible at the level of
governmental and economic policy, as well as in architectural design.

Keynes famously argued that markets crash when the actors within them
behave *too* rationally, becoming risk-averse. To combat this he suggested
that macro-economic policy should structure a *lack* of awareness amongst
actors so as to facilitate an irrational optimism in investment. He effected
this, at a fundamental level, by separating the Bank of England from central government, ensuring that a kind of "functional blindness" existed
between political and economic decision-making. At a more local level, the
UK's National Lottery – which funded many of Arup's high-profile projects of this period – functions in a comparable way; it stimulates irrational
micro-economic behaviour, so as to fund targeted macro-economic stimuli
in the form of "public works" (Keynes's favoured mode of economic intervention). Dutta points us, then, to the role which Arup's iconic projects
played within this broader governmental diagram, at once legitimating,
representing and enacting a political economy of irrational exuberance.
But he also shows how, to some degree, Arup manage to "transcend" this

diagram, being one of the few actors who operate at all of its levels. In the process of delivering these ambitious and complex projects, the firm extended their schedule of services beyond those of mere building design, to include development accountancy, international legal advice and the review and drafting of governmental legislation. That is, over this period, Arup's developed a consultancy platform through which they became capable of reflexively reconstructing their own conditions of practice. As Dutta puts it, from then on buildings ceased to be the *object* of their design, being only the "'front end' of an infrastructural project whose impetus is to transform the modalities of governmentality as such".[8]

6.1.3 Political economy of fire

Fire in London, and its effect on architectural design, is the subject of a book in its own right. The Great Fire of London, whose 350th anniversary occurred in 2016, was perhaps the most influential event to have shaped that city, and the UK's building regulations as a whole. The event led to what are popularly considered our first building standards; the 1667 Reconstruction Act – which required that "No man whatsoever shall presume to erect any house or building, whether great or small, but of brick or stone" – and the Fire Prevention Regulations, of 1668.[9] The men who shaped those rules, and in so doing modernised our building construction practices, infrastructure provision and property law, were perhaps the most influential in the history of the city – Sir Christopher Wren, John Evelyn, Robert Hooke, John Locke and Nicholas Barbon.[10] Indeed, their effect is still so legible within the city that even contemporary commentators can suggest that "the London terraced house is more or less the clauses of [these] regulations turned into bricks and mortar".[11] Other fires in London have gone on to have nationwide effects, too; the Kings Cross fire of 1987 underpins much of our contemporary fire-safety standards. More recently the Grenfell Tower fire of 2016 – the subject of the next chapter – has prompted their comprehensive review.

Much has already been written on the Great Fire and its legacies; as such these two chapters on London offer more minor and more contemporary accounts of the ways in which that city has been shaped by fire-safety regulation. In this first reflection, my focus turns away from regulation itself, though, to questions of de-regulation, a performance-based design. Continuing the line of thought begun above via Koolhaas and Dutta, it on the work of Arup Associates, the "hypnotic window" of computational analysis, the aesthetics of structural expression, and the role of the building industry and its design services as a form of economic stimuli. This chapter extends their accounts, though, by reflecting on these issues through the prism of fire-safety. More specifically, it reflects on the kind of opportunity and agency available to those design practitioners who can meta-engineer the way we *define* safety.

The first section recounts the emergence of fire-safety science in post-war Britain, considering the pivotal role played by Arup Associates. At stake in this section will be the way in which the design ambitions and commercial pressures of architectural practice came to define the problems and concepts of this discipline. The particular focus will be on two initiatives led by Arup, in association with the University of Edinburgh, to free fire-safety engineering from "prescriptive" standardisation by developing an empirical or "performance based" definitions of safety. However, it will note a number of scientific and governmental problems implied by this ambition, suggesting that they function rather by blurring, by making ambiguous, such definitions. The second section reflects on this constructed ambiguity suggesting that, as opposed to being a scientific deficit, it plays a particular political-economic role. Drawing on the work of Higgins, Kitto and Larner it will recognise Arup's work as an example of non-state actors exerting increased control over standardisation, blurring questions of "public" and "private" interest. And with reference to Foucault and O'Malley, it will suggest that the ambiguity constructed by these ambitions be considered part of a trend towards "governing by uncertainty", constructing circumstances for irrational optimism through unequal distributions of risk and responsibility. In the final section, it offers a close study of a mode of computational analysis associated with these initiatives, Arup's *MassMotion* software package. By considering the utopian character of these simulations – the degree to which they act as a kind of wish-fulfilment– it will reflect on how the technicalities of architectural design can be construed as part of a broader process of subject formation.

6.2 Fire-safety and deregulation in post-war Britain

6.2.1 *Magic acts and magic numbers*

The governmental genealogy offered in the Chapter 3 of this book concluded with the Second World War and the nationalisation of both the fire-services and building regulation. This chapter extends that genealogy, and begins with that event. Wartime destruction created both the need and the opportunity to systematically review existing property patterns, construction technologies and their associated urban and architectural paradigms. Within this review, it was recognised that existing building codes – often carried and enforced by local by-law – were a potential barrier to such systematic change. Indeed, like the country's demolished and decrepit building stock, these codes were recognised as a haphazard patchwork, built around outdated practices, and the arbitrary contingencies of past events.[12] We have already noted the lack of empirical "science" behind the "2.5 minute rule", for instance, but such contingencies troubled many of our standards.

That is, at the same time as calling for the universalisation of building regulations, the post-war review of these legal frameworks sought to find a more empirical basis for standardisation. Seeking to free building practices from arbitrary limits the UK government set up the Fire Research Station at Borehamwood in 1949. The ambition of this Station was to develop a scientific basis for the modelling of fire behaviour as a means to overhaul building standards. This work provided the basis for the development of fire-safety engineering as both an academic discipline and a field of design consultancy. David Rasbach, who began his career at Borehamwood, went on to establish and lead the world's first fire-safety engineering programme at the University of Edinburgh in 1974, developing a curriculum which has since been recognised as the "core" of any degree in this field.[13] His successor, Dougal Drysdale, wrote what remains its definitive textbook.[14] Through their work, the UK and Edinburgh established itself as the centre of a global network of fire-safety expertise which today includes the University of Tokyo; Lund University; University of California, Berkeley; University of Maryland; Worcester Polytechnic Institute and University of Queensland.

A disposition *against* prescriptive codification can be seen in the early research in this field, well characterised by the writings of Margaret Law. Law was a colleague of Rasbach's at Borehamwood, and went on to establish the world's first Fire-Safety consultancy with Arup. In "Magic Numbers and Golden Rules" she outlines her critique of existing fire-safety codes, both as arbitrary science and evidence of clumsy government. Of the travel distances inferred from the 2.5-minute rule, she complains, "the regulatory authorities are comfortable with [these] magic numbers. If the distance to a door is no more than 45 m, the building is safe. They need to think no further."[15] This "magic" was hard to de-bunk, though, as it served a broader disposition of government:

> [T]he transfer of technology from researcher to the real world is subject to a ratchet mechanism. Because fire research is almost entirely bound up with safety issues, there is an inherent prejudice in favour of releasing and applying results at the earliest stage if lives can be saved... [while no such pressure exists to disseminate] research carried out which shows that the current approaches to fire safety may be overly restrictive.[16]

6.2.2 Grand gerberettes

Law's writings paint a picture of a discipline which sees itself struggling against government, enrolling the ambitions of contemporary design practice as a means to support a perceived need for empirical fire-science: "as soon as [regulations] frustrate design, we should be able to re-establish the rationale behind the rules and thereby develop new approaches".[17] This attitude resonates both with Arup's "Total Design" philosophy, but also with the commercial interests of a design consultancy and its clients; reading Law's account, the goal of fire-safety engineering appears to construe safety as another case-load to be addressed through bespoke, integrated solutions, balanced against competing concerns and interests.

The way that specific projects and commercial trends shaped the discipline is well described by Barbara Lane, fire engineering practice leader at Arup Associates and visiting professor in fire-safety engineering at Edinburgh University.[18] One of the first signature projects of fire-safety engineering was that of the *Centre George Pompidou* (1971–1977). Piano and Roger's design called for the use of exposed structural steel, something that until then had not been permitted due to the need for fire-insulation (think of Mies's decorative columns at the Seagram Building, completed only a decade before the Pompidou brief). Law had developed a number of ways to achieve the fire-rating of structural steel without insulation; through the massive size of structural members, through water-cooled hollow-sections, or through spatial set-back. At Beaubourg she deployed all of these techniques: the Pompidou's exterior compression columns are hollow and water cooled, and set 1.6 m outboard of the glazing; the slender, solid tensile members are pushed a further 7.6 m away from the fire-load; the connecting "petit gerberettes" are, of course, not "petit" (Figure 6.1). The project is rightly recognised, in these details, as a successful integration of architectural, structural and fire-safety thinking. This was not always seamless, though; it was Law who frustrated Piano and Rogers' ambition for a fully open and uncompartmentalised interior. In order to limit the number of structural elements that might be lost in a fire, she required the building be split into two fire compartments. Concurrent with the Pompidou, however, Arup pushed these logics further in a building of their own design, Bush Lane House (1971–1974), where a hollow-section water-cooled primary structure is pushed outboard of the envelope, creating a completely open and uncompartmentalised floor-plate (Figure 6.2).

6.2.3 Big Bangs and big boxes

Lane goes on to describe how, in the 1980s, two further developments put fire-safety engineers in wider demand. Thatcher's deregulation of the financial services sector – her "Big Bang" – created enormous demand for office space within the City of London. The fashion for atria within these building brought about calls for a commensurate de-regulation of fire-safety design, presenting legislators with challenges for which they did not yet have rules. At Lloyds of London (1978–1986), Arup pioneered the use of Computational Fluid Dynamics to model smoke behaviour. Through this, they demonstrated that the atrium, while allowing for the vertical movement of smoke, likewise provided a reservoir for it, which would allow occupants to escape without succumbing to fumes. Again, fire-safety concerns were not always seamlessly integrated; the building was initially designed as a steel-framed structure, but at the time this could not be proved safe, the steel being famously replaced by concrete late in the process. The corporate atrium

78   IABSE PROCEEDINGS P-61/83   IABSE PERIODICA 2/1983

Fig.3. - Pompidou Center
        Paris

3.5) Centre Pompidou, Paris, France (19)

Architects : Piano and Rogers,
Structural Engineers : Ove Arup & Partners

Much of the structure of this building is exposed externally (figure 3). Where
calculation of the external fire exposure showed protection of the elements to
be necessary to reach the 2 hours fire rating required, protection was provided
generally by water cooling or by shielding although a few parts have conventional
fire protection. The Centre Pompidou has a steel superstructure rising above
a concrete substructure. The main building has six storeys above ground, each
7 m high and 166 m long. The main lattice girders span 44.8 m between short
cantilevers projecting from the main columns, the outer ends of the cantilever
members being restrained by vertical ties. The glazing generally follows
the junction between the lattice girders and cantilever brackets. The main columns
are 1.6 m outside this line and are water filled for fire protection, circulation
being achieved within each column by pumps. The cantilever brackets are 7.6 m
long; thus the outer line of tension "columns" and associated bracing members are
7.6 m from the windows. Calculations showed that in the event of fire, all the
members on the outer plane are protected by virtue of the 7.6 m distance from
the windows; the cantilever brackets are shielded by fire-resistant panels in the
façade. There are sprinklers on the external walls and the cantilevers. Horizontal bracing members close to the windows would be lost in a fire, but with each
floor divided into two compartments, the loss of a proportion of the bracing does
not endanger resistance.

Figure 6.1 **"Pompidou Centre, Paris".** Photographer unknown. Source: Brozzetti,
     Pettersson & Law, 'Fire protection of steel structures: examples of ap-
     plications' IABSE Proceedings P-61/ 1983, p. 78, Figure 3.

travelled the world as a building typology, and in so doing, took Arup with
it. When they arrived in cultures with less developed or looser regulatory
regimes – Russia, the UAE and later China – Arup's appeared not only as
design consultants but also as regulatory advisors, and performance verifiers, so beginning a path towards governmental "meta-engineering".

IABSE PERIODICA 2/1983   IABSE PROCEEDINGS P-61/83   79

Fig. 4 - Bush Lane House
London

3.6) <u>Bush Lane House, London, England (20)</u>.

Architects & Structural Engineers : Arup Associates.

Prior to the construction of this building (figure 4), water cooling had only been used for the protection of vertical columns, since its use for beams raises considerable difficulties in ensuring that adequate controlled water flow occurs and no steam pockets develop. In Bush Lane House, water cooling is used for the external structural steel and protects columns, lattice members, and a critical top horizontal member. Bush Lane House provides eight office floors above a first-floor plant room. Each typical floor is approximately 35 m long x 16 m wide, supported by the lift core and three columns set 11 m   from the extremities of the building. The stainless steel lattice which transmits the floor loads is external to the building envelope and leaves the office space uninterrupted. The steel members are water filled and inter-connected, so that in the event of fire the water circulates and steam is vented at high level or separated in a tank on the roof. This tank also serves as a reservoir to replenish and keep the system full of water. The patterns of water flow, maximum potential steel temperature, and the amount of water storage were all established by calculation.

Figure 6.2 **"Bush Lane House, London"**. Photographer unknown. Source: Brozzetti, Pettersson & Law, 'Fire protection of steel structures: examples of applications' IABSE Proceedings P-61/ 1983, p. 79, Figure 4.

In the UK of the 1980s, the professional context was itself being deregulated. The Monopolies and Mergers Commission and later Warne Report disbanded architect's fee scales and protection of function, opening the market to alternative forms of design consultancy. At the same time, the emergence of Design and Build contracting created new forms of procurement, within which the architect no longer assumed their "traditional" role of contract manager, allowing engineers or quantity surveyors to take the role of lead "designer". Due to their ability to gain exemption from prescriptive codes, and to self-certify designs, firms offering diverse, non-architectural specialisms developed a market advantage. Fire-safety engineering was as an important aspect of this advantage; in the context of Big Box retail and distribution, for instance, the ability to design large, open-plan buildings with exposed structural steel offered significant cost-savings, and gave the discipline its reputation as a form of glorified "value engineering".

6.2.4 Starchitects and sky lobbies

In the 1990s and noughties the development of the "signature" architectural project as a vehicle for sovereign wealth fund investment put Arup in yet more demand. The self-consciously unconventional designs of a Gehry, Hadid, or Koolhaas created technical challenges that further secured a demand for engineered responses. The Seattle Central Library offers an example of this, which accidentally evidences the differing legal stature of architect and engineer: while Koolhaas was ironically complying with the city's zoning laws as a tactic to maximise the permissible volume of the building, Arup was circumventing the city's codes for egress, compartmentation and smoke control – facilitating the large interconnected vertical spaces, and exposing parts of the building's structure – and in turn, establishing itself as a body with greater expertise than that of the regulatory authorities.

Most recently, the aesthetic economy of large, open-plan spaces and unprotected steel structures has been best described through a series of office projects in London. Plantation Place (2004), which has a completely unprotected steel frame and unimpeded floor plates, was the first project to gain regulatory approval through the use of "Dynamic Fire Modeling". This computational mode of simulating fire-spread in buildings was used to demonstrate that, as long as the amount of combustible material within the building is limited, fire will burn out before reaching the heat required to melt structural steel. It is this form of modelling that Arup used to study the structural collapse of the World Trade Center Fire, but also to argue for the safety of its fire-strategy at the Heron Tower (2007–2011). Prior to the World Trade Center fire, regulators had not considered the possibility of simultaneous fires occurring on adjacent floors within a high-rise building: floors are usually "compartments" and designed to stop fire spreading vertically. September 11th proved that this could happen, and Dynamic Fire Modelling was used to argue that it if it did, existing codes were not sufficient to prevent collapse (Figure 6.3). By showing that such risks exist, Arup constructed a market for design-services needed to design them out. And by doing so, they found themselves in a position to do things that would otherwise have been illegal. At the Heron Tower Arup's fire-engineered the design of a tall building that omits fire-proof cladding so as to expose structural steel, and incorporates three-storey "sky-lobbies" which break from floor-to-floor compartments (Figures 6.4 and 6.5). Neither of these would

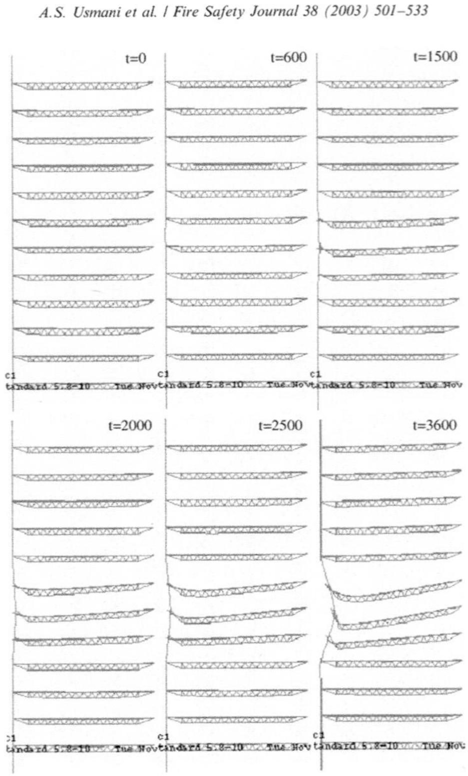

A.S. Usmani et al. / Fire Safety Journal 38 (2003) 501–533

Figure 6.3 "**Model showing collapse, fire scenario C**". Source: Usmani, A. S., Y. C. Chung, and J. L. Torero. 'How Did the WTC Towers Collapse: A New Theory' in *Fire Safety Journal* 38, no. 6 (1 October 2003): p. 523, Figure 18.

be possible following prescriptive standards, nor without arguments based on detailed scenario modelling. That is, the Heron Tower acts to normalise aspects of 9/11. By simulating the conditions of that accident, Arup Associates found ways to recreate that circumstance, and to demonstrate that it can be "safe".

6.2.5 Epistemological limit

The approvals process for Plantation Place and Heron Tower demonstrate some of the recent ways in which Arup Associates are attempting to re-engineer the UK's legislative framework. Arup have developed means for the computational modelling of occupant egress which, together with Dynamic Fire Modelling, suggest a means to overcome the arbitrary limits

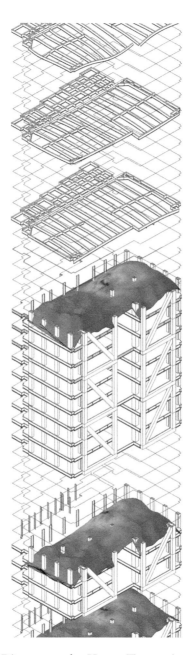

Figure 6.4 **Modelling Disaster at the Heron Tower.** Axonometric of Structural Steelwork at Heron Tower, superimposed with Fire Dynamic Simulation analysis used to assess likely fire-load in the event of a three-storey compartment fire. Chris Tolmie 2020.

Figure 6.5 **CGI visualisation of 3-storey voids, Heron Tower, Kohn Pedersen Fox Associates (2007).** Source: GMJ, reproduced courtesy of Kohn Pedersen Fox Associates

of the "2.5 minute rule". Through the development of agent-based egress simulations – which simulate the behaviour of building occupants in response to a fire-scenario – Arup can simulate the effects of design changes on likely occupant egress time. Arguments for safety can be made by comparing rate of escape with rate of fire-spread, so gaining relaxation on prescriptive guidelines for maximum travel distance. These forms of simulation are supported by current UK building legislation as a means of verifying compliance with its "functional" or "performance-based" standards. Through the use of this form of verification, clients and designers can avoid the need to comply with the standard codes, as long as they demonstrate a solution is deemed "safe".

The ambition for a performance-based standardisation of fire-safety has run into an epistemological problem, though. Despite the ambition of fire-safety scientists, they have failed to offer a more empirical definition of "safety". As discussed in Chapter 3, the definition of "safety" cannot be reduced to a clear legal or technical definition, but rather depends upon specific social and political conditions of possibility. Working in academic abstraction, fire-safety engineers cannot re-define what is considered socially acceptable. This creates an ironic limit inherent within the project of fire-science, as noted by Vincent Brannigan, emeritus professor of fire and Law at the University of Maryland. In "Fire Scenarios or Scenario Fires? Can Fire Safety Science Provide the Critical Inputs for Performance Based Fire Safety Analyses?", he notes how this problem surfaces in the technical challenges of performance-based codification: computational modelling for egress and fire-spread are *themselves* based upon assumptions, standards and codes – indeed, often the same codes upon which prescriptive standards are based.[19] That is, despite the sophistication of fluid and agent-based analysis demonstrated by human, fire and smoke dynamic modelling, the regulatory purpose of this software is still to demonstrate that a building can be evacuated within the duration of the British National Anthem. This is, at a practical level, because fire-engineered solutions are only lawful to the degree that they can be proved to be "as safe" as the equivalent prescriptive codes, which still offers the only legal definition of "safety". But what it suggests more generally is that ill-formed concepts such as "safety" cannot be known other than through the definition of acceptable limits: that the "prescriptive" is epistemologically deeper than the "performative".

6.2.6 *Reflexive tightening*

This does not mean that such regulatory changes have no effect on what can and can't be designed. Performance-based codification allows designers to equate other design features – sprinklers, smoke reservoirs, pressure differentials, the eradication of combustible materials, or enhanced occupant training programmes – with additional escape time. The "regulatory-space" of these codes, therefore, creates a kind of situated freedom, through which designers can exchange one mode of compliance with another. But given the economic and economising nature of its commercial application, this trade-off can have counter-intuitive effects. Since the prescriptive code remains the benchmark of "safety", design freedom (and cost saving) is bought by the creative interpretation of margins of safety, through the introduction of further assumptions. As a result, the material effect of fire-safety engineering is often to legitimate constructional arrangements that could be considered fundamentally less safe: deeper plans, less means of escapes, less fire-protection, less compartmentation, coupled with greater dependence on active management. Furthermore, this ambition to "free" design from regulatory assumptions actually adds to the number of assumptions embedded within the design-model, at the same time as suggesting the need for additional controls on the forms of permitted occupancy. As Brannigan notes, It is logical to assume that, as such regulatory models are mainstreamed, new forms of regulation will be required to ensure that the built environment complies with these models, in terms of use, furnishing and occupancy levels. Thus the creative freedom of the designers is bought at a cost to the freedom of the occupant; the metaphorical loosening of our Regulatory Space implies a reflexive tightening of our literally regulated spaces.

We can see the emergence of these new, *more* highly regulated practices in some of the flagship projects that Arup have recently been involved with. The architectural innovations at Heron Tower, for instance, placed additional burdens on the building's occupants. Chris Stoddart, the first head of the Heron Tower, won "Facilities Manager of the Year" award for his role in educating and monitoring occupant activity. He told the Building Research Establishment that the challenges of managing emergency evacuation in the building demanded: "a Zero tolerance approach to controlling behaviour; Clear command; CCTV; Clear, consistent communication [and]; Strong Management".[20]

6.2.7 Political-ineconomy

Recent fire-safety initiatives, often tied to processes of deregulation, have less to do with improvements in fire-safety, more to do with limiting the economic and aesthetic effects of existing safety standards. And despite not offering improvements in regulatory outcomes, these developments can entail an increase in the *cost* of that regulation, in the form of increased consultancy work in building design, its legislation, its verification and its management. Plantation Place and Heron Tower were only possible due to the close collaboration between Arup, the City of London and its Fire Rescue Services. Eager to ensure the Square Mile remains competitive in the market for office space, the City have required that its fire-fighters and regulators undertake secondments with Arup to ensure they understand the complexity of fire-safety solutions undertaken in these projects.

But this increased cost does not occur only within government, much is displaced to the private sector. That is, while depending upon existing prescriptive standards, performance based forms of standardisation shift detailed decisions about safety to design consultants. The epistemological limits identified by Brannigan are precisely the sleight of hand that allows for this displacement. These new regulatory frameworks scientise the fundamentally social decisions that our standards are based upon, blackboxing them, and so making them even more embedded, invisible. And it is by doing so that they effect a shift in the locus of decision-making. Performance based modes of standardisation shift the space of consequential decisions away from the state – whose agents do not have the expertise to understand detailed fire-safety reports – and into the sphere of design consultation, within which commercial interests hold a powerful sway. In practice performance-based design is only employed when it offers the potential to eliminate prescribed margins of safety through the creative deployment of approximations and assumptions. That is, this change in the technology of government brings with it a change in rationale, and perhaps also what we could call a change in subjectivity; regulation changes from an activity in which we recognise common threats, and develop universalised means, to one through which we make calculated decisions balancing individual opportunities for profit and loss.

6.3 Governing by uncertainty

6.3.1 Black-boxing the social

Much in this account of Arup's work resonates with literatures on standardisation, governmentality and the constitution of a neo-liberal subjectivity. In *Calculating the Social: Standards and the reconfiguring of governing*, Kitto, Higgins and Larner offer an overview of recent social-scientific research on standardisation. They attribute a surge of interest in the topic to questions as to how "governing is achieved in a globalizing world where the state is no longer the main form of regulation, and particularly how public and private entities might most effectively shape conduct 'at a distance'".[21] Summarising the work of this field, they note traits that will strike us as familiar: the rise of international authorities and experts in standard-setting; the global diffusion of the standards they create; the blurring of public and private interests entailed; the "black-boxing" of social concerns within technical guidelines; and resultant questions for democratic accountability. But beyond these general observations – which operate at the level of governmental rationality – these authors call for a more materially focussed analysis of the "work" of standardisation and its relationship to neo-liberalism. They ask if certain types of standards produce certain types of effect, if they reconfigure relations between public and private, and if they privilege specific sites, spaces and agents.

This brief account of Arup's engagement with fire-safety standardisation allows us to sketch a provisional response to some of these questions: The shift in type from prescriptive to performance-based standardisation does seem associated with different social impacts. Where state-based prescriptive standardisation is universalising in nature and intent, performance-based standardisation, which operates through bespoke solutions and privatised verifiers, have targeted impacts for discreet clients. Despite their claim to supplant prescriptive forms of standardisation, performance-based codes in fact depend upon them, or to put that in more bald terms; this privatised mode of "government" does not replace the state, which it ultimately falls back upon as arbiter of "safety". Nonetheless, these mechanisms create a clear privileging of both large-scale corporate clients and of consultants such as Arup; this reconfiguring of legislative practices is disposed both towards the interests of corporate clients, and towards the construction of a market for services provided by their consultants, who come to act as designers, verifiers and advisors to government and other public services.

6.3.2 Creative compartments

These problems are to some degree recognised both by the sector and by government. In a recent report commissioned by the Scottish government, Brian Meacham – associate professor at Worcester Polytechnic, Massachusetts – suggests that while the state of performance-based fire-safety standardisation in Scotland is "not dire", it has a number of associated problems, centring around the verification of fire-engineered solutions.[22] The report – which draws extensively on consultation with Arup – recognises a widespread concern that this mode of standardisation is viewed as a means to save money, as opposed to deliver safe buildings. Further, it finds the UK lacking in expertise within the construction industry, fire-services, regulatory bodies and even within the fire-safety engineering community (which is not professionally certified). This lack of expertise makes it difficult to verify the safety of engineered solutions. And since engineered solutions often achieve only minor deviations from prescriptive requirements, it argues, the practice as a whole creates a disproportionate burden on statutory bodies. Putting this in other words, we could say that while seeming to "free" design practices from the burdens of clumsy government, the practice may save construction costs, but create additional consultancy and governmental costs, and result in an overall net-loss of cost-efficiency.

We might see the recent Private Finance Initiative (PFI) hospital scandal in England, in which a raft of hospitals constructed under PFI have been found wanting in terms of fire-safety,[23] as evidence of some of these concerns. These buildings used fire-safety engineering to allow them to be "creative with compartments", deviating from both national standards and the strict fire-code of the NHS.[24.] Whether the resultant buildings are "safe" or not is not the issue I wish to raise, though; rather, the fact that Arup, who designed a number of these buildings, also acted as the expert witness determining whether those designs are, indeed, safe, would seem to demonstrates the asymmetry of knowledge that characterises this field.

6.3.3 Environmental technology

To connect these practices with trends in neo-liberal governmentality is not hard; the move away from prescriptive to engineered solutions to safety clearly follows a trajectory of privatising previously public functions, through the creation of a market for social goods. The counter-productivities noted above, I think, already offer a powerful critique of this trajectory, which in practice may appear more "clumsy" than those they would supplant. However, my interest here is to suggest a deeper connection that operates not through the governmental *rationalities* of performance-based standardisation, but rather through its blind spots and aporia. That is, just as the previous section employed the way fire in Edo could be construed as useful for a particular govern-mentality, in this chapter I want to suggest that uncertainty over what we define as "safe" likewise serves a broader function within neo-liberal government. The epistemological limits explored above seem a means to allow commercial actors to carve out a space of action, while ensuring that responsibility for that action remains with the state.

One aspect of the history of Liberalism that Foucault offers in the *Birth of Biopolitics* is that of the changed significance of the "marketplace" for successive eras of government: If in the middle ages it was a site for the dispensing of Justice (through the fixing of a "fair price") by the late-twentieth century it had come to be seen as a site through which we recognise ourselves as individual "economic subjects" (and so self-regulate our activity in accordance with "rational" self-interests). Since individual actors must here be construed as "free" to determine those interests, this change entails a shift in the mode of governmental intervention. Governments must try to avoid the direct exertion of discipline (telling us what to do; setting prescriptive requirements), instead acting on the "environment" in which actors "play". The theme programme of neo-liberalism, for Foucault, is therefore not exhaustive discipline, nor exclusionary logic, but rather the "optimizing of systems of difference, in which a field is left open to fluctuating processes".[25] The "environmental technologies" of contemporary government offer "loose frameworks that create the possibility of play". Their purpose is not to determine governmental ends, but to be "open to unknowns, [through a] freedom of interplay between supplies and demands". Governmental action is here limited to the "the regulation of environmental effects [ensuring] the principle of 'non-damage'", and to constructing the "possibility for individuals to regulate the effects of the framework".[26]

6.3.4 Capricious government

The work of Pat O'Malley connects these broad and abstract rationalities to discreet and concrete governmental technologies. In *Risk, Uncertainty and Government* he suggests that risk and uncertainty are not universal or natural phenomena, but rather techniques of governing with specific and divergent political histories.[27] His account of the role of these concepts within neo-liberalism resonates closely with Foucault's "environmentality" of government; the calculative practices that reframe uncertainty as risk facilitate economic speculation around wealth production projects, while providing an infrastructure that limits individual or corporate loss. The construction of risk imaginaries and mitigation technologies creates new and important governmental roles for technical experts, for those people who can, with "reasonable foresight", construct the conditions of "play". And it is in relation to these questions of uncertainty, risk and "reasonable foresight", that I think we can connect Arup's meta-engineering of government back to the Keynesian concerns we began this reflection through. As we have seen, for Keynes the fundamental problem of market economies is that they behave *too* rationally, so tending towards risk-aversion and market collapse. The role of government, therefore, was to maintain – to render politically sustainable – the "capricious" character of our economic games:

> Is our expectation of rain, when we start out for a walk, always more likely than not, or less likely than not, or as likely as not? I am prepared to argue that on some occasions none of these alternatives hold, and that it will be an arbitrary matter to decide for or against the umbrella. If the barometer is high, but the clouds are black, it is not always rational that one should prevail over the other in our minds, or even that we should balance them, though it will be rational to allow caprice to determine us and to waste no time on the debate.[28]

What I wish to argue is that environmental technology of performance-based codification works towards the end of caprice, both by safeguarding against loss (of life, of property), but also by creating opportunities for advantage and profit. Uncertainty plays a fundamental role here. Problems of fire-safety call upon and circle around a "real" uncertainty; the possibility of an actual building fire, the ways in which that fire might develop and spread, the locations within which smoke might pool and the way people might behave in response to these events. These real uncertainties are simulated with more-or-less reasonable foresight and in so doing can be subjected to the probabilistic accountancy of "risk". But at the same time, fire-safety engineering actively *constructs* another form of uncertainty; that question of what we define as "safe". Indeed, this uncertainty is its condition of possibility/impossibility; fire-safety engineering only exists to the extent to which it can call existing standards into question *at the same time* as deferring to them. Engineered solutions are required to demonstrate that they are "as safe as" prescriptive requirements; this formulation defines a space of legal and design flexibility that nonetheless avoids assuming actual governmental responsibility. At the same time as appearing to be a discipline that subjects fire-dynamics and occupant behaviour to empirical analysis, with a view to increasing the safety of our built environment, fire-safety engineering black-boxes the fundamentally unscientific question of "safety" as a means to legitimate often empirically less-safe environments. It is at this level that we can add to Dutta's suggestion that Arup Associates, now through fire-safety engineering, contribute to a Keynesian reconstruction of government: by constructing a space of uncertainty within our definitions of "safety", they make room for capricious decision making. The space that this creates secures a market advantage for some, at the same time as isolating them from particular financial risks.

6.4 Fantasies of fire-safety

6.4.1 Mesmerism and MassMotion

The individual agents are faceless, emotionless. They move at an unnervingly slow and steady pace, neither rushing, nor dawdling, as if in a trance. They maintain a constant distance between themselves and their neighbours, endowed with both respect and patience. They know where they are going; to a place of safety from which to escape a fire, or a terrorist attack. Likewise, they know how to get there: they have internalised a perfect knowledge of the building's layout and are able to determine the quickest route from any location to their final destination. But while acting individually and rationally, they know something of doubt and respond to the dynamics of a crowd. Should a bottleneck form, they can assess the relative speed of those around them, in relation to that of all agents, and re-evaluate their route. That is, acting with an instantaneous and transparent knowledge of the system, and of all other agents, their individual, rational and self-interested decisions aggregate to ensure that total occupant flow is efficiently directed to all available routes (Figure 6.6).

I'm describing *MassMotion*, the most recent egress simulation package developed by Arup's software arm Oasys. The package, used by Arup in the design and verification procedures discussed above, offers "[t]he most advanced pedestrian simulation and crowd analysis tool available anywhere. Capable of simulating hundreds of thousands of people within a matter of hours…".[29] And it is in this software package that we see how the technologies of fire-safety engineering embed the assumptions written into prescriptive standards. The width of shoulders, the rate of movement and the queuing behaviour that is programmed into these avatars are those defined by the regulatory assumptions of post-war building studies, British Standard 9999 and Scottish Building Standard 2.9.3 (Figure 6.7). If we simulate a fire at the Empire Palace theatre using this software, these obedient audience members will escape in precisely 2.5 minutes (Figure 6.8).

6.4.2 Mise En Abyme

I want to dwell on this scene because I I offers, within the drama of fire-safety more generally, a kind of "mise en abyme"; within this book it is a kind of play within a play.[30] In these computational simulations we see recreated the fantasy that eluded the designers of the 2.5 minute rule. Through the use of this simulation software to analyse and modify building designs, we see superimposed two different interpretations of the British National Anthem; a patriotic crowd that moves calmly and slowly to the beat of this tune, and a building that has been designed as an echo of its duration.

I have already suggested a concern that this particular piece of software – and the ambition towards performance based design in general – black-box a kind of ignorance. However, in order to conclude this chapter, I want to suggest that its simulations are also accidentally enlightening; that they offer us clues as to how we should interpret that bigger drama. Moving on from a reflection on matters of fact, then, I wish to consider these simulations as fictions, indeed as *fantasies*.[31] My purpose is not to indulge in fancy; rather, what I want to suggest is that the governmental power of these representations has less to do with their accuracy, more to do with their capacity to make us *want* to believe. Indeed, I will attempt to connect the particular *inaccuracies* of these simulations with particular desires, and so show how they engage us within a process of subjectification. In doing so I will consider three more-or-less sophisticated fantasies, speaking to three more or more-or-less sophisticated audiences, which seem to be nested within these simulations; the fantasies of organic solidarity, of harmless economic games and of a technocratic sovereignty.

6.4.3 Simulated solidarity

Let's begin with the least sophisticated. We can sympathise with the desire of those involved in commissioning, designing and approving new buildings to think that people will be able to escape from them alive. At this level MassMotion functions as a simple act of wish fulfilment. It visualises the conceit of the 2.5 minute rule, allowing us to *see* the calm that is produced by a well-regulated environment. For the concerned client, these videos act like the familiar in-flight safety video, as a means to steady the nerves. In satisfying this role inaccuracy is a positive boon, and doubting questions are best left ignored. It is a rare passenger that asks a flight attendant whether, before ditching mid-Atlantic, with little hope of rescue, does it really matter if I take it actually matters whether they take of their if I take off my high-heeled shoes?

The well-worn irony recognised as the aesthetic hallmark of those videos suggests, no.[32] Indeed, these videos are a perfect example of Beck's "homeopathic irony". When the comedian Vic Reeves announces your emergency evacuation instructions, you suspect that Virgin Atlantic are asking you to worry, but not *too* much.[33] Rather, as Slavoj Zizek has suggested, the purpose of these videos is rather to gentrify catastrophe, which they do by allowing us to indulge "in the fantasy of society as an organic whole kept together by forces of solidarity and cooperation".[34] The simulations offered by MassMotion seem to indulge this same fantasy. Watching them calls to mind all those aspects of occupant behaviour that they *don't* represent; non-reaction, panic, crushing, ineffective attempts to fight the fire, doomed missions to return and save loved-ones. These behaviours would be difficult to model or predict and would raise difficult questions for designers and regulators. The function of this first fantastical dimension, then, would seem to be to equivocate these two difficulties; by accepting these simulations as "reasonable foresight" we accept that any form of behaviour that cannot be readily simulated by pre-programmed avatars is also not "reasonable".

Figure 6.6 **Mass Motion Egress Simulation: Perspective and Seating Plans.** Image shows a simulated evacuation of the Empire Palace Theatre auditorium, in "Agent Follow" mode. Egress of 1759 occupants is completed in 2 minutes 54 seconds. Very similar to newspaper reports of the 1911 fire. Liam Ross and Max Ochel, 2018

6.4.4 Harmless game

This simple fantasy, though, seems part of a more sophisticated one, aimed perhaps more at the building occupants than its owners or designers. It is hard not to notice the homology between the computational logics of MassMotion and those used to model financial markets. The Efficient Market Hypothesis – the investment theory through which stock trading is understood as an effective means to distribute scarce resources amongst mutually exclusive ends – is based on precisely the same set of assumptions. This mode of modelling assumes a total and instantaneous transparency of knowledge between the actors in a system, suggesting that the self-interested micro-economic decisions of individual investors aggregate to determine a "fair-price" for commodities, to balance supply and demand, and ward against catastrophic boom or bust – the celebrated "invisible hand" of Adam Smith. The simulations of MassMotion, along with their associated fire-drills and occupant health and safety manuals, provide another point of contact within which a neo-liberal governmentality asks us to recognise ourselves as "homo economicus", finding within ourselves a rational self-governor. Yes, in the event of fire, this *is* how I will behave. And if I don't recognise myself in this way, I'll become a problem for the facilities manager.

We know that the Efficient Markets Hypothesis is not accurate because of the ability of speculators to "game" the market. The possibility of profit within financial speculation emerges as a result of asymmetries of knowledge. Likewise, case-fires demonstrate that the forms of efficient escape modelled by MassMotion do not play out in reality. Nonetheless, the fantasy provides cover for another kind of "game". Beyond Arup, another leader in the field of fire-safety evacuation modelling is The Walt Disney Company. Using software developed for crowd simulation in their animated films, they have produced *SpirOps*, a system to simulate crowd egress (and queuing behaviour) in their theme parks.[35] In Disney's work there is a direct technology transfer between the simulation of catastrophic crowd dynamics for the purposes of entertainment and their use in commercial and governmental initiatives. And there is something of a transfer of *logic*, too; what family-friendly fantasy movies and fire-egress simulation animations have in common is that everyone escapes *in the nick of time*. The "game", in the latter, is the ability to diverge maximally from prescribed codes – leveraging as much design freedom, and as many cost-savings – while remaining nominally "safe". Fire-safety engineering offers that "loose framework" which allows for a "possibility of play" within building design, while seeming to "regulate its environmental effects", by ensuring a "principle of non-damage". Winning this game is not about improvements in occupant safety – the simulation is a simulation – but about strengthening market dominance through the reflexive re-design of regulatory frameworks.

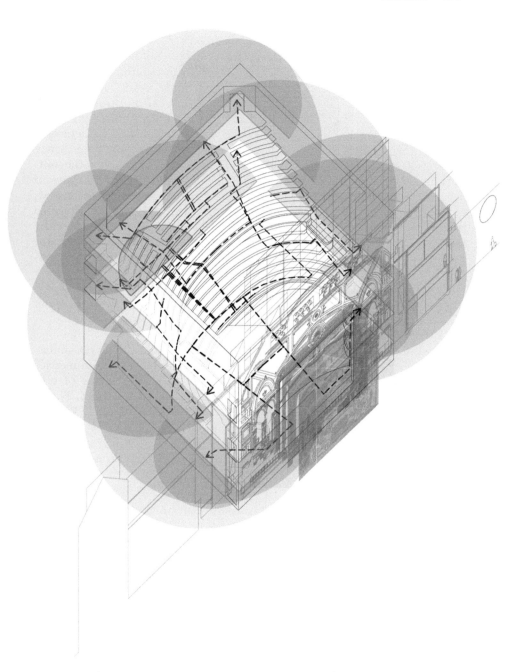

Figure 6.7 **Travel Distance Survey: Axonometric.** Diagram shows seating arrangement, and escape routes (dotted lines). Arcs record remaining available travel distance at exit point. Note that travel distance to stalls level rear right exit is approximately 18 m, the maximum permissible escape distance for slow occupant profile. Liam Ross and Max Ochel, 2018

6.4.5 Technocratic sovereignty

But the ways in which this "harmless game" constructs a "play" within our definition of safety is, I think, only part of a final level of fantasy at work in these simulations. To see it, we have to return to the assumptions that are black-boxed by MassMotion, and more importantly to the *magic* behind its "magic numbers". The avatars calmly queuing to exit a burning ground-scraper in the City are all humming *God Save the Queen*. If the designers of those buildings are clever, they have been able to slow down the tempo, through the deployment of sprinklers, smoke reservoirs, pressure differentials, the eradication of combustible materials, or enhanced occupant-training programmes. But to keep this show on the road, the band *must* keep playing. The original function of this piece of music was to snap us out of one trance, and into another; to shift us from blithe ignorance to patriotic obedience. The simulations of MassMotion continue to act in the same way. That is, at a certain level, 2.5 minutes is not arbitrary science; it *is* magic, it *is* sovereignty. If prescriptive travel-distance regulations governmentalised the space-time of this original decision, fire-safety engineering seems intent on resurrecting its spirit. They do not exorcise the magic of this "magic number", they animate it, become its channel, its medium. MassMotion transubstantiates the Great Lafayette's patriotic bandleader, and he is still mesmerising.

Notes

1 See *The Arup Journal*, no. 2 (2008): 42.
2 The NIST reports suggested that loss of fire-insulation due to the aircraft impact was the reasons the resultant fire was able to topple the structure. This view – in terms of its impact on building standardisation – effectively relegates the incident to the status of a "black swan". See Kristy D. Thompson, *Final Reports from the NIST World Trade Center Disaster Investigation*, NIST, 30 June 2011, https://www.nist.gov/engineering-laboratory/final-reports-nist-world-trade-center-disaster-investigation.
3 G. Flint et al., "Effect of Fire on Composite Long Span Truss Floor Systems", *Journal of Constructional Steel Research* 64, no. 4 (2006): 303–315, and "WTC Ten Years on: Learning from the Unthinkable", *New Civil Engineer*; London, 7 September 2011.
4 Construction Week Online listed Arup Associates in its Top 5 global engineering consultancies, citing 92 office in 37 countries, with over 10,000 staff and a turnover in excess of $1 bn.
5 This concept was the organising theme behind the V&A's recent retrospective of the firms work, "Engineering the World: Ove Arup and the Philosophy of Total Design".
6 See "Post-modern engineering?" in *Rem Koolhaas and Office for Metropolitan Architecture, Content* (Köln: Taschen, 2004).
7 Dutta's essay appears in Governing by Design: Architecture, Economy, and Politics in the Twentieth Century / Aggregate Architectural History Collaborative; Contributors: Daniel Abramson, Lucia Allais, Arindam Dutta, John Harwood, Timothy Hyde, Pamela Karimi, Jonathan Massey, Ijlal Muzaffar,

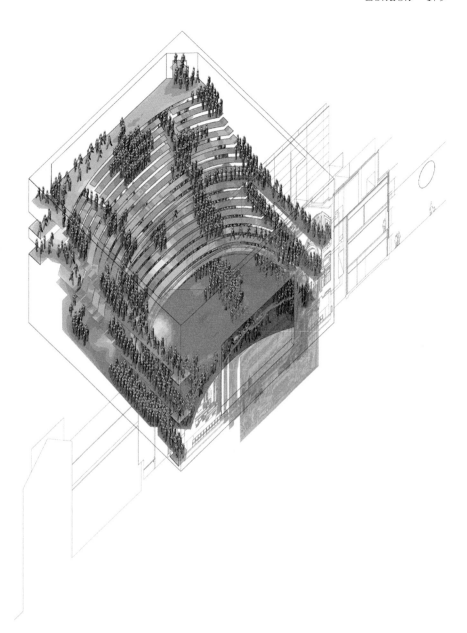

Figure 6.8 **Mass Motion Egress Simulation: Axonometric.** Tone showed in floor plans illustrates "experienced density" of crowd at any point in plan, identifying locations in which bottlenecks and crushing might occur. Liam Ross and Max Ochel, 2018

Michael Osman and Meredith Tenhoor, *Culture, Politics, and the Built Environment* (Pittsburgh: University of Pittsburgh Press, 2012).

8 Dutta refers to a 2004 paper, 'A Review of the Publicity Requirements for Planning Applications', commissioned and published by the Office of the Deputy Prime Minister, authored by Arup Associates. The paper, Dutta notes, was intended to "determine if the current statutory requrements for publicizing applications for planning permissions, listed building and conservation area consent are effective and offer value for money".

9 From the 1667 reconstruction act, collated here as "Proclamation issued by King Charles II. to prohibit the rebuilding of Houses after the great Fire of London, without conforming to the general Regulations therein premised." in 'Appendix: Charters (Charles II) | British History Online', accessed 7 August 2018, https://www.british-history.ac.uk/no-series/new-history-london/pp845-849.

10 See Leo Hollis, *The Phoenix: St. Paul's Cathedral and The Men Who Made Modern London* (London: W&N, 2009).

11 Andrew Saint, 'Lessons from London', in *Cities for the New Millennium* (London: Taylor & Francis, 2001), p. 159.

12 Brannigan makes this argument in Vincent Brannigan, 'Fire Scenarios Or Scenario Fires? Can Fire Safety Science Provide The Critical Inputs For Performance Based Fire Safety Analyses?' *Fire Safety Science* 6 (2000): 207–218.

13 Rasbach's curriculum is David Rasbash, "A Modular Approach to the Subject of Fire Safety Engineering", *Fire Safety Journal* 3, no. 1 (1 November 1980): 31–40. Its adoption as the "core" of any fire safety engineering programme is recommended in S. E. Magnusson et al., *A Proposal for a Model Curriculum in Fire Safety Engineering* 25, no. 1 (1 July 1995): 1–88.

14 Dougal Drysdale, *An Introduction to Fire Dynamics* (Chichester: John Wiley & Sons, 2011).

15 Margaret Law and Paula Beever, 'Magic Numbers and Golden Rules', *Fire Safety Science* 4 (1994): 79–84.

16 Law and Beever. p. 80.

17 Law and Beever. p. 78.

18 The summary offered in this section draws upon Barbara's address at 40 Years of Fire Safety event at Edinburgh University in 1994: Prof Barbara Lane #ed40fire, 2014, https://www.youtube.com/watch?v=zH44JZ1diO8&feature=youtube_gdata_player.

19 Vincent Brannigan, 'Fire Scenarios or Scenario Fires? Can Fire Safety Science Provide The Critical Inputs For Performance Based Fire Safety Analyses?' *Fire Safety Science* 6 (2000): 207–218.

20 His lecture "Managing Emergency Evacuation and Response" was presented at the BRE event *Cities in the Sky*, accessed 10 April 2017, https://www.bre.co.uk/eventdetails.jsp?id=6761.

21 See the editors introduction, "Standards and Standardization as a Social Scientific Problem" in Vaughan Higgins, Simon Kitto, and Wendy Larner, *Calculating the Social: Standards and the Reconfiguration of Governing* (Hampshire: Palgrave Macmillan, 2010). p. 1.

22 St Andrew's House Scottish Government, *Research to Support the Improvement of the Design Verification of Fire Engineered Solutions as Part of the Scottish Building Regulatory System*, Website Section, (2 November 2016), http://www.gov.scot/Topics/Built-Environment/Building/Building-standards/publications/pubresearch/researchfire/resfirdvfes.

23 "FOUR New Hospitals "Have NO Proper Fire Protection" | Daily Mail Online"", accessed 5 April 2017, http://www.dailymail.co.uk/news/article-3764579/If-fire-patients-wouldn-t-chance-hell-FOUR-new-hospitals-NO-proper-fire-protection-problem-47m-two-years-fix.html.

24 "Fire Safety Engineering – Creative with Compartments"", *IFSEC Global*, 11 August 2008, https://www.ifsecglobal.com/fire-safety-engineering-creative-with-compartments/.

25 Michel Foucault, *The Birth of Biopolitics: Lectures at the Collège de France, 1978–1979: Lectures at the College De France, 1978–1979*, trans. Mr. Graham Burchell (New York: Palgrave Macmillan, 2010). p. 259.

26 Foucault. p. 261. Foucault's own example of an environmental technology is US drug enforcement policy of the 1970s, which recognises that supply limitation and scarcity are exacerbating drug-related crime. Through the reduction of enforcement activity and the introduction of subsidised drugs for addict populations, a new "economic" balance is struck between police and drug users.

27 Pat O'Malley, *Risk, Uncertainty and Government* (London: Taylor & Francis, 2004).

28 John Maynard Keynes, *A Treatise on Probability* (North Chelmsford: Courier Corporation, 2004). p. 30.

29 'Oasys Software – MassMotion: Crowd Simulation and Pedestrian Modelling Software', accessed 25 September 2017, http://www.oasys-software.com/products/engineering/massmotion.html.

30 The phrase *mise en abyme* originates from heraldic design; it is a sign set within ("placed in the middle" of) another sign, and so changing its meaning. Within the history of Western art we see it in many forms; picture frames caught within the frame of a picture, or plays set within other plays. It is a device used to create a moment of reflexive self-awareness in an audience; a theatre troupe stages a play, to tell one audience member (called Hamlet) that they understand the bigger plot he himself is hatching. At the same time, another audience, the spectators, are prompted to reflect upon the play they are watching (also called Hamlet), and to consider the bigger dramas it might point to, beyond the walls of the theatre.

31 It would be possible to describe the 2.5 minute rule in similar terms; it was "fantastical" for the British Fire Prevention Committee to assert that people would remain calm, in the event of fire, if they were able to escape within the specified time. I use this lens here, though, because it seems to me that one of the things that is novel about MassMotion, as opposed to the 2.5 minute rule that it is based upon, is its particularly visual medium, that it will us to imagine – far more than any prescriptive standard – what it is like to escape from a burning building. This seems to me an important part of its rhetorical power.

32 Tanya Dua, "A Brief History of Cheeky In-Flight Safety Videos", *Digiday*, 27 May 2015, http://digiday.com/marketing/brief-history-cheeky-flight-safety-videos/.

33 'Safety Video Saturday – Virgin Atlantic – Economy Class & Beyond', accessed 11 December 2017, http://economyclassandbeyond.boardingarea.com/2010/09/11/safety-video-saturday-virgin-atlantic/.

34 Slavoj Žižek, Elizabeth Wright, and Edmond Leo Wright, *The Žižek Reader* (Oxford; Malden: Blackwell Publishers, 1999). p. 91.

35 See Mei Ling Chu, "A Computational Framework for Egress Analysis with Realistic Human Behaviors", 2012, https://cife.stanford.edu/node/955.

7 Grenfell
Trial by fire

7.1 The Grenfell Tower fire, 2017

7.1.1 Deregulation on trial

The origin of the word "test" is the Latin *testa*, a "piece of burned clay, earthen pot, or shell". Its contemporary English usage originates from the roll such pots played in "assaying", in melting ore to test the purity of metal. Fire has also been used as a means to test the "mettle" of people. The medieval "trial by fire" was a means to test the conviction of a defendant by testing their faith. The rationale was that, if they were innocent, they would trust God to protect them from burns while running barefoot over hot coals. Through the concept of the test, the trial, the assay and indeed the essay, we are reminded that fire is a part of the infrastructure of science and law, a means to reveal hidden qualities in people and things through the differential effect it has upon them.

At the time of its occurrence, the Grenfell Tower fire was popularly conceived of as a "trial" for the then Prime Minister, Teresa May, the "Hurricane Katrina moment" of her waning premiership. Occurring in the early hours of 14th June 2017, the fire consumed a tower-block in the Royal Borough of Kensington and Chelsea, causing 72 deaths and 70 injuries. The casualties were mostly council tenants and mostly from ethnic minority backgrounds. Grenfell was the most deadly accident in Britain since the end of the Second World War, and ten times as deadly as the Great Fire of London. That high death toll was attributed to the rapid external spread fire through a cladding system that had been recently installed by the local council. That council, which is Conservative led, had previously sought to demolish the tower and its surrounding estate to create room for new development. The cladding was therefore widely perceived as an amenity for affluent neighbours, rather than the tenants, a means to limit the negative impact of a post-war social housing project on neighbouring property values. Evidence for this view was the fact that tenants had long expressed concerns about fire-safety failings in the tower to its management, the Kensington and Chelsea Tenants Management

DOI: 10.4324/9781003026297-7

Organisation. These concerns, many of which were material on the night of the fire, appear to have been ignored. Indeed, the tenant association group predicted the fire, suggesting it was the only way that problems in the building, and with its governance, would be revealed: "Only an incident that results in serious loss of life ... will allow the external scrutiny to occur that will shine a light on the practices that characterise the malign governance of this non-functioning organisation".[1]

If the chapters of this book have each begun with moments of "Infrastructure Inversion", moments in which fire reveals the politics of standardisation, Grenfell is the most exemplary of such moments in recent British history. In its immediate aftermath fire-safety standards became the stuff of political protest and headline news. On June 17th, protesters marched on Downing Street to criticise the government's response. *The Sun* headline read "It Was Murder". *The Guardian* reported that "Grenfell fury spills onto street", making "Calls for ban on combustible cladding". *The Independent* called the event "'Justice for Grenfell' The march for answers". The *Daily Mail* asked "Were green targets to blame for fire tragedy?" "Why were families told to stay in their flats?" and "How many more tinder-box towers are there?" Conservative papers accused opposition ministers of spreading "fake-news" and stirring up "mob-unrest", while noting that the "Queen Calms Shaken Nation".[2]

At the first Prime Minister's Question Time following the event, Jeremy Corbyn sought to enrol the event in a broader policy critique, suggesting it was evidence of "the disastrous effects of austerity", "the terrible consequence of de-regulation", and of the government's "disregard for working class communities". He sought to do this by connecting the event to the *Regulatory Reform (Fire Safety) Order,* an act that had recently abolished mandatory fire-safety checks on new buildings. That act was the keystone policy of a deregulatory agenda pursued by successive governments since 1997, initially through Tony Blair's "Better Regulation" Taskforce, then through David Cameron's "Red-Tape Challenge". But Corbyn's "essay" quickly floundered; investigations revealed that the fire brigade had carried out numerous fire-safety checks at Grenfell, but had no authority to comment on cladding construction.

The fire has prompted a number of other investigations, likewise intended to judge whether regulatory failing were responsible for the event. The first to conclude was *Building a Safer Future: The Independent Review of Building Regulations and Fire Safety.* Commissioned by the government, and Led by Dame Judith Hackett, it published its findings in May 2018. *The Grenfell Tower Public Inquiry*, ordered by Teresa May, and led by Sir Martin Moore-Bick, is ongoing at the time of writing. Already the largest and most costly in British history its first phase report, published in October 2019, sought to establish the facts as to what happened on the night of the fire. Lessons learned from the fire await a second phase, which is yet to conclude.

The fire in the Grenfell Tower is therefore different to those discussed already in this book; it is not possible to know the full scope of regulatory reform this event might prompt, let alone study the effect of that reform in the *longue durée*. My ambition in this chapter is necessarily focussed on what we do know at this time: details of the fire itself, related investigations into regulatory failings and the government's initial response. This chapter is an attempt to use details we have about the fire as a means to assess the rationale of the government's response; it is an attempt to "test" Hackett's report through the initial findings of the Public Inquiry. It begins by outlining the govern-mentality of *Building a Safer Future*. Proposing that Grenfell be used as an argument against prescriptive standards, as a means to further deregulation, that document is taken to represent the government's own preferred response. The chapter continues to consider evidence presented at the Public Inquiry, concerning the ignition and spread of fire through the cladding system. It suggests that by following fire as it moved through that physical structure, it is possible to identify failures in the fire-safety claims made about its components, and so identify failings in our regulatory frameworks. Through a digression on the significance of the "test" in Latour's sociology, it suggests that we can use this method to assess the rationale of Hackett's report, also. The chapter concludes with a reflection on the government's later decision, contra Hackett, to impose a ban on combustible cladding. Using terms familiar from the work of Leigh Star, it reflects on the different forms of knowledge that fire-safety regulation needs to negotiate, and why in this case prescriptive codes appeared the only means to do so. The ambition of this essay, then, is similar to Corbyn's; it also means to connect the Grenfell Tower fire to the neo-liberal govern-mentality, and to deregulation, if here by a more socio-technical route.

7.2 Ownership of risk in *Building a Safer Future*

7.2.1 *Legal complexity*

Building a Safer Future was, in many ways, a scathing critique of the UK's building regulations. According to Hackett, our regulatory frameworks are not "fit-for-purpose". The complexity of those frameworks are, in her view, a key part of that problem. Hackett takes care to map out graphically (Figure 7.1) the multitude of current legislation that pertains to fire-safety, across the various stages that make up the life-cycle of any building project; the Building Act, the Building Regulations, Health and Safety at Work Act's, the CDM Regulations, Fire Safety in Construction regulations, the Regulatory Reform (Fire Safety) Order, the Housing Act and specific Housing Health and Safety regulations. She shows how each of these legal frameworks overlap in time, drawing differently on a wide array of stakeholders: the owner, consultants, contractors and builders, planning and building standards authorities, approved inspectors, residents

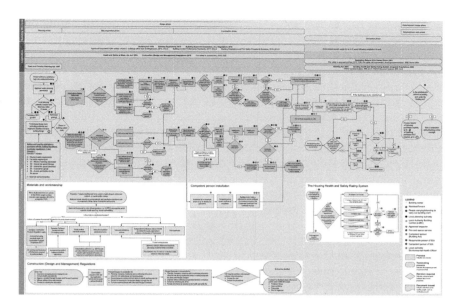

Figure 7.1 **"Map of the current regulatory system for high-rise residential buildings".** Source: Hackitt, Judith. 'Building a Safer Future: Independent Review of Building Regulations and Fire Safety: Final Report'. Her Majesty's Stationery Office, 2018. p. 14 www.gov.uk/government/publications

and the fire-and-rescue service. Taken together she a finds these frameworks "highly complex – involving multiple routes, regulators, duty holders and differing (and overlapping) sets of legislation".[3] She suggests that this system constructs a lack of clarity over discreet roles and responsibilities, leading to an ignorance or indifference towards governmental goals. Hackett acknowledges that recent deregulatory initiatives, discussed in the previous chapter, have contributed to this situation. She recognises that private sector certification, the ambiguity of performance-based standards and the lack of supporting governmental expertise have created a "competition of interpretation" that drives a "race to the bottom", through which individual actors have sought to "game the system". Nonetheless, Hackett fundamentally supports "outcomes based" regulation; she is opposed to the creation of additional prescriptive standards. Indeed, Hackett suggests that we already have too many prescriptive codes, which in turn attribute too much responsibility to government. For Hackett, this was the root cause of the Grenfell fire, a culture of ignorance and indifference in those who actually commission, design and manage buildings.

It was because of this view that Hackett's report was met with immediate political and media critique, being dubbed a "disappointment... betrayal and whitewash".[4] For opposition MP's and most journalists, it seemed clear that the root cause of the fire was the prevalence of combustible cladding at a height that could not be extinguished. There was a widespread sense that a ban on such combustible cladding was required. Hackett's refusal to propose one was read as a refusal, by government, to acknowledge responsibility for the event. Defending her report in light of its reception, she argued that "simply adding more prescription, or making amendments to the current system, such as restricting or prohibiting certain practices, will not address the root causes", which again she contended were the result of poor engagement with and enforcement of existing guidelines.[5] There has been much speculation as to why Dame Hackett did not move for such a ban, with claims of a conflict of interest. Her appointment was controversial; in a previous role, Hackett led a body that approved and promoted cladding and insulation similar to those used in the tower.[6] Those concerns notwithstanding, the govern-mentality of her report is clear. What Dame Hackett calls for is a transfer of responsibility away from government, whose role should be limited to one of setting broadly defined performance standards. It should set out the "ill-structured" goals defined by our Mandatory Standards, but not engage in offering the detailed guidance used to demonstrate compliance with those goals, which should be left to experts, and be open to innovation. What this would support, she suggests, is a clearer "ownership of risk"[7]; what our regulatory framework should define is not particular rules, but rather "clear responsibilities for the Client, Designer, Contractor and Owner to demonstrate the delivery and maintenance of safe buildings". From that perspective, banning flammable materials would be counter-productive; a new regulatory framework, she argues, must be,

> truly outcomes-based (rather than based on prescriptive rules and complex guidance) and it must have real teeth, so that it can drive the right behaviours. This will create an environment where there are incentives to do the right thing and serious penalties for those who choose to game the system.[8]

Incentives and penalties are particularly important for Hackett. Our regulatory frameworks become effective not by offering more guidance, but by identifying moments of failure. It is events like Grenfell, and its Public Inquiry, that shape this "environmentality" of governance. Prosecutions for regulatory failings are what make the system strong. From this perspective, it is imperative that the Public Inquiry identify a guilty party, in breach of code, and to discipline them.

7.2.2 Interlocking components

What Hackett proposes is a new regulatory framework that would make attribution of responsibility more clear. She recommends a consolidated set of regulation for High-Rise Residential (HRR) buildings, one that selectively gathers existing guidance in one document. She proposes this by suggesting that High-Rise equals High-Risk; that tall buildings comes with specific attendant fire-safety concerns. The truth of this assumption, questioned by expert witnesses to the Public Inquiry, is beyond the scope of this study.[9] What I wish to dwell on in Hackett's report is a socio-technical metaphor she employs about the design of regulatory frameworks. If the regulation of high-rise residential buildings is to secure the engagement of those involved in their construction she suggests that it must be designed in the image of those buildings. It must recognise "the reality of most high-rise buildings, which operate as a complex inter-locking system".[10] The root cause of the Grenfell fire was, in her opinion, that responsibility for fire-safety was not properly defined, it "fell through the cracks". The key ambition of her proposed framework is to make it clearer who and what component in that building carries the responsibility for fire-safety, so as to understanding precisely where and when they fail.

I draw attention to Hackett's metaphor – that our regulatory frameworks must be constructed like our buildings – because it seems to recognise the way changes in construction practice have changed their attendant fire-safety risks. We can see this by comparing the original structure of Grenfell Tower with that of its renovation. The original tower was built, owned and managed by the state, largely out of a single, non-combustible material, concrete. The physical risks that this structure created, and the way that it distributed them, was quite simple. We could say that, in socio-technical terms, it was quite monolithic. Since that tower was built processes of procurement and construction have changed dramatically. Buildings are more complex materially, they employ more components, but they also distribute responsibility in more complex ways. The Grenfell recladding project is an example of this. It involved a wide-range of different interlocking building components, design, certified, supplied and installed by a wide range of different actors. These physical and legal complexities, both noted by Hackett, are related. Contemporary modes of procurement and certification are means to break up the liability for construction into smaller component parts, to isolate actors from certain risks while still allowing them certain rewards. What Hackett seems to recognise, if tangentially, is that such practices can in parallel increase fire-risk.

7.2.3 Socio-technical agreements

I draw attention to Hackett's metaphor for another reason; it also brings some of the concerns raised by Grenfell into dialogue with the concerns of this book. By suggesting that our codes and standards must recognise the "reality" of contemporary construction, Hackett allows us to reflect on standardisation through terms drawn from Latour's sociology. For Latour, scientific theories (and here govern-mentalities) should never be judged in terms of their own rationale, their internal logic, but rather through their contact with "reality". What Latour means by "reality" is not a transcendental truth or external nature, but rather the sum total of socio-technical agreements, those networks of human and non-human cooperation, that we find ourselves immersed within. The "reality" that Hackett draws our attention to, then, is that intersection of overlapping and intersecting legal responsibilities that are carried by, and enrolled within, the overlapping and intersecting components that make up any contemporary building. Latour calls these networks "reality" to draw attention to a particular way that we experience them. As already noted, he suggests that those network tends to become visible, tend to be thematised, when they fail, or when they resist. *Res*, the Latin for "thing", is the root of both the word "real" and "resist".[11] As Grenfell demonstrates, Latour suggests that these networks of responsibility only really get noticed at those moments in which our technical delegates fail to act as expected; "reality" is something we only experience in moments of surprise.[12]

This is, of course, just another way to describe a moment of "infrastructure inversion", but one that I think helps us define what we might hope to discover in this particular case study. For Latour, it is the unforeseen accident, the unexpected overlap of interest or actancy, that either strengthen or weaken our socio-technical bonds. Events like the Grenfell Tower fire pose, in his terminology, a "trial of strength" for existing rationalities; they are a "reality test" that reveal new fault-lines or powers of consolidation between people and things.[13] We have already noted how in the aftermath of Grenfell political parties and media outlets used the events to shore up or critique existing policy platforms. My ambition in this chapter is similar. I want to consider how fire revealed the "reality" of Grenfell's cladding, the way its material components failed to act as expected, so revealing weaknesses in our regulatory systems. By doing so I hope to suggest how that event has acted as a "trial" for particular ways of thinking about governing, leaving some weakened and some strengthened.

7.3 Proprietary knowledge in the laboratory

7.3.1 *Following fire*

I am confident that the fire started in the Kitchen of Flat 16 (Level 4), in the area near the window. The fire most likely spread to the cladding via gaps or holes which formed in the polymeric window framing boards that surround the kitchen window, and also through the weatherproofing membrane and thermal insulation, all of which were installed during the 2012–2016 refurbishment. The fire most likely then penetrated into the back of the cladding cavity and ignited the polyethylene filler material within the aluminium composite material (ACM) rainscreen cladding cassettes that form the majority of the building's exterior surface. The fire appears to have spread to the cladding, and started escalating up the East Face of Grenfell Tower, before the first fire service personnel entered the kitchen of Flat 16 and attempted to extinguish the fire within the building. The primary cause of rapid external fire spread was the presence of polyethylene filled ACM rainscreen cassettes in the buildings refurbishment cladding system. Other factors that may also have contributed to the fire's spread include: the use of combustible products in the cladding system; the presence of extensive cavities and vertical channels within the cladding system; and the use of combustible insulation products within the window framing assemblies.[14]

The above quote is an extract from the expert witness report provided to the Grenfell Tower Inquiry on 4 June 2018 by Luke Bisby, Professor of Fire and Structures at the University of Edinburgh. Luke was asked by the report to identify where the fire started and how it spread through the building. The above is his summary. Bisby's findings were not controversial; his report confirmed the widely held view that the fire most likely spread through flammable filler material located between the original concrete structure and the refurbishment windows (Figure 7.2). The phrase I wish to stress here is "most likely". In the introduction to his report, Bisby spends some time noting the "extraordinarily complex technical challenge" of determining the precise trajectory of any fire through forensic examination. Furthermore he notes that, at the Grenfell Tower, that job is made all the more difficult by the nature of the cladding, which is itself "a highly complex system, consisting of multiple materials and products, many of which are combustible".[15] If there is anything surprising in his report it is the amount of time it spends outlining this forensic and material complexity. He describes how the fire spread to the cladding first, but also how many different ways it travelled there, and how many other ways it could have gone; fire certainly travelled through gaps between the window and the structure, but it also travelled through an extract fan, through filler around the fan opening, by burning through an infill panel, and through the open window itself (Figure 7.3).

Explaining the process through which fire propagates, Bisby outlines the process of *pyrolysis*, or "fire separation". As things burn, they are separated into their component parts. For instance, wood does not "burn" directly; it's cellulose decomposes when exposed to heat, turning into a gas which then oxidises in the atmosphere, releasing heat that then continues this chain reaction. In an analogous way, fire separates and decomposes constructional arrangements; the cladding panels and window arrays used at Grenfell do not ignite directly when exposed to a flame. But should a sustained fire take hold near to them, those material assemblies begin to delaminate, melt, deform, exposing their flammable interiors. That is, fire poses a particular threat to materials and constructional arrangements; it

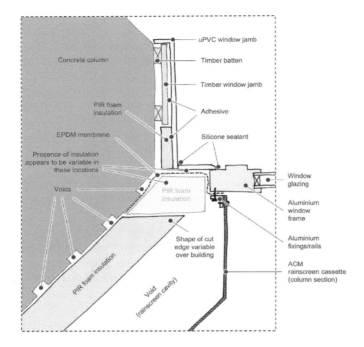

Figure 7.2 "Detail drawing showing the approximate location within the external cladding build up from which melted, dripping, burning PE is considered most likely to have first originated based on the evidence available at the time of writing". Source: Bisby, Luke. 'The Grenfell Inquiry: Phase 1 Expert Report'. Grenfell Tower Inquiry. University of Edinburgh, 2018. p. 128. https://www.grenfelltowerinquiry.org.uk/evidence/professor-luke-bisbys-expert-report. (accessed, August 24, 2021)

decomposes them, creating and exploiting gaps between their component parts. What is conspicuous about Bisby's description of the fire is the sheer quantity of potential lines of failures. The refurbishment project included a wide range of different components, many of which were plastic, and many of which were flammable, resulting in a material assembly that was thermally "thin".[16]

7.3.2 Probability of one

The question of how the fire originated was posed to another expert witness, José Luis Torero, then John L. Bryan Chair in the Department of Fire Protection Engineering at the University of Maryland. Again, his report begins by noting the complexity of the task presented: "Fire evolves in space and time leading, in many instances, to a complex sequence of events and

Figure 7.3 "Excerpt from [MET00004480] showing West Face. This shows various potential routes for fire and smoke ingress, including broken window glazing, deformation of window surrounds, and missing extract fan units (with the extract fan mounting panels remaining largely intact)". Source: Bisby, Luke. 'The Grenfell Inquiry: Phase 1 Expert Report'. Grenfell Tower Inquiry. University of Edinburgh, 2018. p. 202. https://www.grenfelltowerinquiry.org.uk/evidence/professor-luke-bisbys-expert-report. (accessed, August 24, 2021)

multiple processes and activities occurring simultaneously". And again, if there is anything surprising in the report it is Torero's insistence that the fire could have originated in any number of ways. The source had been popularly attributed to a malfunctioning fridge within the kitchen of flat 16 (Figure 7.4), but Torero finds no evidence to confirm or contradict that existing view: "[A]t the date of submission of this report, there is no conclusive evidence that constrains the cause, origin and initial stages of the fire to a single timeline or set of events".[17] Torero does confirm that smoke from a malfunctioning refrigerator could have melted the nearby kitchen window, exposing flammable components within the buildings external cladding; uPVC loses it mechanical properties at around 90°C, whereas the smoke from such a fire would be likely be 100–200°C. However, he goes on to demonstrate that the same result could have been caused by a pan-fire, or, indeed, the malfunction of almost any common appliance (the Lakanal House fire, of 2009, which also spread via a window, to the

Window
opening   Fridge-freezer   Cooker   Toaster   Washing machine
(displaced)   Microwave

Freezer   Fridge

Figure 7.4 **"Approximate arrangement of kitchen of Flat 16".** Source: Bisby, Luke. 'The Grenfell Inquiry: Phase 1 Expert Report'. Grenfell Tower Inquiry. University of Edinburgh, 2018. p. 33. https://www.grenfelltowerinquiry.org.uk/evidence/professor-luke-bisbys-expert-report. (accessed, August 24, 2021)

external cladding, was started by a faulty TV). As such, he suggests that the specific source is not only unknown but also irrelevant:

> From a design perspective, a fire of 300 kW occurring in a residential kitchen, and in the proximity of the window, should be considered to have a probability of one. A fire of this nature will happen in a residential unit and therefore the building is required to respond appropriately.[18]

If Bisby and Torero appear circumspect about pinning down the precise origin or route of the fire, their attitude might be understood with reference to literatures on fire-safety investigations and standards. In "The Regulation of Technological Innovation: The Special Problem of Fire Safety Standards" Vincent Brannigan reflects on a problematic tendency in forensic fire science. He suggests that, under pressure to identify clear points of responsibility, forensic fire investigations often conflate the source of ignition with the cause of catastrophe. When done accurately,

> analysis of disasters shows just how complex the chain of causation can be in a specific accident. But regulators face an even more complex

task since they have to analyze and interrupt these chains of causation before they occur and across the entire spectrum of scenarios.

A focus on the ignition is, he suggests, usually an attempt to divert attention from that complexity, and so from the failure to regulate fire spread. By stressing the irrelevance of ignition, and the multitude of possible routes, Bisby and Torero seem to support Brannigans critique. But their testimony might also cast doubt on the possibility and value of identifying and prosecuting a single point of failure responsible for such catastrophes. The ambition to do so might conflict with that of identifying wider, more complex, and more structural concerns.

7.3.3 Legislative pyrolysis

As the fire moved through the filler materials, infill panels, insulation and cladding system at Grenfell Tower, it tested the strength of their fire-safety claims. That is, a key question for the Inquiry, and for government, was whether those components met with relevant fire-safety standards. That question is a legal proxy through which to identify who should bear responsibility for the event. The conservative government in the form of Phillip Hammond was quick to state that the cladding used on the building was banned for use in the UK.[19] He was backed up in this claim by what was then called the Department of Communities and Local Government (DCLG) – the body responsible for building regulation in England – who released a statement that: "Cladding using a composite aluminium panel with a polyethylene core would be non-compliant with current building regulations guidance. This material should not be used as cladding on buildings over 18m in height."[20] These statements would seem to insulate government from any claim of regulatory negligence, and facilitate prosecution of the contractor. The clarity of those claims quickly came apart, though. The contractor Rydons claimed that the design "met all required building control, fire regulation and health and safety standards".[21] This ambiguity was not helped by the Royal Borough of Kensington and Chelsea, the owner of the tower, client for its renovation and also the body responsible for warranting its compliance with building standards. Shortly after the fire they revealed that a warrant had never been issued for its refurbishment: designs had been submitted to, and reviewed by the council, but "a formal decision notice was not issued for the plans".[22]

The ambiguity that allowed Phillip Hammond and Rydons to make contradictory claims are examined in detail by investigative journalists Peter Apps, Sophie Barns and Luke Barrat, reporting for *Inside Housing*. They show that such ambiguities are, unfortunately, written in to our building standards. In England and Wales, the performance specification for external fire spread is defined by mandatory standard B4 (1), of *Approved Document B*. This regulation states that "The external walls of the building shall adequately resist the spread of fire over the walls".[23] In hindsight it might seem self-evident that the cladding used at Grenfell Tower – a Reynobond composite comprising two 0.5 mm-thick aluminium sheets fixed to a 6 mm-thick core of polyethylene – fails to satisfy this standard. Polyethylene has an extraordinary fire-load; "If you look at a one metre by one metre square section [of cladding] that will have about three kilograms [of polyethylene], the equivalent of about five litres of petrol."[24] But that material can be shown to meet the prescriptive requirements associated with standard B4. Paragraph 12.6 of Approved Document B states that the external surface of an external wall will meet that standard if it achieves a "Class O" rating for surface spread of flame. Reynobond's aluminium cladding systems were certified to achieve that rating by the British Board of Agrément, through a test that involves exposing their aluminium face to flame. When exposed at its centre, the aluminium coating did not reveal the polyethylene core, and so was classed as a permissible "surface". The interior of that surface was simply not visible to this means of testing, and as such could be ignored by those who later specified it. As some would put it, "It's not within the imagination of the [industry] that the panel can come away and expose the flammable materials behind."[25] After Grenfell DCLG did appear to become more imaginative: in order to sure up what might seem like a regulatory failure, it released a statement noting,

> For the avoidance of doubt the core (filler) within an aluminium composite material (ACM) is an 'insulation material/product', 'insulation product', and/or 'filler material' as referred to in Paragraph 12.7 … of Approved Document B.[26]

The significance of this statement is that insulation products are subject to the more onerous demand of demonstrating "limited combustibility", being capable of surviving for at least 2 hours in a 750°C furnace. It would seem too late, on 22 June 2017, to avoid that doubt, and the need for parentheses within this statement – to change the name of what it sought to define – doesn't help. It's possible to call a cladding panel an insulant, even if it has no insulating function, but that doesn't lend to clarity. It is also hard to believe that lack of clarity was a surprise; as their later testimony would confirm, the flammablity of this product was well known to its manufacturer, but its certification was also useful for a government and a building industry required to achieve the energy saving targets agreed to through the Kyoto Protocol, which are hard to meet without such high-performing insulants. Nonetheless, the uncertainty allowed for in this standard would seem to have allowed this dangerous cladding to be used while making it difficult to prosecute clear responsibility for its specification.

7.3.4 Rivets that are present and absent

If this evidence supports a concern that our prescriptive standards are not fit for purpose, the Grenfell fire provides reasons to be concerned about "outcomes-based" standards, also. The polyisocyanurate foam insulation used on the tower, Celotex RS5000, was subject to the more onerous requirement of "limited combustibility". While this material does not meet that requirement on its own, its manufacturers successfully argued that it can "adequately resist the spread of flame", through performance-based codes. These forms of regulation were first developed by the Building Research Establishment (BRE), with the view to testing how whole material arrays, as opposed to individual buildings components, perform in fires. This form of standardisation operates through the use of full-scale mock-ups, which are themselves subject to a standardised test, defined by *British Standard 8414: Fire performance of external cladding systems. Test method for non-loadbearing external cladding systems.* That test requires that the mock-up wall resist the spread of flame across its height for at least 30 minutes (Figure 7.5).

The construction and testing of full-scale mock-ups is time-consuming and expensive. It would be impractical to test every material assembly in use in buildings across the UK today. As such, this route to approval has gradually been subject to short-cuts and modes of deregulation. Today, wall assemblies can be approved on the basis of "desktop studies" – studies that argue that an assembly would survive a BS8414 test based on tests of similar assemblies – and those studies can be completed by any "suitable qualified fire specialist". Furthermore by 2016 it had become common practice for non-governmental bodies – such as the Energy Saving Trust, Dame Hackitt's former employer – to suggest combinations of materials, including those used at Grenfell, that might be used without the need for desktop studies. Such practices allowed the widespread use of components that on their own would not meet the requirement of "limited combustibility" without tests of any kind. This fact was recognised by Teresa May when, days after Grenfell, she announced that "a number" of other high-rise residential tower blocks within the UK might use a similar cladding system to that used at Grenfell. The effect of this announcement was the immediate evacuation of households from estates in Camden, the triggering of waking watches for effected buildings that continue to this day, and the beginning of an ongoing process to replace unsafe cladding, and to determine who should bear the cost of that replacement. Following that announcement, the DCLG launched a series of tests, via BS8414, to determine the safety of ACM cladding more generally. 299 of the 312 social-tenure high-rise buildings tested by January 2018 had failed those tests and were deemed in need of re-cladding. Figures within the private sector – where this form of cladding and insulation is also widespread – are not known.[27]

The methodology of BS8414 subsequently came under scrutiny as a result of Grenfell. The closest full-scale test to the wall build-up used at Grenfell Tower had been completed by BRE in 2014. This tested Celotex RS5,000 in combination with a fibre-cement rain-screen, a more thermally "thick" cladding. However, shortly after Grenfell, BRE released a statement

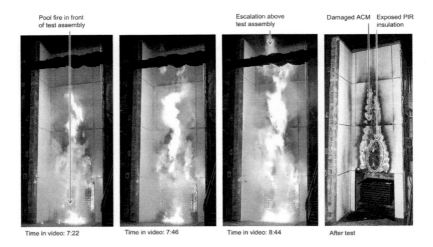

Figure 7.5 "Annotated extracts from DCLG video [CLG10000380] showing the progression of the fire during an 8.5 m tall BS 8414-1 [16] test on a cladding arrangement that used similar rainscreen (Test DCLG1), cavity thermal insulation, and cavity barrier products to the Grenfell Tower cladding refurbishment external cladding build up". Source: Bisby, Luke. 'The Grenfell Inquiry: Phase 1 Expert Report'. Grenfell Tower Inquiry. University of Edinburgh, 2018. p. 148. https://www.grenfelltowerinquiry.org.uk/evidence/professor-luke-bisbys-expert-report. (accessed, August 24, 2021)

withdrawing those test results. They had been made aware by the manufacturer of "anomalies between the design specification for the cladding system and the actual cladding system they installed to be tested."[28] BRE were keen to stress that they took no responsibility for the way in which the cladding system was constructed; this was strictly the responsibility of the manufacturer. If and how Celotex rigged that test is not clear; the results of *BS8414* tests are confidential and proprietary. However, we can make an educated guess on the basis of research commissioned by the Association of British Insurers. This body – no doubt wary of its own collective liability – asked the Fire Protection Association to compare the parameters of *BS8414* with the "real-world" conditions that it simulated. They found it to be unrepresentative in a number of ways: domestic fires often include plastics, and so burn hotter than the test recognises; cladding systems are often tested as sealed units, when in reality they have ventilated cavities which provide conduits for fire-spread; and the test uses material in "manufacturers conditions", when in practice they will be compromised by further openings, such as those required for vents and windows.[29] All of these issues were identified by expert witnesses as material within the rapid spread of the Grenfell fire. But more damningly ABI's report – which was submitted to Dame Hackitt and seems tacitly acknowledged in her introduction – alleges that some manufacturers "game the system" in precisely the way that BRE's statement suggests, testing constructional arrangements that are not as per the published design specification. Specifically, they draw attention to a practice of riveting components in an assembly together, intentionally stopping them from delaminating when subjected to heat.[30] The implication of their report is that far more than 312 towers are in need of inspection, via tests more onerous than those that have already found 96% of those tested to be unsafe.

7.4 Reality Test

7.4.1 *"Discipline" and government*

From the evidence reviewed above, the Grenfell Tower fire does support a number of the claims made in Dame Hackett's report. Grenfell has shown that our regulatory framework is not fit for purpose – indeed, that it is being intentionally "gamed". Celotex is not the only manufacturer alleged to have rigged fire-safety tests for materials used at Grenfell Tower. Providing evidence to Phase 2 of the Inquiry, Arconic president Claude Schmidt likewise admitted that rivets were used in test assemblies despite their absence within design specifications. He recognised that when his product was tested in a cassette application it failed those tests dramatically. The Inquiry was presented with emails that showed test results of the specified application should be kept "VERY CONFIDENTIAL", and Schmidt admitted awareness that those specifying the product had been misled. That the two products material to the spread of fire at Grenfell both appear to have rigged fire-safety tests in the same way supports the ABI's assertion that such practice is widespread, and Hackett's recognition that manufacturers "game" the system. What this specific case does not seem to support, though, is Hackett's assertion that "outcomes-based" regulation is any less prone to misunderstanding or abuse. Abuse of testing procedures undermined both prescriptive and performance-based forms of certification for materials used in Grenfell's facade. Both were subject to forms of verification that transferred responsibility away from those bodies created to assume it – Ministers, Local Authorities, the BRE – into proprietary procedures conducted by actors for whom a competition of interpretation is incentivised.

Returning to "neo-liberalism" and its role in the Grenfell fire, we can recognise that Hackett's report is based on an assertion that the market will discipline itself if an environment of rewards and punishments are put in place. So far, the Inquiry has not provided evidence that would allow us to judge that assertion. The Public Inquiry is not an inquest – its findings are not legally binding – and all criminal investigations are on hold until its conclusion. Nonetheless, it has revealed how resistant some actors will be to prosecution. Arconic representatives initially used blocking statutes to avoid giving evidence, statutes specifically designed to prevent French nationals giving evidence against themselves abroad; prosecuting national laws in the context of a globalised industry is not simple. Closer to home, the British Government has shown limited appetite to discipline those responsible for installing dangerous cladding on other buildings. That issue was addressed in the Fire Safety Bill passed into law in April 2021. While the bill offered limited financial support for those replacing cladding at a height over 18 m it nonetheless defined the responsibility for that replacement as sitting with leaseholders. Despite an amendment approved in the House of Lords to this effect, the government specifically rejected any proposals that would ensure this liability was "owned" by those who designed, approved, installed or manufactured that cladding.

By following fire as it spread through the components and legislation that held Grenfell Tower together, I think we can also offer a more general critique of Hackett's govern-mentality. What we saw in Bisby and Torero's reports, and in Brannigan's argument, is that in any fire it is difficult to pin down singular points of failure. Fire is an actant that networks whether we like it or not. It spreads, and in so doing, spreads risk. Grenfell and catastrophes like it depend upon and reveal a multitude of failures, any one of which is both necessary and contingent. Cladding and insulation components were not the only ones to fail in the fire, just as Celotex and Arconic are not the only manufacturers to have abused our regulatory processes. Even if we choose to focus on this headline failure, what it points to more broadly is the failure of our standardised tests, that is, of the need to discipline government itself. BS8414 did not only allow individuals to "game the system", as part of a neo-liberal "environmentality" it tacitly supported that "gaming"; penalty and reward are the organising poles of a competition, and the space for competition that BS8414 creates is the "black box" of proprietary testing. With 72 dead, and an ongoing Inquiry, Grenfell made that game publicly visible, but also politically untenable, at least for a short time.

7.4.2 Ill-structured solutions

I present the above argument in the hope of drawing lessons from Grenfell, but also to contextualise the apparent U-turn made by the UK Government shortly after the release of Hackett's report. In June 2018, the Ministry for Housing, Community and Local Government launched a consultation on banning combustible cladding on high-rise residential building, a ban that was put into place November of the same year. Pressure to do so had been mounting in the media, but its strongest advocate were architects. The Royal Institute of British Architects (RIBA) set up an Expert Advisory Group on Fire Safety, whose published recommendation included a repeal of the Regulatory Reform (Fire Safety) bill, the abolition of desktop studies for demonstrating performance compliance, as well as further clarification of Approved Document B4, suggesting the inclusion of new prescriptive guidance, specifically a ban on combustible cladding at height. These recommendations corresponded closely to the political mood after Grenfell, but are directly opposed to those of Hackett's review, and the opinion of other experts testifying at the Inquiry.

Engineer Angus Law and sociologist Graham Spinardi reflect on those differing opinions in "Performing Expertise in Building Regulation: 'Codespeak' and Fire Safety Experts". They note the wide range of different kinds of knowledge that the problem of fire-safety gathers; the first-hand experience offered by tenants caught up in fires; the practical knowledge of fire-fighting offered by rescue teams; the empirical and theoretical knowledge offered by those who study or model fire behaviour. They note that, in relation to these stakeholders, those who design buildings and regulate design have a different form of understanding; they are not experts in fire, but in "codespeak", in the language of regulation. Despite this being a particularly abstract form of knowledge, they recognise it as having particular virtues: "Although distanced from fundamental empirical experience of fire, codespeak is powerful because of its relative clarity and certainty, and legal status."

Again, we see that those actors involved in the design of fire-safety regulation seek to shape those regulations in relation to their own concerns and knowledge positions. There is a pronounced difference between the way engineers and architects, for instance, think about the problem of fire. Engineers are disposed to model and measure, they think in terms of equations and accuracy. As we saw in the last chapter, this disciplinary perspective tends to prefer "engineered" solutions, and so performance-based standards, because that mode of regulation operates through their own govern-mentality, and generates a need for their own services. Architects, by contrast, are neither fire-safety experts nor qualified to conduct such calculations. Their work balances a wide range of competing concerns, usually through the resolution of spatial parameters. As such, they are disposed towards prescriptive standards, which allow them to retain control of fire-safety, through their own skill-set. Debates as to the relative virtue of these two modes of regulation are often shaped by a competition between these two disciplinary perspectives, as each stakes out their claim to "own" the problem of fire-safety.[31]

Reflecting on why the RIBA's approach was given precedence over that of other experts, Law and Spinardi offer a more general reflection on the virtues of prescriptive codification, in terms we have engaged with already in this book. They do so by first recognising that fire-safety is an "ill-structured problem". The governmental objective is clear and simple; "that the external walls of buildings shall adequately resist the spread of fire". But the detailed definition of what constitutes "adequate", and the variety of ways that that might be achieved, is complex and prone to controversy. The problems revealed by Grenfell, explored above, related to this broader problem of adequately defining "safety". The promise of performance-based standardisation is to avoid representational simplification, to reproduce the problem at scale 1:1; to move from the "ill" to the "well-structured". Nonetheless, the Grenfell fire has revealed that process to be fraught with opportunities for sophistry. In this particular circumstance, where the complexity of and competition between knowledge positions is itself a problem, recourse to simpler modes of standardisation appeared necessary. Law and Spinardi note that the familiar terms involved – a ban, on combustibility – alongside the authority traditionally ascribed to architects, worked together to make this policy position the most powerful one. This is not without its problems. We don't know what the long-term effects of the Grenfell Fire, or the ban on combustible claddings, will be, but in the short term both have led to a reduction in the energy performance of many buildings, as combustible high-performing insulation is removed and replaced with less combustible but less effective alternatives. Its not clear what the long-term impact of a reduced ability to use high-performance insulants, particularly in a high-rise retro-fit context, but this certainly raises challenges in terms of our ability to meet reductions in energy consumption. The ambition of this chapter, though, has been to demonstrate the way Grenfell has offered a trial, a test, for our current fire-safety standards, and for those associations that exist between fire-safety science and deregulation, and between architecture and prescriptive standards. In the immediate aftermath of Grenfell, the former appears weakened and the latter strengthened.

Notes

1 'Grenfell Resident Who Raised Fire Concerns Labelled Troublemaker, Inquiry Told', *The Guardian*, 21 April 2021, http://www.theguardian.com/uk-news/2021/apr/21/grenfell-resident-who-raised-fire-concerns-labelled-troublemaker-inquiry-told.

2 Conservative papers redirected the story against the protestors. *The Daily Telegraph* headline was "Militants Hijack Inferno Protest", with a second headline noting "Corbyn-Backers Spread 'Fake News' about blaze toll". Corbyn also made a sub-line in *The Sunday Express* for "stirring up mob unrest", but that paper led with "Queen Calms Shaken Nation" and Teresa May's "vow to take charge". See Josh Hamilton, 'Grenfell Fire and Fallout: A Lesson In Media Framing', *The Jist* (blog), 18 June 2017, http://www.thejist.co.uk/politics/uk/grenfell-fire-fallout-media-case-study/.

3 Judith Hackitt, *Building a Safer Future: Independent Review of Building Regulations and Fire Safety: Final Report* (Her Majesty's Stationery Office, 2018), www.gov.uk/government/publications. p. 14.

4 'Grenfell Tower Fire Review Branded "Betrayal and Whitewash"', accessed 27 July 2018, https://inews.co.uk/news/politics/grenfell-tower-review-branded-betrayal-and-whitewash/.

5 '"Radical Reform" of Building Regulatory System Needed, Finds Dame Judith Hackitt – GOV.UK', accessed 26 July 2018, https://www.gov.uk/government/news/radical-reform-of-building-regulatory-system-needed-finds-dame-judith-hackitt.

6 Hackitt is the former director of the Energy Saving Trust, a body which publishes a list of "approved products" that "meet UK regulatory requirements". This list includes polyisocyanurate foam insulation boards similar to those used on the Grenfell tower refurbishment. For concern over Hackitt's appointment, see Robert Booth, 'Grenfell-Style Cladding Could Be Banned on Tower Blocks, Government Says', *The Guardian*, 17 May 2018, sec. *UK news*, http://www.theguardian.com/uk-news/2018/may/17/grenfell-style-cladding-could-be-banned-on-tower-blocks-government-says.

7 Hackitt traces this principle back to the Health and Safety at Work act, of 1974: "The principle of risk being owned and managed by those who create it was enshrined in the UK health and safety law in the 1970s, following the review conducted by Lord Robens, and its effectiveness is clear and demonstrable". See Judith Hackitt, 'Building a Safer Future: Independent Review of Building Regulations and Fire Safety: Final Report' (Her Majesty's Stationery Office, 2018). p. 6. www.gov.uk/government/publications.

8 Hackitt, 'Building a Safer Future: Independent Review of Building Regulations and Fire Safety: Final Report'. p. 6.

9 Colin Todd's expert witness report casts some doubt on this association between tall buildings and fire risk; indeed, it states clearly that "High Rise does not mean High Risk". The incidence of mortality in high-rise buildings, due to fire, is *not* higher than those in other forms of accommodation. If there are greater "risks" within this particular kind of building – centralised, tall accommodation for social tenants – they are political, rather than technical. That is, I think it is possible to say that Hackitt here follows, and legally reinforces, a popular concern about high-rise social housing, one which has been reinforced – even in "progressive" discourse – through Grenfell. As evidence we might cite Simon Jenkins column in the Guardian, which has used Grenfell to claims that high-rise residential buildings "are antisocial, high-maintenance, disempowering, unnecessary, mostly ugly, and they can never be truly safe". Ironically, The Grenfell Enquiry reports allow us to prove that this last assertion, at least, is false. Andrew O'Hagan perhaps betrays a similar trajectory; his extensive article on Grenfell, for the London Review of Books, is titled "Tower", and notes an association between tall buildings and Heaven. That is, one likely consequence of Grenfell will be an increased social and political concern about the real and perceived risks of high-rise accommodation, a concern which architects might well help to shape. See Colin Todd, 'Report for The Grenfell Tower Inquiry: LEGISLATION, GUIDANCE AND ENFORCING AUTHORITIES RELEVANT TO FIRE SAFETY MEASURES AT GRENFELL TOWER', 2018. p. 15. Also 'The Lesson from Grenfell Is Simple: Stop Building Residential Towers | Simon Jenkins | Opinion | *The Guardian*', accessed 29 June 2018, https://www.theguardian.com/commentisfree/2017/jun/15/lessons-grenfell-tower-safer-cladding-tower-blocks. Also 'Andrew O'Hagan The Tower LRB 7 June 2018', accessed 25 July 2018, https://www.lrb.co.uk/v40/n11/andrew-ohagan/the-tower.

10 Hackitt, 'Building a Safer Future: Independent Review of Building Regulations and Fire Safety: Final Report'. p. 3.

11 Here I am paraphrasing from *Laboratory Life*:

> If reality means anything, it is that which 'resists' (from the Latin 'res'—thing) the pressure of a force. The argument between realists and relativists is exacerbated by the absence of an adequate definition of reality. It is possible that the following is sufficient: that which cannot be changed at will is what counts as real.

See Bruno Latour and Steve Woolgar, *Laboratory Life: The Construction of Scientific Facts* (Princeton: Princeton University Press, 2013). p. 260.

12 Here I draw from *Politics of Nature*:

> We are thus going to associate the notion of external reality with surprises and events, rather than with the simple "being-there" of the warrior tradition, the stubborn presence of matters of fact. Humans are not specially defined by freedom any more than they are defined by speech: nonhumans are not defined by necessity any more than they are defined by mute objectivity. The only thing that can be said about them is that they emerge in surprising fashion, lengthening the list of beings that must be taken into account.

See Latour. p. 79.

13 Latour defines the idea of a "trial" in the essay "Irreductions", embedded within *Pasteur*. The concept is closely tied to that of "reality", as defined above.

> Whatever resists trials is real. The verb 'resist' is not a privileged word. I use it to represent the whole collection of verbs and adjectives, tools and instruments, which together define the ways of being real… The real is not one thing among others but rather gradients of resistance. There is no difference between the 'real' and the 'unreal', the 'real' and the 'possible', the 'real' and the 'imaginary.' Rather, there are all the differences experienced between those that resist for long and those that do not, those that resist courageously and those that do not, those that know how to ally or isolate themselves and those that do not.

Bruno Latour, *The Pasteurization of France* (Cambridge, MA: Harvard University Press, 1993). p. 158.

14 Luke Bisby, 'Professor Luke Bisby's Expert Report, Grenfell Tower Inquiry', accessed 27 June 2018, https://www.grenfelltowerinquiry.org.uk/evidence/professor-luke-bisbys-expert-report. pp. 2–3.

15 Bisby, 'Professor Luke Bisby's Expert Report, Grenfell Tower Inquiry'. p. 2.

16 Thermally "thin" materials are those that respond to pyrolysis quickly, and so ignite easily, having either high conductivity or low heat capacity. It is conventional to use this term to describe the pyrotechnic behaviour of individual materials, but this can be misleading. As we will see below, it is possible to construe ACM cladding as relatively "thick", in the sense that aluminium does not readily ignite. Rather, I suggest here that we can think of whole assemblies as thermally "thick" or "thin", and that this provides a useful way – for instance – to understand why the Grenfell refurbishment burned down, and the original tower did not. See Bisby. p. 15.

17 Judith Hackitt, *Building a Safer Future: Independent Review of Building Regulations and Fire Safety: Final Report* (Her Majesty's Stationery Office, n.d.), www.gov.uk/government/publications. p. 2.

18 Torero. p. 3.

19 'Hammond: Grenfell Cladding Was Banned in UK', *BBC News*, accessed 4 July 2018, https://www.bbc.co.uk/news/av/uk-politics-40318318/chancellor-philip-hammond-says-grenfell-cladding-was-banned-in-uk.

20 Robert Booth, 'Grenfell Tower: 16 Council Inspections Failed to Stop Use of Flammable Cladding', *The Guardian*, 21 June 2017, sec. UK news, http://www.theguardian.com/uk-news/2017/jun/21/grenfell-tower-16-council-inspections-failed-to-stop-use-of-flammable-cladding.

21 'Grenfell Tower Fire Probe Focuses on Cladding | Construction Enquirer', accessed 27 July 2018, https://www.constructionenquirer.com/2017/06/15/grenfell-tower-fire-probe-focuses-on-cladding/.

22 Booth, 'Grenfell Tower'.

23 Department of Communities and Local Government, *Approved Document B: Fire Safety, Volume 1 Dwellinghouses*, 2013 edition (Place of Publication Not Identified: National Building Specification, 2013).

24 Here I am quoting from evidence given by Tony Enright, a fire safety engineer, cited by *Inside Housing* in their analysis of the Grenfell Tower "paper Trail". See *Inside Housing*.

25 '"Flaw in Industry's Thinking on Panels"', *Inside Housing*, accessed 4 July 2018, https://www.insidehousing.co.uk/news/news/flaw-in-industrys-thinking-on-panels--51019.

26 In the review of regulatory failings I am providing here, I draw heavily on existing and excellent media coverage. Outstanding among this was the coverage offered by *Inside Housing*. It is in their coverage that the DCLG memo quoted from here was unearthed. See *Inside Housing*, 'The Paper Trail: The Failure of Building Regulations', *Shorthand*, accessed 4 July 2018, https://social.shorthand.com/insidehousing/3CWytp9tQj/the-paper-trail-the-failure-of-building-regulations.

27 'Expert Panel Recommends Further Tests on Cladding and Insulation', *GOV.UK*, accessed 4 June 2018, https://www.gov.uk/government/news/expert-panel-recommends-further-tests-on-cladding-and-insulation.

28 'Statement Regarding Celotex BS8414 Cladding Tests', *BRE Group* (blog), 31 January 2018, https://bregroup.com/press-releases/celotex-statement/.

29 'Scale of Fire Safety Testing Failures Laid Bare ABI', accessed 4 June 2018, https://www.abi.org.uk/news/news-articles/2018/04/scale-of-fire-safety-testing-failures-laid-bare/.

30 Robert Booth, 'Cladding Tests after Grenfell Tower Fire "Utterly Inadequate"', *The Guardian*, 24 April 2018, sec. UK news, http://www.theguardian.com/uk-news/2018/apr/25/cladding-tests-after-grenfell-tower-fire-inadequate-claims-insures-report.

31 While The preparatory research for this section was developed in parallel to engaging with two forums for such discussion. The first was the Holyrood Magazine 'Building Regulations in Scotland – Ensuring People's Safety' event. The second was a cross-party group on architecture and the built environment, held at the Scottish Parliament, on September 21st 2017. In both events, which involved contributions from engineers, architects, regulators, fire-safety experts, manufacturers, clients, it was notable how each stakeholders understood Grenfell from a sectoral perspective. For architects, Grenfell was seen as the result of the lack of authority architects currently held; it was only by re-establishing a singular point of authority within building design that such errors could be prevented. On the other hand, fire-safety engineers typically used the event to call for a further professionalisation and reinforcement of their own position as experts, seeking to extend that role to encompass oversight of all matters of design. These meetings, in themselves, demonstrated how powerful a "boundary object" fire is, and how many different stakeholders seek to enrol it into their own concerns.

8 Conclusion

Fire-space

8.1 The actancy of standards

This study sought to describe and analyse practices of fire-safety standardisation through concepts and concerns drawn from two related disciplines. Informed by Governmentality Studies the problem of fire-safety has been understood as one that is shaped by its historical and geographical context, experienced differently from place to place and time to time. This study has considered a range of circumstances through which the problem of fire-safety emerged, and been used as a means problematise and rationalise the scope of governmental action. Through that process, fire-safety initiatives have been described as means through which practices of becomes enmeshed with particular ways of knowing, particular technologies, and particular subject positions. In the case of Scotland, for example, this study showed how the problem of fire-safety emerged in and was shaped by specific characteristics of the city of Edinburgh. Scotland's fire-safety standards were shown to have developed and changed in relation to that changing urban morphology, being shaped by its construction practices and technologies. Those standards were shown to develop in relation to new rationalities of government, each coming with their own ways of seeing and knowing; fire shifted from being a problem of personal responsibility, or of corporate risk-sharing, to form the basis of municipal and then state-led measures. Each of those initiatives was seen to produce and depend upon tools and identities, from the horse-drawn squirt and the fire-fighter to the Goad map and the insurer, which, in turn, shaped their effectiveness.

In analysing standardisation, this study has focussed on questions of translation. It has paid particular attention to the way fire-safety standards are abstracted from, and re-inscribed into, built form. Drawing on Infrastructure Studies and actor network theory, it has considered the built environment as a "technical delegate" of government, one that brings with it its own "actancy". Studying The Grenfell Tower fire, for instance, it showed how buildings and their performance in fire reveal problems not visible to existing regulatory practices. The section on travel distance sought to demonstrate how, through the process of spatial abstraction and transcription, new ways of

DOI: 10.4324/9781003026297-8

thinking about fire-safety can be produced. As a whole, this collection was structured through an attempt to study the different kinds of surprise that occur through processes of standardisation. Through the effects of set-back regulation in Lagos it sought to consider the fire-safety problems that can be created by fire-safety standards. Through practices of egress simulation it sought to identify how particular modes of regulation "black-box" knowledge, and create moments of situated agency for those who work closely with them. Through its study of Edo/Tokyo's Fire Regime it sought to reflect on how fire-safety becomes entangled with particular kinds of historical imagination, and the active role that design plays in reinforcing or reimagining those histories.

The concept of the "Boundary Object" has been important to those studies. Fire-safety has been recognised as an "ill-structured problem", one that is understood to intersect with a wide range of stakeholders, and one that is understood differently and with differing levels of resolution by each of them. The process of standardisation has been conceived as a means to come to terms and stabilise that problem, to define certain aspects of common agreement so as to support coordinated action. This conceptualisation brought with it a way of assessing the success of particular standards. Standards were seen to fail when they fail to enrol all actants gathered by a common problem, when they fail to accommodate the concerns of particular stakeholders, or the characteristics of particular materials, technologies and practices. Sometimes this was seen to occur where standards become too specific, dominated by the rationale of one particular stakeholder. This was suggested in the case of certification based on computational analysis of fire-dynamics and occupant egress; through such processes the definition of "safety" came to be controlled by, and accessible to, a very small group of experts. On the other hand, standards have been seen to fail where they remain too broad, leaving the problem too ill-defined. This was recognised as the case in the UK's Mandatory Standards, and the room for interpretation they create. At the same time, it could be used to describe problems seen in both Tokyo and Lagos, where fire-safety initiatives remain either incomplete, or came to be used for other purposes.

8.2 Abstraction and standardisation

Written by an architect, the ambition of this study was to address the problem of fire-safety to architects, to assert their role as stakeholders within it. That ambition was prompted by the Grenfell Tower fire itself, but also by the ambivalence many practitioners note in relation to processes of building standardisation, their concerns about "professional identity" and "role ascription". As a response, these studies have sought to highlight the agency that buildings and building designers have in shaping governmentality. Their ambition was to open literatures on fire-safety and governance to an architectural audience. To conclude though, this chapter seeks to situate those studies in relation to recent literatures on fire-safety and governance, and to suggest what it contributes to them. It does so first by reflecting on what other scholars have sought to abstract from urban case-studies of the sort presented here.

An important contribution to the literature on urban fire-safety has been made by Lionel Frost, referenced explicitly in Chapter 5 of this study. Through case studies of particular urban fire-safety measures, Frost seeks to abstract broad design or planning principles. In the US, for instance, he identifies an "Atlantic" fire-regime that achieves fire-safety through the use of non-combustible construction materials. This makes buildings expensive, but also allows for a dense, more "European" urban form. By contrast a "Pacific" fire-regime achieves fire-safety through spatial separation, allowing for cheaper construction, but demanding a more diffuse, sub-urban configuration. As such, a distinctively east-coast and west-coast approach to fire-safety might be seen to characterise the urban morphology of the US. Extending this thinking to the global scale, Frost suggests that for "the West" non-combustibility has been a key concern allowing investment in real-estate to become a more durable commodity. In "the East", the limiting of potential losses associated with fire has been more important. Beyond these geographic oppositions, Frost posits a transition from less to more durable built forms as a key yardstick of "Modernity". For other scholars, these generalisations are problematic and to be avoided. For Jordan Sand, likewise discussed in Chapter 5, they do not assist us in understanding the social and political specificity of fire-safety initiatives. For Greg Bankoff, they ignore the complexity of really existing cities, which are not only hybrid with respect to the paradigms Frost identifies but also suggestive of alternatives. For Cornel Zwierlein, these abstractions run the risk of reinforcing problematic categories, such as "East" and "West", "Modern" and "Pre-Modern".

Through their focus on particular cities the studies collected here have sought to pay close attention to historical and geographical specificity, sharing those concerns outlined above by Sands, Bankoff and Zwierlein. In that sense, each chapter is an isolated contribution to a more plural history of urban fire-regimes. Nonetheless, this collection has also paid attention to the way fire-safety knowledge moves, the way it is abstracted from its original context, and allowed to travel. Through the chapters collected here we have followed fire-safety thinking on a number of journeys: from Edinburgh to Tianjin, from Britain to Lagos, from Paris to Edo, from New York to London, as well as from desktop studies to as-built configurations. These journeys have also occurred through time, considering how governmentalities of fire-safety change from often feudal origins, to moments of colonial encounter, through the experience of the Second World War and through processes of globalisation and neo-liberalisation. Standards have been presented as documents that allow us to make such journeys through space and time. That is the key contribution of this collection as a whole is perhaps it focus on the way standards allow fire-safety thinking to move and change. The remainder of this chapter is an attempt to clarify and conceptualise that specific contribution. It recounts certain aspects of the journeys we have travelled by way of standardisation. In doing so, it employs a final concept drawn from Actor Network Theory as a means to conceptualise the way that govern-mentalities transform as they are translated through space and time.

8.3 Thinking with fire

This collection began by recognising the foundational role fire has played in architectural theory. Recounting his myth of the discovery of fire, Vitruvius suggests that that "first fire" created the conditions of possibility for social gathering, as well as the first prompt for coordinated of action and agreement. On that basis, like many before and since, Vitruvius suggests that we recognise fire as the original "spark" that created not only architecture but language and society, culture and the city. This mythical origin story resonates, in part, with Gaston Bachelard's phenomenology of fire, which likewise suggests a close relationship between fire and thought. Bachelard is keen to stress that the comfortable warmth created by fire was not simply a utilitarian end, but also the prompt for reflection on our own condition of comfort. The warmth offered by a log fire, he contends, was the primordial context for a specific form of thought, for "reverie"; fire provides the "infrastructure" for a form of thought that is freed from utilitarian end. But it also offers that thought a common object of wonder, and metaphor to be employed within explanatory schemes. It is on this basis that Bachelard proposes a "psychoanalysis of fire", identifying poetic "complexes" that fire has burned into our patterns of thought, even those that profess to be "objective" and "scientific". Fire tinges thought with craftiness; as for Prometheus, knowledge is something to be stolen. Fire tinges thought with desire; as for Eros, it is something that enflames our passions. Fire tinges thought with death; as for Empedocles, it speeds things up, accelerates time, moving us towards an ultimate conclusion. But beyond these specific complexes, Bachelard also suggests that fire lends reverie a particular "shape", one that distinguishes it from other patterns of thinking.

> The Dream proceeds on its way in a linear fashion, forgetting its original path as it hastens along. The reverie works in a star pattern. It returns to its centre to shoot out new beams. And, as it happens, the reverie in front of the fire, the gentle reverie that is conscious of its well-being, is among those which best hold fast to their object or, if one prefers, to their *pretext*.[1]

Prompted by Bachelard, it is tempting to "psychoanalyse" some of the episodes recounted in this collection. There is something Promethean in the work of Arup Associates, and the advocates of performance-based regulation; for these actors, simulated fires, in laboratories or on computers, appeared as a means to "steal" the legitimacy of fire, and so to "capture" existing regulatory frameworks, directing them towards their own ends. The Scotland Act, through the connection it drew between "common women" and house fires, might be read as the legal codification of an association between fire and sex, through their mutual inflammatory potential. And perhaps, in accounts of a perceived fatalism with "Asian" or specifically Buddhist approaches to fire, we see an equivalent to, or the projection of, an Empedoclean complex.

8.4 The spatiality of fire

The aspect of Bachelard's analysis I wish to dwell on here, though, is the "shape" he associates with fire-side reverie. I wish to dwell on this shape because within Actor Network Theory it has been used as a means to describe the "spatiality" of techno-scientific knowledge. This argument is made by John Law and Annemarie Mol in "Situating Technoscience: an Inquiry into Spatialities". Relating closely to concerns outlined above in relation to fire-safety knowledge, that paper begins with a reflection on the geographic specificity of Science. They suggest that the fundamental insight offered by ANT has been to "spatialise" science:

> The process of tracking down 'science' in the laboratory rather than in theory not only implied that normative epistemology gave way to ethnographic realism. It also brought the sciences down to earth. No longer the result of being transcendental, science needed to be localised.[2]

Law and Mol contend that what Latour and others have demonstrated is that knowledge is fundamentally "local"; it makes sense in relation to a given context. As such, moving knowledge is hard work; if a given fact is to keep making sense, it must carry aspects of its broader context with it, so as to assist other in making sense of it. The myth of fire as the origin of society, for instance, would make less sense if it were moved outside of a culture that does not depends upon fire for thermal comfort; the explanatory power of fire is reduced when its utility is associated only with food, and not with shelter.[3] Law and Mol's own example is that of a ship, sailing between Lisbon and Calicut in the 15th century. The ship itself is a relationship of facts and artefact, bulwarks, spars, sails, maps, people, practices, the wind and seas. This spatial arrangement must hold itself together if the ship is to reach its destination. On its first encounter with another context, however, that ship will be understood very differently. If it wants to be understood on its own terms, it will need to carry with it a broader set of cultures and practices from Portugal and seek to reproduce them in India. And what is true for this ship is no less true for any "object" of technoscience: for corrugated steel, computer simulations, metric units, the concept of gravity. By redescribing Latour's schema in these terms, Law and Mol seek to identify a spatiality latent within Actor Network Theory; the basic analytic move of

ANT is to study the relationship between "networks" and "regions". Networks are understood as relationships that can be made stable as they are moved: "objectified" relationships, those that Latour calls the "immutable mobiles". Regions are the geographic spaces through which such objects can be moved, the contexts within which they come to be recontextualised.

Law and Mol outline this spatial schema to suggest its limitations. Do technoscientific objects always remain stable as they travel, and if they don't, does that mean that they have failed? Law and Mol suggest not, and that further spatial metaphors assist in understanding the variety of ways in which knowledge moves and changes. It is here that they turn to the topological thought of Bachelard and Serre. Some technical objects, they suggest, are "fluid" in their character. The Zimbabwe Bush Pump, for example, is not physically immutable; its component parts are often replaced with alternatives as needs must. Those pumps also move between varied knowledge frameworks. Intended by its inventor to achieve a defined standard of water cleanliness, it does not do so in every circumstance. However, the authors recognise that standards of cleanliness change from place to place, while remaining meaningful to local actors. The pump occupies a "fluid" spatiality, inasmuch as it remains the same, and it continues to work, despite incremental shifts in its physical make-up and understanding.

Law and Mol draw on Bachelard's phenomenology of fire to describe a fourth "spatiality" of knowledge. Sensitive to the Empedoclean drive, they note that moments of abrupt destruction are also vectors along which scientific cultures travel; disaster and war are extreme modalities of cultural exchange. As such, certain kinds of technical objects make sense not because they form an "immutable" constellation in themselves, but rather because they relate to and invoke a common "absence". This is what they seek to describe through their term "fire-space". Techno-scientific objects have a fire-like spatiality, they suggest, when they move and change through processes of abrupt destruction and substitution. Artefacts make sense in relationship to facts that they supplant and replace. Concepts and tools continually change, but like Bachelard's fire-side reverie, they hold fast to a common shared pretext.

> Three attributes: continuity as an effect of discontinuity; continuity as the presence and the absence of Otherness; and continuity as an effect of a star-like pattern in this simultaneous absence and presence: this is what we imagine as the attributes of shape constancy in the topology of fire.[4]

8.5 The "flicker" of standards

The example Law and Mol offer for such an object is a formula – indeed, a standard. It concerns the maximum strain permissible in airplane wing design, understood through the property "G", or "Gust Response". G is here defined by the equation: $G = (V \times L) / W$. Of course, like any algebraic equation, this formula gives presence to a set of absences; V is the velocity at which a plane flies, L is the "Lift Slope" of the wing, and W is the Wind Load. By controlling the relationship between these varied actants, the formula hopes to ensure that the wing holds together. But the absence Law and Mol refer to is another one. The point of the formula is to facilitate safe design, and so reduce the number of accidents during test flights, but it nonetheless depends upon accidents that have already occurred in prior test flights. The formula represents and replaces the experience of brave or unfortunate pilots who agreed to test planes with a variety of wing types, flying very low, and at very high velocity, until they were either sick or blacked out – or their aircraft disintegrated.

> Look at it. *Present* is a figure of tolerable G. It is there, on the paper. But that figure depends precisely upon what is *absent* – a sickened and frightened pilot. *Depends* upon that which is absent (so it is present) but (in an additional twist) at the same time depends upon *making* it absent: because there is certainly no room for a pilot and his vomit in the network of relations pencilled on a sheet of paper by an aerodynamicist in a clean office. G in the expression achieves its significance because of that flickering between two impossible alternatives: that the pilot is absent; and that the pilot is present.[5]

We have been looking at that same flicker throughout this book. We saw it first when studying travel-distance codes in Edinburgh. On many different pieces of paper we saw a repeated figure, that of 2.5 minutes, the definition of tolerable egress time. That figure evoked an absent one: a heroic conductor and the calm he is supposed to have created. To make sense, the former figure depended upon but sought to replace the latter. There is no room for heroism within the process of standardisation, or in the standardised built environment. Nonetheless, the problematics explored in relation to the 2.5 minute rule were the result of that "flickering" between two impossible alternatives: the conductor must be present, the conductor must be absent. In the Grenfell Tower fire, we saw that flicker in reverse. On paper the BS8414 test results conducted by BRE in 2014 confirmed the safety of Celotex RS5,000 insulation panels. What they did not make visible, what was black-boxed, was that that safety depended on a rivet that was present in the test assembly, but absent in the design specification. There was no room for failure in that fire-safety test – that failure could only be allowed to occur later, after those panels had been attached to the Grenfell Tower, and to other buildings across the world. Until the Grenfell Tower fire, the legality and marketability of RS5,000 depended upon two impossible alternatives: that the rivet was present, and that the rivet was absent.

Beyond identifying this particular "flicker", we can use Law and Mol's schema of "fire-space" to define more precisely the insight provided by this collection. This collection has not discovered a common technologies and rationalities of urban fire-safety, applicable across differing geographic and historic contexts. Rather, it has described a series of regionally specific "regulatory spaces", legal frameworks that have developed in close relationship to their context. Those spaces have certainly shared similar components; we have seen a number of urban fire-safety initiatives that seek to limit fire-spread through requirements for non-combustible construction or prescribed spatial separation. But those technologies of fire-safety have meant different things in different places. Where they have been translated from one context to another, they have had to be re-contextualised; they have "shot out new beams", established new forms of agreement. Buildings and building design have played a key role in this process of moving and shaping govern-mentalities. The process of building standardisation has sustained that "flickering exchange" between the rationalities and technologies of fire-safety. Standards are moments of abstraction; concrete characteristics of the built environment are selected and taken to be of universal value. Future buildings concretise that abstraction, inscribe it into reality. This process allows ideas about urban fire-safety to be moved, but also to change. Interpreted in new contexts, those standards come to mean and do different things. Those actors that are brought together by the pretext of fire-safety gather around an object that they nonetheless seek to displace, to replace, to out-law. Galvanised by the risk of fire, they nonetheless seek to extinguish it. That is, we could use Law and Mol's term to describe the subject of this book as a whole. It has, in sum, been an attempt to describe "fire-space", to describe exchanges between problems of governance and of building design prompted by the problem of fire. It has studied those exchanges through processes of standardisation, through moments in which governmental concepts are abstracted from, and then re-inscribed into, our built environment. The following paragraphs summarise the stories told in each chapters of this book with a view to highlight those moments of "flickering".

8.6 From grand Dieu to Yin Yang

Our first story began with a fire that broke out in a theatre in Edinburgh, and a conductor that played a tune. That tune had originally been written down by a magazine editor in London who – responding to the exigency of a Scottish rebellion – sought to use it to enrol the English regions in displays of patriotic obedience. But once established, that obedience proved itself useful in other ways; years later, in a pacified Edinburgh, it struck up an uncanny relationship with the geometry of a particular building, and so became enrolled in the drama of public safety. Because the song and the building were the same *length*, they were able to form a network, one that was strong enough to support the construction of a new regulatory frameworks defining the first geometric limitations on plan depth. Those frameworks were understood to offer a reified form of calm, through the technical delegate of building design. In Scotland, that calm came to be reconstituted in the form of door widths, corridor lengths, and plan geometries. But while these technical delegates seek to replace the need for quick-witted conductors, they cannot do without them entirely. As our experience of fire and our sense of patriotism wanes, new forms of rehearsal are required in order to ensure our obedience. These social and architectural equations facilitate a trade-off between the real and reified forms of obedience: additional design freedom can be bought through the adoption of a zero-tolerance approach to staff management. In parallel, the same codes allow fire-safety thinking to travel, and to generate collateral effects. In Tianjin, the same travel distance codes are used to discover an accidental architectures of tacit way-finding, at the same time as generating a surplus symbolic value. Adherence to them provides a means to demonstrate openness to the "West", or at least to international exchange. That symbolic value is offered imaginary reinforcement by the fact that those same standards can be used to create a visual metaphor for the happy convergence between communism and capitalism. Fire-safety knowledge continues to be globalised, by way of glossy visualisations depicting American designs for a building in China that realises British Standards.

8.7 From sovereign cession to passive ventilation

In Lagos a spark flew from a pistol, setting light to a thatched roof. The distance that spark flew was translated into a formula, defining an area of fire-safety setback. What that spark meant originally was the presence of an indigenous armed militia. And what that distance meant originally was a legal rationale for Sovereign cession, in the form of "slum clearance". But in the process of its governmentalisation, that rationale becomes tied to other concerns, initially those of enforced colonial dependence. For later generations of planners, though, its meaning would change; the space cleared by that spark would offer a means to prevent the spread of disease, to create a distant image of Welwyn Garden City, or to ensure universal passive ventilation. In parallel, on the ground, that same standard would make room for a wide range of other uses. It creates the footprint for Mosques, for the homeless and for the shadow labour that makes life liveable for poorly paid policemen, accommodating but reinforcing the marginality of these uses. The coexistence of these different understandings depends on two impossible alternatives: that the setback remain empty, or that setback be filled in. The incompatibility of those alternatives suggests a *realpolitik* that recognises greater potential risks than fire. In their struggle to occupy that space on the ground, another abstraction is being concretised, the concept of a "public good".

8.8 From ramparts to towers

In Edo, the houses of the urban poor burned down, and burned down, and burned down again, until they brought with them the castle of their Shogun. But by being burned down, that castle found a way to extend itself, to become bigger and stronger. Always a physical mechanism for capital concentration and generalised impoverishment, the govern-mentality of that building came to be translated into the domain of city planning. Through sumptuary law, fire-risk became encoded within more wide-spread and formalised mechanisms designed to control access to land ownership and capital. At the same time as expanding his authority, the shogun also found himself giving ground – quite literally – to an emergent merchant class. The problem of urban fire-safety defined a legal and physical space within that class could grow; merchants could build their "castle" only where the laws of property and land could be brought into relationship by the dense mud of fire-proof construction, and only on the margins – economically and spatially – of an economy that was still based on the continuous consumption of cheap flammable buildings. Despite being rebuilt dozens of times, a spectre of Edo's feudalism continues to hang over contemporary Tokyo; salarymen still labour their entire lives to pay off a ground-rent whose value is determined by the constructed pyro-seismic risk of a disposable building stock. The intervention of European commentators has done little to change this state of affairs; indeed, they may have sustained it. In Tokyo, fire-safety has come to be associated with "the West", and the most risky buildings are perceived as the most Japanese. In Tokyo's "risk imaginary", national history and future catastrophe conspire to frighten an economy into a continued habituation with loss. This vicious circle is only broken at its point of greatest intensity – when concrete high-rise buildings become simply too expensive to demolish.

8.9 From terrorist attack to obedient avatar

American Airlines Flight 11 and United Airlines Flight 175 collide with the twin towers of the World Trade Center, in New York. They carry with them a mass of combustible materials, unanticipated by existing building regulations, and leave a three-storey hole in the building's fabric, stripping its structure of fire-proof cladding. The question as to which of these reasons caused the building's collapse will decide whether this event should be anticipated by future building regulations. The high political and economic cost of this event supports a series of detailed post-fire analyses, ones that, in turn, validate new modes of computational modelling for fire dynamics. One of those analyses will attribute the building's collapse to a loss of fire-proof cladding, arguing that buildings should be designed to retain structural integrity without such cladding. This argument, and those modes of modelling, has the effect of normalising aspects of the World

Trade Center crash; they are used to gain regulatory approval for buildings that are designed with three-storey voids within them, and that omit the use of fire-proof cladding. Those new modes of modelling are developed in London; they translate the credibility offered by 9/11 to a new regulatory context, where they are used to critique prescriptive standards for fire-safety. One of the rules they are used to critique is based on the original fire considered here, the Edinburgh theatre fire. But to replace that fire, these modes of modelling also *depend* upon it; they translate its assumptions into avatars, simulated humans that are more reliably obedient. Those avatars don't submit the abstractions of that previous formula to empirical testing, rather they "black-box" them. Nonetheless, those simulations are convincing for certain audiences, and offer another means of translation; they allow the equation of heterogenous technologies – ceiling heights, sprinklers, pressure differentials, levels of combustibility and management programmes. In doing so, they support the design of buildings, of a wide variety of shapes, all over the world. At the same time – for Arup Associates and the City of London Corporation – the capacity and rhetoric of design flexibility provides a means to consolidate specific forms of commercial consultancy, and specific forms of governmental regulation, in a specific place.

8.10 From the Great Fire to the Grenfell fire

On Grenfell Road we discovered an archaeology of urban fire-safety. That street had originally been lined with London's vernacular row-houses, themselves the result of the Great Fire of London, and the building regulations imposed in its aftermath. Destroyed by high explosive bombing during the Blitz, that site made space for a new urban and governmental technology: the post-war social-housing tower-block. Describing the original structure of Grenfell Tower, we found it to be socio-technically monolithic, and highly resistant to fire; commissioned and built by the local authority, its concrete structure and cladding were both thermally "thick". But for some, the durability of that tower might have been seen as a problem by some. This type of council-owned building has outlasted the governmentality that created it, coming to be seen as a costly asset that exerts negative pressure on the value of neighbouring private properties. The 2014 2012-16 recladding project was and answer to that problem, one that was socio-technically more complex. The procurement, construction and regulation of that cladding involved a wide range of mostly for-profit stakeholders, creating a complex and interlocking set of responsibilities. The cladding itself was likewise built of many components parts, all of which were thermally thin. The structure was prone to many lines of possible failure, both legally and physically. The 2017 fire revealed a number of those lines of failure, most dramatically in relation to the cassette and insulation panels. Those components failed in the fire, but also revealed failings in associated processes of regulation. The BS8414 tests used to test whether those components were safe failed to identify a divergence between their perfor-mance as tested, and as built, suggesting a widespread problem with this standard. But more generally, that fire was seen to act as a test for a particu-lar govern-mentality, one that sought to deregulate design by passing more responsibility to those who design and build our buildings. The verdict of the Grenfell Tower Public Inquiry and any subsequent criminal proceedings will form an important part of that test.

8.11 Star patterns of standardisation

While this book has focussed specifically on fire-safety standards, the con-cept of "fire-space" might be used to describe any form of standardisation. Processes of standardisation gather stakeholders around shared concerns or problems. They are defined by a central pretext, a "boundary object" in Leigh Star's terminology. Standards are defined by specific groups of stakeholders in specific circumstances, constructing local networks of agreement. Those networks are expanded as standards are applied in new contexts. That process entails a momentary "flicker". The act of legislating, of writing rules, is one through which concrete specificities are abstracted from their context in an attempt to universalise them. The act of regulating, of acting in accordance with such rules, is a process through which those abstractions are re-concretised in new contexts. Govern-mentalities are born of and translated through that process. And while that process aspires to universality, to ubiquity, it is perhaps better understood as a process of networking locations; in the standardisation stories told here we have seen how standards have been used to broker agreement between specific stake-holders in specific places – between the governors of Britain and Nigeria, the urban planners of Japan and "The West" or the engineers of New York and London.

The process of standardisation has been seen to operate through that drama of absence and presence that Law and Mol use to characterise "fire-space". In regulating action, standards make present something that was absent, the detail of a destroyed building or of an aircraft wing. Each time they are enacted they invoke that original concern, invoke it in order to make it absent. Fears concerning the future are dramatised to ensure they do not occur. As such, the process of standardisation seems to trap us between two simultaneous yet impossible alternatives. On the one hand, standards seem to arrive too soon; they outline ambitions that diverge dramatically from the present conditions. Reading them, we can't help but be struck by the sharp disjunction between what is written on paper and what we see around us. At the same time, standards seem to arrive too late. Built on precedent and prior knowledge, they describe a future that is caught in the past, one that seems distracted from challenges to come. But that tension is what gives standards their meaning. Standards are fundamentally utopian; they make sense in their divergence from lived reality. We experience them, and they act, inasmuch as they conduct our conduct otherwise. The circumstance in which everything already acts as it ought to is also the moment in which this form of government would appear superfluous.

When standards work, they do so in a fire-like way, they allow govern-mentalities to move and change. When applied in new contexts, they need to be made sense of afresh. New groups of stakeholders reinterpret and adapt govern-mentalities in response to their own needs and circumstances. Old utopias are supplanted by new ones, colonising the redundant infrastructure of solved or forgotten problems. Standards are liable to be "captured", occupied by other interests, addressed to new ends. Nonetheless, inasmuch as they retain a relationship to that original concern, they can be "tested". As such, moments of innovation retain a relationship with that shared central pretext.

8.12 Governing by accident

Law and Mol developed the concept of "fire-space" as part of an ambition to "situate" science, to bring science "down to earth". Deploying it here we use it as a means to "situate" govern-mentalities. That ambition resonates with one outlined in Chapter 2. Paraphrasing Rokpe we defined Governmentality as a process that concerned "shifting the centre of gravity of governmental action downward".[6] That is, for Foucault, that term carries with it an ambition to shift reflections both in and of government away from assertions of sovereign Right towards an increasing practical imbrication with the health, safety and welfare of the population. Again summarising the stories told in this collection, we can see this as the common trajectory of each chapter. When *The Gentlemen Magazine* published "God Save The King", it did so as a direct assertion of the sovereignty of George II, a call for obedience in the face of the Jacobite uprising. However, by enrolling the obedience elicited by this tune in further governmental networks, fire-safety might be seen as one of many means by which that authority claim came to be re-cycled, through rational and technological mediation. Through that process, the authority claims of government came to be enmeshed within a set of highly contingent relationships between particular personalities, fires, buildings, standards and simulations, and as such was shaped by and advanced the interests of a wide range of other interest groups. The reduction of Lagos by HMS Bloodhound and Teaser, and the resultant cession of that city by the British Crown, were simple acts of sovereign violence. But the fire-safety standards that British settlers then imposed upon the city began to governmentalise that authority, exposing it to re-direction and occupation. Again, those regulatory mechanisms came to be claimed by diverse interests and concerns, and their material carriers appropriated by other users. The sumptuary laws of Edo, which denied the urban poor access to widely available means of fire-safe construction, were likewise means to enrol buildings and fire within the maintenance and representation class privilege. But the effects and side-effects of those laws, as they went on to shape the city, became a mechanism through which the ruling class had to give ground, physically and legally, to an emergent merchant class.

For scholars of Governmentality Studies and Science and Technology Studies the ambition to bring political and scientific discourse "down" to the level of its socio-technical networks is critical and self-conscious. That was not always the case for those actors narrated in the studies collected here. The shifts in govern-mentality summarised above have often been ones that seem to occur by accident, or to use Beck's phrase, via the "back stairs of side-effects". They have been prompted by unexpected or unforeseen events, usually misfortunes or mishaps: a ship that strikes a reef and is sunk, a botched trick that kills a magician, a cook-pot that is knocked over and burns down a city, a passenger plane that is hijacked and flown into a skyscraper. But at the same time, they have depended on another kind of accident – on properties and qualities of objects that are usually considered inessential, coincidental, contingent: a corridor that happens to be the same length as a piece of music, the unintended symbolism of a travel-distance diagram, the passive ventilation benefits of prior "slum clearance", the expense and durability of structures required for high-rise construction, the economic and aesthetic value of removing fire-proof cladding. Like Ropke and Beck's phrases, the word "accident" describes a downward trajectory. Its root is the Latin *cadere*, "to fall". Accidents are things that bring us "down to earth", that reduce our "centre of gravity". If the studies collected here do help to "situate" governmentality, to concretise it, I suggest they do so at the intersection of those two types of "accident". Accidents often prompt programmes of governmentalisation, but those programmes are also held together by accidental overlaps between the interests and actancy of diverse stakeholders, both human and non-human.

Thought in this way, we might suggest one reason that buildings and building design play an important role in governmentalisation. Buildings are closely associated with accident; most accidents happen in the home, and of those that occur at work, most occur within the construction sector. The design of the built environment conditions most of the accidents that befall us. But more importantly, the design of the built environment is a matter of concern for a particularly wide range of stakeholders. The Public Inquiry following the Grenfell Tower fire is the largest in British legal history for that reason. It has the largest number of "core-participants" assembled for such an event. 519 individuals, 18 commercial organisations, 8 public bodies and 2 trade unions have so far been deemed to be of direct and significant interest to the Inquiry. They are the survivors and the bereaved, those involved in the event of the fire itself, but also those responsible for the design, construction and regulation of the building process; tenants and tenants associations, the emergency services, architects, engineers, contractors, suppliers, manufacturers, utility providers, the local authorities, regulators, government departments, mayoralties and their lawyers. That is, buildings are a particularly powerful kind of "boundary object"; we gather inside them, but they also gather us around them, as matters of common concern.

8.13 Resistance and change

Law and Mol use fire as a metaphor to describe the shape of our knowledge frameworks, but the studies included in this collection concern a kind of knowledge that is also about fire. By describing the "fire-space" of Fire-safety standards we therefore take Law and Mol's metaphor literally. Again taking the Grenfell Tower fire as an example, a few final thoughts might be offered as to how fire itself has a shaping effect of governmentality. Law and Mol use fire as a metaphor to describe socio-technical objects that makes sense in relation to moments of abrupt change or loss, and fires create precisely such moments within our buildings and cities. As such, fire might be seen to shape our thinking through its particular destructive power. Urban fires are a highly visible kind of destruction. Cities and fires go badly together because they have something in common; they both want to go up, they both tend towards the vertical. This is why fires in tall buildings are particularly dangerous; additional fuel is available in the direction that fire travels and grows fastest. But this is also what makes towers and fires powerful signals; they are things that stand out in stark contrast to the horizontality of the ground. The Grenfell Tower fire was a kind of beacon, it was visible far and wide, and it spoke differently to many different constituencies. We could say that urban conflagrations of this type are "signal" events, rising above the noise of the everyday, being recognised as meaningful.[7] As such, fires provide ready prompts from which to build broad programmes of governmental change.

Fires are also associated with renewal because they destroy some of those things that might otherwise resist change. By damaging or destroying our buildings and cities, they get rid of those obdurate remainders of prior govern-mentalities. As such, fires provide a powerful prompt for both urban renewal and governmental change. They remove cost barriers to change, they write off forms of material investment in the status quo, as well as those forms of reputational investment that are their twin. Fires destroy credibility, they disassemble networks of relationship that connect particular ways of thinking and acting, so creating the circumstance in which they might be re-imagined.[8] The Grenfell Tower fire, for instance, didn't just destroy that building, and the lives of those who lived within it; it also discredited those involved in its refurbishment, those who supplied the materials to build it, those who commissioned it, and those who warranted it as safe. The purpose of events like the Inquiry is to control that broader process, and to begin to shape what occurs in its aftermath. Fire has a close physical and metaphorical relationship with that process of destruction and re-birth; that is what is explained by the mythological figure of the Phoenix.

The Phoenix is a myth, though, and change is rare. One reason for that is that the network of agreements defined by law are often more obdurate than those we set in stone. The cost barriers to re-writing a building standard can be far greater than those of making changes to, or even completely replacing an individual building. The cost of Grenfell Fire, for instance, has often been compared with the cost-saving that led to it. The Royal Borough of Kensington and Chelsea are said to have saved around £300,000 by substituting Reynobond ACM cladding panels for the original and safer specification. As of May 2021, they have spent an estimated £406 m on their response to the fire, including an estimated £221 m acquiring properties to rehouse surviving residents. But the broader costs associated with that event are far higher. The cost of the Public Inquiry, charged with determining what changes should be made as a result of the fire, has at present cost an estimated at £117 m.[9] In response to the first regulatory change, that of banning combustible cladding at height, the UK Government has allocated a sum of £5 bn to subsidise the process of replacing non-compliant cladding. Estimators suggest that the actual cost the leaseholders will be closer to £50 bn.[10] To calculate the total cost only that single regulatory change we would also need to consider the cost implication for manufacturers, suppliers and designers, not just for leaseholders, and to consider the cost to government itself. These costs are indices of the scale and breadth of material investment that codes and standards negotiate. The forms of agreement they mediate are far greater than those embodied in individual buildings. A single line of code might therefore be said to have more "materiality" than any building, it might offer far more resistance to change.

The possibility of and resistance to change is demonstrated tragically by the Grenfell Tower fire. Edward Dafarn, co-founder of the Grenfell Action Group, not only predicted that fire but also its necessity. He did so expressing anger at the Kensington and Chelsea Tenants Management Organisation for a perceived failure to address tenants' fire-safety. One year before the fire he blogged that "Only an incident that results in serious loss of life of KCTMO residents will allow the external scrutiny to occur that will shine a light on the practices that characterise the malign governance of this non-functioning organisation." Today that body exists only to remain accountable to an Inquiry that is much broader in remit than Dafarn assumed. Some of the shifts in govern-mentality recounted in this collection have, as with Grenfell, been the result of tragic accident. They have occurred when fire and buildings interact to reveal fault-lines in particular ways of thinking. Others have been the product of design. They have occurred when regulators recognise problems and respond with new forms of legislation, and when architects and engineers develop create buildings that offer new solutions to old problems, or create new problems. Taken together, these processes have been presented as a means of investment and cooperation through which govern-mentalities are made real and tested. The chapters collected here have been presented as examples of the way that buildings, by accident and design, contribute to shifts in govern-mentality. The practice of building design may be caught up in a complex and widespread governmental context, but the studies collected here have sought to demonstrate that individual buildings can and do reflexively shape that context.

Notes

1 Gaston Bachelard, *Psychoanalysis of Fire*, New Edition (Boston: Beacon Press, 1977). p. 14.
2 John Law and Annemarie Mol, 'Situating Technoscience: An Inquiry into Spatialities', *Environment and Planning D: Society and Space* 19, no. 5 (1 October 2001): 611.
3 Myths of the origin of fire from tropical cultures frequently associate this with the discovery of cooked food, but seldom extend that its significance as far as Vitruvius does. See Sir James G. Frazer, *Myths of the Origin of Fire*, 1st ed. (London: Routledge, 2019).
4 John Law and Annemarie Mol, 'Situating Technoscience'. p. 616.
5 John Law and Annemarie Mol. pp. 617–618.
6 Michel Foucault, *The Birth of Biopolitics: Lectures at the Collège de France, 1978–1979: Lectures at the College De France, 1978–1979*, trans. Mr. Graham Burchell (New York: Palgrave Macmillan, 2010). pp. 148, 157.
7 In this paragraph I am testing some of the key concepts Latour develops in *Laboratory Life*. "Noise" is a key terms that Latour and Woolgar suggests is a necessary circumstance for the construction of scientific "facts":

> Let us start with the concept of noise. For Brillouin, information is a relation of probability; the more a statement differs from what is expected, the more information it contains. It follows that a central question for any participant advocating a statement in the agonistic field is how many alternative statements are equally probable. If a large number can easily be thought of, the original statement will be taken as meaningless and hardly distinguishable from others.

  By using it here, I mean to infer analogously the importance that Noise plays in the construction of govern-mentalities, and so the importance of surprising events that stand out from it. See Latour and Woolgar, *Laboratory Life*. p. 240.
8 Cost is another important concerns for Latour and Woolgar, one which they associated with the broader concept of "credibility". That is, economic cost is one of the many forms of investment which pose resistance to change, and as such secure agreement. We used credibility to define the various investments made by scientists and the conversions between different aspects of the laboratory. Credibility facilitates the synthesis of economic notions (such as money, budget, and payoff) and epistemological notions (such as certitude, doubt, and proof). Moreover, it emphasises that information is costly. The cost-benefit analysis applies to the type of inscription devices to be employed, the career of scientists concerned, the decisions taken by funding agencies, as well as to the nature of the data, the form of paper, the type of journal, and to readers' possible objections. The cost itself varies according to the previous investments in terms of money, time, and energy already made. The notion of credibility permits the linking of a string of concepts, such as accreditation, credentials and credit to beliefs ("credo," "credible") and to accounts ("being accountable," "counts," and "credit accounts"). This provides the observer with an homogeneous view of fact construction and blurs arbitrary divisions between

economic, epistemological, and psychological factors." By using it here, I mean to draw attention to the forms of cost and credibility that are entailed in constructing particular govern-mentalities. See Latour and Woolgar. p. 238.

9 'Grenfell Costs Surpass £500m as Council Bill Revealed', *The Guardian*, 21 May 2021, http://www.theguardian.com/uk-news/2021/may/21/grenfell-costs-surpass-500m-as-council-bill-revealed.

10 'Estimators Price Cladding Replacement at 10 Times Government Budget', accessed 29 July 2021, https://www.theconstructionindex.co.uk/news/view/estimators-price-cladding-replacement-at-10-times-government-budget.

Index

Note: *Italic* page numbers refer to figures and page numbers followed by "n" denote endnotes.